PUT THE
MOOSE
ON THE
TABLE

LESSONS IN LEADERSHIP

FROM A CEO'S JOURNEY

THROUGH BUSINESS

AND LIFE

PUT THE
MOOSE
ON THE
TABLE

RANDALL TOBIAS

Chairman Emeritus—Eli Lilly and Company
Former Vice Chairman—AT&T

WITH TODD TOBIAS

INDIANA
University Press

Bloomington & Indianapolis

The photographs on pages 4, 5, 23, and 29 are property of AT&T. Reprinted with permission of AT&T.

This book is a publication of
Indiana University Press
601 North Morton Street
Bloomington, Indiana 47404-3797 USA

http://www.iupress.indiana.edu

Telephone orders   800-842-6796
Fax orders   812-855-7931
Orders by e-mail   iuporder@indiana.edu

The paper used in this publication meets the minimum
requirements of American National Standard for Information
Sciences—Permanence of Paper for Printed Library
Materials, ANSI Z39.48-1984.

Manufactured in the United States of America

Library of Congress Cataloging-in-Publication Data

Tobias, Randall
Put the moose on the table : lessons in leadership from a CEO's journey through
business and life / Randall Tobias ; with Todd Tobias.
p. cm.
Includes bibliographical references and index.
ISBN 0-253-34239-2 (cloth : alk. paper)
1. Organizational change. 2. Industrial management—United States—Case studies.
3. Tobias, Randall. 4. Executives—United States—Biography. I. Tobias, Todd. II. Title.
HD58.8 .T62 2003
650.1—dc21
2002015748

1   2   3   4   5   08   07   06   05   04   03

*For my
five oldest grandchildren,
Connor, Ella, Emily, Annie, and Ashley,
who already know the challenge and
excitement of continuous
change.*

*The five oldest Tobias grandchildren (left to right):
Connor and Emily Button, the children of my daughter
Paige; Ella Tobias (front), the daughter of my son Todd;
and Annie and Ashley Ullyot, the daughters of Marianne's
son Jim. Photo courtesy of Kathy Blankenheim.*

CONTENTS

INTRODUCTION

You do not like them.
So you say.
Try them! Try them!
And you may.
—Dr. Seuss, *Green Eggs and Ham*

In the spring of 1849, David Tobias, a first-generation Welsh immigrant, purchased a small, unpretentious plot of land near the Muscatatuck River in southern Indiana and built a water-powered mill on its banks. The Tobias Mill, as it would come to be called, was powered by a large waterwheel and housed several grinding stones and saw blades used to convert corn into corn meal, wheat into flour, and trees into lumber.

When he was old enough, David's son, Theopolis, was trained to run the family business, which he did, until his son, Harry, eventually took over.

By the turn of the nineteenth century, the steam engine had become the new technology. Thanks to the wide availability of steam power, and other technological breakthroughs, it became more convenient and cost-effective for farmers to convert their grain right in the field rather than haul their crops to the river's edge, as had been the custom. That was the beginning of the end, and the mill eventually ceased operation.

Sometime during the summer of 1949, one hundred years

The Tobias Mill, constructed in 1849 on the Muscatatuck River in southeastern Indiana, by David Tobias, an immigrant from Wales and my great-great-grandfather.

after that first land was acquired on the Muscatatuck River, Roy Tobias, the great-grandson of David Tobias, brought his seven-year-old son to visit the former site of the family mill. I remember the visit well; I was that seven-year-old-boy. Aside from the mill's foundation, there was not much left to see. And even though I was too young to realize it at the time, what I experienced that day was a lesson I have carried with me through school and college, marriage and children, and a business career spanning nearly four decades. That lesson is quite simple:

> **In business as in life, one thing is**
> **absolutely inevitable—continuous change.**

In just a hundred years, my own family had gone from the poverty of Wales to the promise of the Indiana frontier. They saw

Introduction

a prosperous family-owned mill made obsolete by the advent of steam power. Later, they experienced changes in the economics of a small family farm which made it both necessary and acceptable for subsequent generations to find yet other ways to make their living.

Since the dawn of the industrial revolution, and probably long before that, generations have seen a collection of professions fall by the wayside because of the very nature of the entrepreneurial spirit they once embodied. The Tobias family learned this reality the hard way. Indeed, the Hoosier experience of my own family, over more than 150 years, has been one of continuous change. As clear evidence of that point, today, unlike in 1849, you are not likely to find a working miller in your neighborhood.

But almost as inevitable as change itself are the plaintive cries of disbelief that invariably lie in its wake. As each successive generation experiences the sting of change, a familiar refrain ensues anew: "Look what's happened to us!" they say, as if change were a concept unique to their particular moment in history.

What *is* unique to the business world today is that the very notion of change is, well, changing. That is to say, change in today's workplace is even more inevitable, more prevalent, and is happening at an exponentially faster clip than ever before. Chances are that by the time you finish reading this book, Wall Street analysts will be touting the upside potential of a new stock in one industry or a promising IPO of another that no analyst had ever heard of at the time you *began* reading this book. As a result, last week's up-and-comer will risk becoming tomorrow's punch line. And so it goes. Change is no longer an occasional exception, it's a pride-swallowing, business-as-usual, embrace-it-or-perish rule.

But the changing face of corporate America doesn't affect only a company's shareholders. It affects a far more important corporate asset—its people. I graduated from Indiana University in 1964 and began working for AT&T's Indiana Bell Telephone Company shortly thereafter. Employees who began their career in that period could, on the basis of their capacity, interests, ambitions, and opportunities, more or less discern the trajectory their career path would take. Or at least that they hoped it would take. Those of us embarking on corporate careers then had the naïve arrogance to assume that post–World War II growth and prosperity had put behind us any threat of crippling industrial transformation. At the very least, we were certain it couldn't happen to our generation. And now that we had gained employment, that important decision was over; we could proceed with our careers as planned. Once hired, without consciously realizing it, we felt, in a word, *secure.* And nowhere more so than at AT&T. Can you blame us? After all, for those of us joining the Bell System, as it was then known, the apron strings of Ma Bell had held steadfast for well over a century. We knew we weren't going to get rich, but working for the phone company offered the satisfaction of being part of an extremely prestigious and successful organization and, above all, certainly represented security and stability. Little did we know. . . .

On January 8, 1982, AT&T and the U.S. Department of Justice announced an agreement to enter into a consent decree. Two years later, the Bell System was shattered, literally overnight, like a mirror dropped to the floor. What remained were eight jagged pieces, some catching more light than others, but all realigned in what turned out to be a frightfully disjointed composite. The age of security was dead, as if it ever really existed. And as we tried to make sense of what implications this event held for our future, we couldn't help but feel an overriding sentiment: "Look what's happened to us!"

With almost total certainty, employees entering the American workforce today, regardless of the industry, will have been hired to do jobs that will have a shorter life cycle than their careers. In all probability, by the time they begin to consider retirement, the jobs they were first hired to do will not exist in anything resembling

Introduction

their original form, if at all. What was once a prognostication is now a fact. The business world today is governed by a constantly evolving set of changing ground rules. A dire reality? Hardly. In fact, the sooner the leaders of tomorrow recognize that change itself represents the very core of competitive advantage, the sooner they will taste success. Change is a lot like fire. Manage it, turn it to your advantage, and you will bask in the warmth of its glow; ignore it or manage it poorly, and one thing is certain—eventually, you will get burned.

The fascinating thing about the current business environment is not simply that everything is constantly new but that everything is constantly renewing. I'm sure there will always be managers who seek competitive advantage by slowly avoiding or even denying the presence of continuous change. But they are destined to be left behind by those who will find ways to convert change into opportunities and benefits for their companies and their customers, employees, and shareholders. How one responds to change plays a major role in defining the future for one's business or a career—in determining likely success or failure. Among other things, responding to the unrelenting pressure of change provides an ongoing test of one's character and values.

If there is one word that characterizes my life, it is *change*. And this book is an effort to capture the leadership lessons I've learned over the course of my life and my career in the corporate world. But it's more than that. It's a reflection on experiences throughout all of my life, many exhilarating, some painful. It's about life in a small town, growing up in rural Indiana, and the uniquely Hoosier part-time jobs along the way. It's about the wonderful years at Indiana University and those that followed as an army artillery officer. It's about my telephone-company experiences in the years leading up to the disaggregation of the Bell System—first at Indiana Bell, then at Illinois Bell, then at AT&T headquarters—and later at the "new" AT&T, ultimately as Vice Chairman. It is also told in part through the lens of my experiences as Lilly's leader—accepting the job as CEO of the company at a time when the pharmaceutical industry was under attack from Washington, the company stock price had dropped precipitously, employees were protesting the ouster of my predecessor, takeover rumors were in the air, and patients in a trial for a very promising new drug suddenly began experiencing liver failure.

What's most important, I think, is that it's about the things I learned the hard way, such as through the trauma of trying to manage change in the absence of a clear and compelling strategic vision after the breakup of the Bell System in the early 1980s, and in the aftermath that lasted well into the 1990s.

Put the Moose on the Table is certainly not just the story of one company, or even two. It's also a personal story, including some personal tragedy, to be sure. But mostly, I believe it's a success story, with lessons of how success sometimes has its roots in earlier failure.

It's about leadership lessons and experiences from a time of unprecedented change and challenge in the world of American business. It's about turning change to advantage, told from the point of view of one who's had the enormous privilege of a ringside seat to some pretty serious corporate transformation.

One of the early lessons I learned is the importance of open communication. That doesn't happen automatically in the corporate world, or in life. It takes real effort to make it so. Have you ever been in a meeting, or even a personal conversation, where some unpleasant or difficult issue was known to everyone in the room and was significantly impacting relationships or standing in the way of resolving the problem at hand, but no one felt comfortable or even empowered to raise that subject? Too often, these kinds of issues are not addressed directly when they should be. Too often, people simply pretend the issue doesn't exist and try to somehow work around it, often with very negative consequences.

Introduction

There's a device I've used over the years to encourage people to deal with each other more openly, and it is the basis for the rather unusual title for this book. Imagine that there is a real live moose standing in the boardroom, or for that matter in your own family room. It's huge. It may be mean-spirited. It's quite homely. It has a very unpleasant smell. It's hard to imagine that everyone would carry on as if the moose simply did not exist.

Instead of the moose, imagine that the intrusion in the room is actually an unaddressed and unresolved issue that also has an unpleasant smell and is mean-spirited or ugly. "Let's put the moose on the table" is simply a way of saying to everyone involved, let's address this issue as openly and as honestly as we would feel compelled to do if we had a real live moose to confront. Somehow, describing an issue in that way seems to make people feel more comfortable in speaking as openly as they know how. That's exactly what I've tried to do in writing this book.

Put the Moose on the Table is an unvarnished look at one man's journey through corporate change—and life—in late-twentieth-century America. It's about a passage that began in the cornfields of northern Indiana and moved on to executive suites and corporate boardrooms in Chicago, New York, Basking Ridge, Miami, San Jose, Palo Alto, Dallas, Houston, Bartlesville, Indianapolis, and beyond, with more than enough overseas miles logged on corporate missions to fly—literally—to the moon and back.

The ideas and instincts I brought to Lilly came from a lifetime of varying experiences, ranging from the influence of my parents in establishing an underlying set of values to early work experiences as a grocery-store clerk to my time as a student at Indiana University to my nearly thirty-year career with AT&T. They were, I believe serendipitously, a useful combination of experiences for what later needed to be done during my years at that great pharmaceutical company. While they're certainly not the silver bullets for someone else to use in any situation, at any place, and anytime, I do believe there are conclusions to be drawn and lessons to be learned—both positive and not—from my experiences. The fact is, my leadership role in corporate America has, by and large, centered on the issue of striving to turn change—in all of its varied manifestations—into competitive advantage while trying always to do what's right. And that is the essence of this book.

I truly hope this story will both engage you and provide you with a few ideas to take away and apply to your own organization or career, or to some other aspect of your life. At the very least, I hope it will raise some questions for you to ponder. I don't presume to have come up with all of the answers, or to have always made the right decisions. Clearly, I didn't. But I do believe I've always tried to move forward, always seeking to do the very best I could in the process. And I guess that's the point. For me, constant transformation, embracing new ideas, taking calculated risks, and always moving on have, in the end, characterized the way I've tried to live my life—in all of its aspects.

I've often said that leadership is far more complicated than simply being an effective manager. Among other things, it's about leaving behind indelible footprints.

These are mine.

Randall Tobias
McLeod, Montana
November 8, 2002

PUT THE
MOOSE
ON THE
TABLE

ONE

Prescription for Disaster

Primum non nocere. [First, do no harm.]
—attributed to Hippocrates

The Note

There's a framed note that hangs on my office wall. Has for years. It's yellowing a bit around the edges, as it's now some two decades old. Over the years, I've lined my walls and shelves with this type of work-related memorabilia. And over the years, as the focus of my life has evolved, many of these awards and photos have come and gone. But somehow, as I mark each new chapter in my life and find myself in the new office space that such a change invariably provides, this particular keepsake always seems to find its way along for the ride. It's never too far from view.

While this reminder of days long past has begun to show its age, its implicit message rings as true today as it did the day it was written, December 16, 1981. It reads:

Randy,
I am very, very sorry to have delayed you this way. The discussion here now is exceptionally important and I cannot cut it off. I don't want to do a half job on your subject so let's postpone it.
I apologize.
CLB

———

1

The note written to me by AT&T CEO Charlie Brown during the December 16, 1981, AT&T board meeting while the board was discussing Brown's recommendation to enter into an agreement with the U.S. Department of Justice that would break up the Bell System.

To the average person, this cryptic note, written in marginally legible and now fading cursive, probably doesn't convey anything special. Its meaning is most likely lost . . . until, that is, one reads the newspaper clipping that's framed beside it. That article, from the *New York Times*, is headlined "Historic AT&T Settlement As Seen by the Participants." It begins:

WASHINGTON, January 10—Seventeen directors assembled in the dark, wood paneled boardroom of the American Telephone and Telegraph Company on December 16. They listened quietly as Charles L. Brown, the chairman, presented a report that would lead to the dismemberment of the largest company in the world and to the reshaping of the telecommunications industry.

An accompanying article, from the same day's *Wall Street Journal*, continues:

Starting on time at 10:30 A.M., Mr. Brown quickly scrapped a planned presentation on marketing. . . .

That morning, Charlie Brown, the venerable, soft-spoken leader of the Bell System, a man whose stoic countenance had earned him the secret nickname "Ol' Steely Blue Eyes," made not only the biggest single decision in the history of the company but also arguably the biggest single decision that any American business leader would render in the twentieth century. The board of directors, gathered at AT&T headquarters in Lower Manhattan that morning, listened intently as Brown asked for approval to accept the terms of the divestiture settlement that had been painfully worked out with the Justice Department. He asked for permission to break up AT&T, the largest, most powerful corporation in the world.

Although the term was not yet part of the mainstream vernacular, Charlie Brown demonstrated that morning the qualities of leadership we so commonly refer to today as those of a *change agent*: the ability to build a consensus to support a decision he'd concluded had to be made; the ability to effectively communicate that vision to the company, press, and shareholders; the ability to act swiftly and decisively. The list goes on. Much has been written about that decision and its far-reaching legal, political, and economic ramifications. But what has gone missing from such narrative accounts of that morning's events is that, unknown to anyone until now, Ol' Steely Blue Eyes demonstrated an instinctive but

The January 1982 press conference announcing the agreement to break up the Bell System: (left to right) Deputy U.S. Attorney General for Antitrust William R. Baxter, AT&T Chairman and CEO Charles L. Brown, and AT&T General Counsel Howard Trienens. Photo courtesy of AT&T.

unconscious gesture of leadership that I would literally carry with me from office to office for the rest of my life.

As the decision to break up Ma Bell's empire was being debated by the company's most senior leaders behind the closed doors of the twenty-sixth-floor corporate boardroom, just outside sat a nervous, recently promoted thirty-nine-year-old executive, maybe the youngest corporate vice president in the history of the company—waiting to make his first appearance before the AT&T board of directors with a presentation on marketing. He had not slept much the previous night in anticipation. It would have been easy for Charlie to send an assistant to shoo me away. It would have been easier yet, and totally understandable, for him to have for-

The AT&T boardroom on the twenty-sixth floor of 195 Broadway in Lower Manhattan, where the company was headquartered at the time of the breakup of the Bell System. The portrait of Theodore Vail, the company's first CEO, is visible on the wall overlooking the board table. Photo courtesy of AT&T.

gotten about me altogether. Instead, amid the intensity and high drama of that monumental meeting, Charlie carved out a small, unnoticed moment of time to jot a quick note, apologizing for the inconvenience this change of agenda had created. With the typical understatement that so defined his style—"*The discussion here now is exceptionally important*"—this gesture by the chairman and CEO of AT&T made an indelible statement about the importance of treating subordinates with the same grace and respect one showed the company's board members. And it underscored the profound and lasting significance that leading by example, even through the simplest of gestures, can have on employees caught in the midst of a changing environment. Charlie Brown was an extraordinary leader.

The Bell System was about to embark on a series of dramatic changes. Its leaders, and indeed its people in general, were dedicated and caring and quite good at what they had done for more than one hundred years. But as it charged headlong into the uncharted waters of a deregulated, competitive environment, many of its senior leaders, of that generation and the next, would prove ill prepared to lead AT&T through the unforeseen internal and external changes the company would confront in the years ahead.

That meeting marked the end of an era, in more ways than one. Many more meetings would ensue in the weeks and months and years that followed, spawning increasingly tired conversations about how best to steer the company through the wreckage wrought by the terms of divestiture. Trouble was, more and more frequently, as the senior leadership gathered to rehash the same old debates about the company's future, and as the level of stress continued to grow, fewer and fewer notes found their way to sleep-deprived employees—the ones waiting just outside. And a company whose success was once driven by the loyalty of its people began to pay a very dear price.

These lessons were certainly not lost on me.

Occam's Razor

There's a precept known to scientists as Occam's Razor[1] that posits the notion that all things being equal, the simplest explanation is most likely the correct explanation. In business, I have found the same holds true for the simplest questions or the simplest actions—they are often the most important and can yield the most

---

1. William of Occam (1284–1347) was an English philosopher and theologian. Occam emphasized the principle of Aristotle that *entities must not be multiplied beyond what is necessary*. This principle became known as Occam's Razor. This rule has been interpreted more broadly to mean that the simplest of two or more competing theories is preferable—that a problem should be stated in its basic and simplest terms.

---

significant results. On the morning of Monday, June 28, 1993, I walked into the executive conference room near the chairman's office at the Indianapolis headquarters of Eli Lilly and Company, unknowingly about to put this theory to the test.

As I entered the room that morning, all conversation came to an abrupt and collective halt, in the way it does when people who have been talking about you suddenly feel they've been caught in the act. It felt as if the steps carrying me toward the unfilled chair at the head of the table were being made in the shallow end of a swimming pool. In spite of the many welcoming smiles and nods, the unspoken tension in the room was thick. Many of the attendees were well known to me from my seven years on the company's board. But this was a whole new relationship for all of us.

A great deal had happened since these same faces had routinely gathered with their former leader in this very conference room earlier in the prior week. On Friday, June 25, Eli Lilly and Company sent a shock wave through Wall Street, to say nothing of its own rank and file, by announcing that company President and CEO Vaughn Bryson was resigning and that the Vice Chairman of AT&T, Randall Tobias, was leaving AT&T to become Lilly's new Chairman, President, and CEO. The move was being characterized in the press as a "boardroom coup." A few days later, I received a call from my longtime friend, former Vice President Dan Quayle, who had just returned from a trip to China. He wanted to tell me about running into a group of Indiana tourists who were also visiting China. When they asked him if he'd heard about "the coup," he at first assumed that something might have just happened in Thailand, which at the time was experiencing political turmoil. He was amazed to learn they were referring to events back home at one of the state's most stable and respected corporations.

When news of this change began to ripple through the company, employees gathered in hallways, in the campus courtyard in the heart of Lilly's downtown headquarters, and outside every entrance. To the uninitiated driving past Lilly's offices that afternoon as thick torrents of rain lent a somewhat ominous hue to the brick-paved approach out front, the goings-on probably seemed more akin to a 1960s protest rally than what one would expect to find at a global pharmaceutical company during regular business hours. There was a sea of lights and cameras from all of the local television stations, murmurs of bewildered and sometimes angry comments, and more than a few tears being shed. Speculation was soon running rampant that "this telephone guy" was being brought on board to lay off large numbers of employees, just as AT&T had done in its own change-induced downsizing efforts.

In the absence of information to the contrary, this theory seemed logical enough. Initially, the only statement being issued to the press was one that seemed to have been worded carefully to say nothing. To Lilly employees, however, the terse wording of the press release seemed to say *everything*. According to company Chairman Richard D. Wood, "Vaughn Bryson, the company's President and Chief Executive Officer, has announced his retirement due to differences with the board over management philosophy. . . ."

Vaughn Bryson had spent his entire professional career at Lilly. In recent years, as an executive vice president, he'd been working mostly outside the company's core pharmaceutical business, providing oversight to the Elizabeth Arden cosmetics company, the Elanco plant science and animal health businesses, and the medical device businesses. While the financial community had grown increasingly nervous in his twenty months at Lilly's helm, Bryson had been a popular leader among employees—and understandably so. Of his contributions to the company over that period, his attempts to overhaul the corporate culture are what he will be remembered for. During his brief tenure as CEO, he was instrumental in launching efforts intended to define and remove outdated bureaucratic processes and to encourage more open communication between management and employees.

Employees were interpreting the news that Bryson was stepping down because of his "management philosophy" to mean that the board didn't like the way its now-former CEO was trying to make Lilly a more open place to work. It was widely assumed that a renewed formality, a "command and control" approach at the hands of an AT&T hatchet man, along with cost-cutting in the form of layoffs, would soon be the order of the day.

But at that moment, it was not the company's culture that had the board's attention—it was the absence of a clearly articulated and compelling vision for the future of Lilly's businesses. It was the laundry list of uncertainties the company was now facing. Certainly there was no lack of change-driven activity on the part of the company's leadership. Indeed, there seemed to be a near obsession with throwing out the old simply for the sake of throwing out the old. But activity without a compelling vision, without a persuasive strategic focus, was not the answer. And perhaps most disconcerting to the board was the lack of a convincing plan to stem the slide in the company's stock price. There'd been virtually no communication between the CEO and Wall Street. These conditions would clearly require changing prescriptions. To the board's way of thinking, time was running out.

In the 117 years since its founding, Eli Lilly and Company had amassed an extraordinary record of achievement. Until early 1992, through a period encompassing the entire twenty-year tenure of the former CEO, Dick Wood, the company had demonstrated stellar financial performance, perhaps best characterized by an unbroken record of consecutive quarter-over-quarter earnings growth that was, in duration, second only to that of one other company among the Fortune 500. But over the course of the preceding year and a half, the company's market value had steadily declined, from $24 billion to $14 billion, prompting one newspaper headline-writer to ask, "Is the Gilt Off Lilly?"

With the massive scale of the proposed Clinton health-care

reform threatening to dramatically alter the entire nature of the pharmaceutical industry, and with evidence suggesting that unwelcome merger partners might be lurking just over the Hoosier horizon, the board had reason to be concerned about the long-term independence of the company. Had they known, employees and the entire Indianapolis community would have shared that concern, for the loss of an independent Lilly from the Indiana economy would have surely brought far-reaching consequences to nearly every aspect of the area's well-being.

Certainly the problems facing the company were largely not the creation of its current management. But the solutions would have to be. And after several months of focused effort and anguished debate, the board had reluctantly concluded that those solutions were not going to be forthcoming without a change in leadership.

But on the afternoon of June 25, 1993, as the driving rain began to puddle, any understanding of the board's long-pondered reasoning for replacing the CEO was drowned out by broad-based support for the recent cultural initiatives that employees were rallying around.

On Saturday, the day after the announcement, I received an unexpected call at my home in Bernardsville, New Jersey. It was to be the first of many that day.

When I officially accepted the job as Lilly's CEO twenty-four hours earlier, my naïve hope was that as serious as Lilly's issues were, I would have a few days to at least keep one foot in my former world to effect an orderly transition from my AT&T responsibilities. While I saw the new challenge as a unique and quite unexpected opportunity to make an important contribution to a company I had respected all of my life, and in so doing conclude my corporate career back home where it had started, I still had some unfinished business to complete before I could fully engage. I was in the middle of wrapping up a deal for AT&T that was generating its own share of media attention. In the weeks before

the Lilly announcement, AT&T had garnered worldwide head-
lines by announcing that it had reached an unprecedented agreement with the government of China. That agreement was intended
to begin a process whereby AT&T would provide significant equipment, technology, and know-how for beginning the task of totally
modernizing the telecommunications infrastructure of the People's
Republic of China. The potential value of the arrangement was
pegged at about $5 billion.

This deal was, arguably, as important for its symbolic cachet as
it was for the potential financial benefit it represented for the company. The agreement between AT&T and the highest levels of the
Chinese government was thought to signal the dawning of a new
era for the company in that megamarket. A major bastion of resistance to AT&T's brand of American capitalism had seemingly mel-
lowed, and a new frontier of international opportunity was now
open for business. My colleagues, Blaine Davis in the United States
and Mei Wei Chang in Beijing, along with my small but mighty
band of globalization zealots within AT&T, had done extraordinary work to bring the project to the point where we were able to
push it over the top. As Vice Chairman of AT&T, Chairman of
AT&T International, and the leader for this effort, I had become
the poster boy for this landmark deal. An image of China's Prime
Minister (now President) Jiang Zemin and me shaking hands was
splashed across papers around the globe, including the *New York
Times*. And in a follow-up story, the *Times* underscored the far-
reaching significance of this deal by pulling its "Quote of the Day"
from coverage of the agreement and its relationship to the annual
congressional debate on whether to renew most-favored-nation
trading status for China. "We have long known that the pen is
mightier than the sword. We must now understand that the fax
machine is mightier than the rifle," I was quoted as saying. This
entire project was something I cared about a great deal, and in
which I had invested an enormous amount of personal time and

China Premier (now President) Jiang Zemin and me shaking hands after a meeting in the Great Hall of the People in Beijing.

effort. Selfishly, in light of my imminent departure, it was also an important capstone to my twenty-nine-year AT&T career. Before departing, I wanted to be certain that my people around the world were taken care of and that the necessary steps had been taken to ensure continuity after my departure, so that project follow-up would be carried out with the same dedication that had brought us to this point.

When I picked up my phone in New Jersey that Saturday morning, it quickly became apparent that not only was I already fully involved as Lilly's new leader, but I was also about to address my first major crisis. I can't remember which call came first, but in rather quick succession I had substantive discussions with, among others, Lilly's head of research and the head of media relations. While the perspectives varied somewhat, the vast majority of the calls that morning were placed with more or less the same intention—to inform me about an incredibly negative turn of events regarding a drug that I knew literally nothing about.

As an outside director on Lilly's board since 1986, I was familiar with the company's lines of business, major initiatives, and core products, but when it came to the specific details concerning the compounds in clinical trials, I was the first to admit that I had a great deal to learn. That morning, I received a crash course. With each new call, I was learning in greater detail about a potential product called FIAU—an abbreviation for the chemical compound fialuridine. FIAU was a very promising drug, well along in clinical trials, and was believed to have enormous potential in the treatment of hepatitis B. The trials had been taking place in collaboration with the National Institutes of Health (NIH) and were showing every indication of success. The duration of the study was designed to be six months, in hopes of prolonging the temporary inhibition of the hepatitis B virus seen in a previous one-month study at NIH. In fact, subjects in the study were largely patients who had participated in that earlier trial. In all, fifteen subjects were enrolled in the trial, eleven of whom were previously exposed to FIAU.

Early Saturday morning, the principal investigator at the NIH notified Lilly that one of the patients needed to be hospitalized because of profound liver failure. Within hours, a joint decision to stop the trial was made by the NIH investigator and Lilly medical personnel. The other fourteen patients were contacted during the weekend and instructed to stop their medication and report to the NIH as soon as possible. By Monday morning, it would be evident that several other patients had early signs of liver toxicity and were in grave danger. Clearly, the company's new Chairman, President, and CEO, who had not yet carried those titles for a full day, needed to come to grips with the implications of these unexpected circumstances and address the issue in person.

Assuming, of course, that he would not first be run out of town by his disgruntled employees.

The transition I was about to take on was also a sobering reminder that success and praise in the corporate world often have a shelf life about as long as that of a gallon of milk. Wall Street, whose analysts in the prior weeks had been very generous in describing my role in AT&T's China achievement, now did not see the logic in selecting a lifelong telephone executive to lead a turnaround of the fortunes of a pharmaceutical company. "A strange choice," said one analyst, perhaps summarizing the opinions of most. And Lilly employees, when asked to comment on their new leader, were even less forthcoming. They cared very little about the highlights of my former jobs. What they cared about was the status of their own.

Much to my relief, on the following Monday morning, my first official day of work as a full-time Lilly employee, there was no angry mob waiting for me outside the building's entrance. Instead, my new assistant, Marsha Farley, was in the lobby to usher me to the office where, up until the preceding Friday, she had provided support for Vaughn Bryson. I took further solace in learning that my predecessor had in fact vacated the office over the weekend—a step that, under the circumstances surrounding his unusual reaction to the board's decision, was not a foregone conclusion. Almost immediately upon my arrival in the executive suite, I was informed that "the meeting" was about to get under way.

As I began the long walk from the doorway of the executive conference room to the one remaining empty seat at the head of the table—a distance I later calculated to be all of ten feet—all eyes from the two dozen or so in attendance moved in the tracking, collective stare found often at tennis matches and funerals. The mood in the room felt considerably more like that of the latter. As I established eye contact with those in the packed room, the first words out of my mouth struck me almost instantly as being charged with far more irony than I had intended: "Good morning. For those who don't know me, I'm Randy Tobias. . . ."

After brief introductions, which had seemed appropriate because there were a few unfamiliar faces in attendance—mostly physicians and research scientists who'd never had exposure to the board—I informed the group that I regretted having to meet under such doleful circumstances and that I was there principally to listen and observe. I asked them to proceed with the meeting as they would normally have done.

Rebecca Kendall, an admirer of Bryson's, was in attendance that morning as the lawyer directly responsible for the legal issues. I would later promote her to General Counsel, making her the first woman to reach the company's seniormost ranks, and we would become close friends. But not that morning. Years later, she shared the thoughts that were going through her mind at that moment: "The circumstances under which Randy became Chairman and CEO were pretty incredible and traumatic for this organization. There were many, many people who had strong feelings about it. I had worked for Vaughn when he was President of Elanco, and I was a strong supporter. I was not pleased to see him leave. So I was thinking to myself, 'We'll see what this guy is made of, because I bet none of his telephones ever killed anybody!'"

I'm confident hers was a shared sentiment.

The meeting got under way with the medical people outlining what was known and what was not. This was an extremely unusual circumstance for the company. In fact, of those in attendance who had worked for the company for their entire careers, no one could recall an incident of this magnitude ever occurring before in a clinical trial. Something like this just didn't happen.

From time to time when the discussion got bogged down with technical language, Dr. Mel Perleman, who was chairing the meeting, was very gracious about taking the time to help me understand the broad strokes of what was going on. (He was then the head of Research and Development at Lilly, a member of the board of directors, and perhaps the most outspoken proponent within the board for Vaughn Bryson's continued leadership.) In fact, under the circumstances, I felt that all were going out of their way to make me feel welcome—or at least not unwelcome. After the medical and scientific presentations, after the lawyers had their say and the public-relations people noted their concerns, and after Dr. Perleman summarized what had been decided and the assignments that had been made, all eyes, once again, found their way to the head of the table.

It was a great deal to digest. I was sure I didn't begin to understand all of the inner workings and all of the implications of what had gone wrong in this trial. But from experience, I knew I didn't necessarily have to have all the right answers. Rather, as the new leader, it was now incumbent on me to ask the right questions and to set the right tone. When I walked into the room that morning, there was one issue in particular that had leaped ahead of all others in my mind. And even in light of everything just described, it was still the issue I was focused on.

"I would like to thank everyone who presented this morning for all you're doing to deal professionally with this extremely serious matter," I began. "I trust you'll proceed to handle all of this just as you would have done before I arrived, and that's exactly what I want you to do. I'll want to talk further with some of you in order to better understand the issues, but for now, I would like to express just one point of view. . . ."

Was the "hatchet man's" bottom line–oriented management philosophy about to emerge? A hush came over the room.

"I want to be sure we are focused on doing the most we can for these patients and their families," I said. "Certainly I want to understand the potential legal and financial exposure that could result from this situation. But the patients are our top priority. I would like their well-being to be the driver of our decisions, first and foremost. We must center our actions around how we can best address the needs and interests of these patients. We need to make arrangements to fly their families to the NIH immediately, if that's what they want. We need to express our intention to pick up the bills for all expenses incurred as a result of their illness. We need to communicate, in short, our desire to help in any way we can. Not only because we have a responsibility to do those things, but more importantly, because it's the right thing to do."

Without consciously realizing it, I had delivered my first speech as Eli Lilly and Company's new leader. The theme was one I would continue to emphasize until I would eventually step down five and a half years later. Success in corporate America, especially in a changing environment, begins and ends with a company's commitment to treating all of the people it touches with respect. Success in corporate America begins with leading by example and doing what's right.

I'm sure I was not then fully aware that the palpable tension which had been hovering in the room for the past hour was suddenly and measurably eased. Indeed, I might not have completely understood until the time of my I retirement, when Dr. Jennifer Stotka, the gifted young physician who had been the principal presenter that first day, brought tears to my eyes with her own recollections of the import of my words at that meeting. She would later remind me that one of the most basic and frequently cited quotations in medicine is the Latin phrase *primum non nocere* ("first, do no harm"). The focused attention on the patients and their family members was something she had grown accustomed to seeing in hospital rooms. She just wasn't sure if the "telephone guy" would be thinking in quite the same way in this particular boardroom.

Over the years, everyone in that room had heard about or known about corporate executives trying to dodge potentially explosive situations such as this one by making sweeping suggestions about the company's values and then handing the matter over to others in the company to make the issue quietly disappear. That was not the way the people in this room wanted to practice their values. And neither did I.

I suspect it was not only what I *said* that morning that seemed to engender the trust of all involved but also what was left *unsaid*. In the simple gesture of doing what my experience had taught me was the only logical path, I was instinctively moving the company past the potential trapdoors—the easy ways out. And as my new colleagues witnessed my first stake being put in the ground, they saw boundaries being established based on values and proper priorities. They also saw I was not going to manage every detail from my office. It was clear that the rest of what needed to be done was being left to those with the competence to handle it well, within the boundaries I had established. The participants that morning recognized that the newly anointed chairman intended to treat them with respect and not only subscribed to the rhetoric of the company's holy trinity of long-standing values—people, integrity, excellence—but recognized the importance of truly walking the talk.

Of course, in a room full of scientists, I should have figured that the less-is-more approach would have the resonance it did—Occam's Razor and all.

I had survived my first hours on the job, pretty much unscathed.

In the weeks ahead, five of the fifteen patients involved in the trials would die of severe liver toxicity. Initially, we took our knocks from some politically oriented observers. A few voices began to demand congressional hearings. But the public, the financial markets, and the medical and scientific community seemed to understand that Lilly had been involved in very complicated trials; the company had acted professionally, responsibly, and compassionately; and every effort had been made to do what was right, including determining factually what had gone wrong.

Two years later, the Institute of Medicine of the National Academy of Sciences issued a 280-page report exonerating Lilly's actions completely by calling the deaths "uniquely and totally unpredictably unavoidable." The report also pointed out that there was a good deal of new science discovered as a result of this tragic experience.[2]

But none of that stopped us from making good on our promises to the patients involved. It was the right thing to do.

I have often wondered what the findings and perceptions might have been had we behaved differently that morning. Sooner or later, I believe the company would have paid a price. Lilly would have been viewed differently by Wall Street and by our shareholders. Employees would have come to view their company and its senior officers quite differently.

As I made my way back to my new office that morning, I searched among the just-arrived boxes stacked outside my door for the one marked "personal." Without much difficulty, I found what I was looking for and quickly went about hanging it on a recently vacated nail—on a wall not too far from view of my desk. It was a framed note . . . yellowing a bit around the edges.

---

2. Most importantly, our actions following the FIAU trials were embraced and applauded by the people who were most directly affected by them. In July 2001, one of the patients from that clinical trial spoke to the *Washington Post* on condition of anonymity. Known simply as "Patient #10," the FIAU trials participant told the *Post*: "I hold no grudges against anyone." The *Post* reporter went on to say: "To this day, Patient #10 has no regrets. Far from it, he says, for he would do it all again. He would sign the consent form and submit his body to a potentially dangerous treatment, knowing with chilling clarity what can happen—what did happen—when the unexpected risks of medical research overwhelm even the most important possible benefit itself."

TWO

The Ghost Ship

*From that moment forth they were forced
to roam the mighty seas for all eternity,
a ghost ship, without a destination.*
—from the legend of the *Flying Dutchman*

Good-bye to Ma Bell

The years immediately following the breakup of the Bell System were, for me, simultaneously very exciting and extremely painful. On the one hand, it was an opportunity for those of us in the leadership of the new AT&T to pick up the often incongruous pieces we'd been given of the fractured Bell System and try to cobble them together in some meaningful way. On the other hand, I don't think anyone, inside or outside the company, properly estimated the magnitude that challenge would pose to virtually every part of the business.

From my years at AT&T, I have many dear friends and countless treasured memories of extraordinary experiences. Nonetheless, this is a period in my life that I will largely remember for the constant uncertainty, confusion, and disagreement—from my arrival at AT&T headquarters in the spring of 1981 through my retirement as Vice Chairman of the company some twelve years later. And there was good reason.

The Ghost Ship

Being part of the new AT&T was somewhat like working for a large U.S. airport and being told by government authorities that you are monopolizing aviation in your area. To remedy the situation, you're being compelled to agree to a consent decree dividing the airport into two separate companies. You'd been part of the leadership of this very successful airport. You knew what you were doing and you had pride in your achievements. The people with whom you worked were almost like family. Now you would be part of a new and more limited company, consisting only of the taxiways, the runways, the control tower, and the air traffic control system. And you will no longer be able to work hand-in-hand with those of your former colleagues whose new company will operate only the airport terminal facilities, the parking lots, the ticket counters, the luggage handling, the boarding gates, and the rest of the passenger-related facilities. Under these circumstances, it will also not be obvious what business you are now in or which business model will bring you competitive advantage and strategic success. And under those circumstances, it will also not be obvious what place your long-standing philosophies, values, and traditions will have in the company, because, in essence, you no longer have a history.

"Physically, technically, and operationally, the telephone system was never meant to be structured the way it was after the breakup," says my longtime friend and colleague, former AT&T Vice Chairman Morry Tanenbaum.[1] "I remember walking into company buildings where part of the equipment now clearly belonged

---

1. Tanenbaum retired in 1991 as one of AT&T's most senior executives, Vice Chairman of the Board and Chief Financial Officer. But prior to becoming an executive, he had an equally distinguished career as a Bell Laboratories scientist. He pioneered the use of silicon as a commercial semiconductor material and was also a leader of the Bell Labs group that discovered the first practical materials for superconductor magnets. He is a member of the National Academy of Engineering.

to the long-distance business and part of the equipment clearly belonged to the local telephone company, and everything else was sort of tied together. We had to decide frame by frame who was going to get what and where we were going to draw the line. In most offices, we literally painted a big solid yellow line across the floor. On one side was the new AT&T and on the other side was the new Baby Bell."

In the absence of a new and clearly defined companywide vision, decisions at the new AT&T were quite often implemented on the basis of a set of assumptions for an industry that no longer existed. The rules of the game had changed, but for many of the company's senior leaders, a specific brand of corporate learning and telephone culture had seeped into their very souls. Asking them to think in new ways, to deny a lifetime of corporate heritage, was like asking them to change the color of their eyes.

Initially, there was a further complication. With the absolute best of intentions, Charlie Brown had decided to play two somewhat conflicting roles in the divestiture process. On the one hand, he was the designated Chairman and CEO of the new AT&T, responsible for its competitive success going forward. On the other hand, he was, and would remain until January 1, 1984, the Chairman and CEO of the old Bell System. His continuing responsibility for the well-being of every element of the enterprise was something he took very seriously, and he was determined that his old job would come first until the divestiture process was accomplished.

"Not many people outside the company know what a . . . mess—I think that's the best word I can use—AT&T was immediately after the breakup," says former Chairman and CEO Robert E. Allen, AT&T's eventual leader and my boss from 1986 to 1997. "What I mean is that the leadership of AT&T at the time of the breakup was so focused on being certain that the operating companies were going to be spun off healthy that . . . only a very small

The members of AT&T's senior executive body, called the Office of the Chairman, in the mid-1980s (left to right): Vice Chairman Chuck Marshall; General Counsel Howard Trienens; Chairman and CEO of AT&T Information Systems Bob Allen; Chairman and CEO Charlie Brown; Chairman and CEO of AT&T Communications, me; Vice Chairman Morry Tanenbaum; and President Jim Olson. Photo courtesy of AT&T.

part of our planning was focused on what the new AT&T would be in the post-divestiture environment."

Certainly the consequences of the divestiture seemed onerous to everyone involved at AT&T. But we had all been trained to believe that vertical integration was a powerful and necessary element in the success of the Bell System, which, up to that point, it might well have been. Through the lens of the only experience we brought to the table, the choice of the elements of the old company that would come together to form the new AT&T seemed a logical and workable combination—the Bell Laboratories, Western Electric, AT&T Long Lines, the long-distance components from the operating telephone companies, and the customer equipment businesses. My friend and former colleague John Zeglis, one of the lawyers most directly involved in the divestiture agreement and now the CEO of AT&T Wireless, recalls the driving factors foremost in the mind of AT&T's Chairman at the time the settlement agreement with the Justice Department was devised: "Two things drove the decision of Charlie [Brown] and the board to settle the case. One was very business oriented, and that was Charlie's view that what counted most was a technological integration, as he called it, from the Labs to the equipment to the manufacture of the equipment to the deployment in the network. And related to that was . . . [becoming convinced] that as long as any of our competitive businesses like long distance was tied to a monopoly business, we would never get out of the antitrust courts and we would never get out of our old consent decree which prohibited us from selling computers. Those two factors, Charlie believing in technological integration and [AT&T General Counsel] Howard [Trienens] believing you've got to take the competitive businesses and [separate them from the monopoly businesses] if you want to be free to enter the computer business—this is really what drove the board to agree to the breakup."

Initially, the leaders of the individual elements of the new AT&T were very focused on their own requirements. Bell Laboratories, the company's research and development organization, and Western Electric, the company's manufacturing arm, did not see themselves as internally impacted by the changes, even though their relationships with their principal customers—the telephone companies—were changing dramatically and ominously. On the other hand, the leaders of the newly created AT&T network organization had a major job to do. They had to make internal sense out of their new organization, merging into the existing Long Lines organization people and facilities from virtually every operating company in the old Bell System. At the same time, they had to quickly prepare, as part of a separate government decision, for what was to be the equivalent of a nationwide election. AT&T's long-distance customers would not automatically continue with the company without overtly selecting AT&T. In the view of the Federal Communications Commission (FCC), many of AT&T's customers had that relationship only through inertia—only because AT&T had once been the sole choice. Under the terms of a plan devised by the FCC and intended to level the playing field, every telephone customer in the country would be required to choose a long-distance carrier from among AT&T, MCI, Sprint, and dozens of others. In one of the more draconian provisions of the plan, those customers who made no choice at all (perhaps because they were perfectly happy with AT&T) would eventually be divided among AT&T and the other competing companies in direct proportion to the distribution of customers who did make a choice. John Smart, the senior officer in charge of getting customers to choose AT&T, remembers this time as chaotic: "We had to remarket our message to millions of existing customers to get them to affirmatively reselect AT&T, or [we would have risked] a devastating market-share loss. Most customers, unaware of the FCC's plan, thought we were nuts."

With the integrated Bell System's historic effort to make telephone service as widely available as possible, it had been essential to keep the price of basic local telephone service as low as possible. This was done by making enough profit on long-distance calls to enable the total business to be profitable, because the company's telephone equipment—telephones, private branch exchanges (PBXs), and the like—had never been priced to be profitable on their own. But standing alone, they had to be. So the management of that part of AT&T's business had a major, arguably impossible task ahead, with no clear path to success.

That's where I found myself at the time of divestiture—as Presi-

Speaking to a group of AT&T employees at a sales recognition event in the mid-1980s.

dent of one of those businesses, AT&T Consumer Products. I'd been in that role essentially since 1981, and officially since the beginning of 1983, when the FCC required the Bell System to set up a "fully separate subsidiary" to handle everything then known as customer premises equipment. Only problem was, I had been President of that business in name only. As with many organizations where economies of scale were thought to be important and where speed and flexibility were not seen as important competitive capabilities, the Bell System's overarching organizational architecture was highly "functional." That meant, quite simply, that organizations were focused internally on the performance of common activities rather than externally on the value-added chain of activities that ultimately delivered products and services to customers. The research and development people still reported to Bell Labs, for example, and the manufacturing and distribution people still reported to Western Electric. Culturally, we were a long way from breaking out of our devotion to functional organizations. Initially, only the sales and marketing people reported directly to me, but there was plenty to keep me busy there. The sales organization consisted mostly of high-cost retail stores in major malls, and there was much to be done there to develop a viable sales channel. It would be months before I could get the various managers who were driving major pieces of the consumer products business to sit down around the same table as a team to develop and own an integrated strategy. I didn't have time to pay much attention to the problems in other parts of the company, nor did anyone else. Across AT&T, even though the picture was not a pretty one, our focus was largely on fighting the business problems we faced and not each other. For the most part, we were still enjoying the challenge.

"In the very early years after divestiture, there was a collegial atmosphere, we were focused, and it was an exciting time," says Sam Willcoxon, former Executive Vice President of the company, and the man who taught me everything I know about AT&T's network and more. "But then as three, four, or more years went by, there [was] a lot more infighting and internal competitive pressures. . . . As a consequence, things began to change in a way that I think was deleterious. During that time frame, I saw firsthand conflicting versions of what [people thought] the strategic direction for AT&T should be."

It became apparent fairly quickly that the strategies of some parts of the new company were at odds with the needs of others. "In the years immediately following divestiture, I think most people felt that AT&T was by and large a good place to work," says Ed

Block, the company's Vice President[2] of Public Relations at the time of divestiture and one of the most skilled and thoughtful practitioners of that art I've ever had the privilege to know. "I think generally people felt good about their own individual organizations but were uneasy about the organization overall. Some of that uneasiness, I think, stemmed from the enormous size of the company and the difficulty the various units faced working together."[3]

The Vision Thing

As we tried to make strategic sense out of the new enterprise as a whole, many had growing difficulty getting any real traction on our chosen path. There were other options, to be sure, but none of the alternative choices seemed clearly compelling without a willingness to make some potentially painful tradeoffs. The terms of the deal had been devised in a way that would enable AT&T to maintain its technological integration and to enter the computer business. As that vision gradually became less compelling, there was almost no stomach at the top to revisit what at the outset had seemed a logical set of starting assumptions.

At the same time, I don't believe that the leadership as a whole was ever totally comfortable with the direction the company was heading, but it *was* the direction we were heading. For those who championed an alternative strategic path, there were always at least as many others who wanted to head down yet another path. Some

---

2. To better put this role in context with the roles of other AT&T officers who were interviewed for this book, the reader should know that after Ed Block's retirement, the AT&T executive title system changed. His former position became Executive Vice President.

3. Kathy Martine, now Vice President of AT&T Consumer Services, worked for me as an executive assistant while I was Vice Chairman of AT&T. She remembers watching the process by which decisions were forged and a consensus built. "I learned that sometimes the best way to get something done is not by hitting people over the head with a two-by-four. Sometimes you have to work behind the scenes and use a lot of diplomacy. I'm not very patient, and that was an extraordinary learning experience for me."

The members of the AT&T board of directors in late 1992, just prior to my departure to become Chairman and CEO of Eli Lilly and Company. I am seated in the right foreground, next to AT&T Chairman and CEO Bob Allen. Just behind Allen is Lou Gerstner, who at about the same time left the AT&T board and his post as CEO of RJR Nabisco to become Chairman and CEO of IBM. Photo courtesy of AT&T.

were blindly focused on the assumptions that had driven the divestiture decision. Some were motivated by a genuine conviction of what was best for the company. A few were driven by their own self-interest, regardless of how well that might match the company's needs. But above all, no chosen vision was ever articulated in a way that clearly and compellingly captured all minds and hearts. Therefore, the leadership was never able to act as one. In short, we were never completely committed either to a single vision of what business or businesses we were really in or to the relationship of those businesses to one another: Computers? Long-distance services? Telecommunications equipment? Integrated solutions?

Software-defined networks? Entertainment and information? In what combinations? With what implementation strategy? Toward what ends? Tragically, we had seen the dawning of the information age coming for years. Now that it was finally here, where was our place in it?

Who was to blame for all of this chaos? The answer, quite frustratingly, is *take your pick*. Steve Coll, now the Pulitzer Prize–winning managing editor of the *Washington Post*, attempted to answer that very question some years ago when he was a fledgling journalist at the *Wall Street Journal*. In his book *The Deal of the Century*,[4] he attributed the breakup of the Bell System to the following:

> Precious little in that history [*US vs. AT&T*]—the birth of MCI, the development of phone industry competition, the filing of the Justice lawsuit, [MCI CEO William] McGowan's deceptive entry into regular long-distance service, the prolonged inaction of Congress, the aborted compromise deals between Justice and AT&T, the Reagan administration's tortured passivity, the final inter-intra settlement itself—was the product of a single, coherent philosophy, or a genuine, reasoned consensus, or a farsighted public policy strategy. Rather, the crucial decisions made in the telecommunications industry during the 1970s and early 1980s were driven by opportunism, short-term politics, ego, desperation, miscalculation, happenstance, greed, conflicting ideologies and personalities, and finally, when Charlie Brown thought there was nothing left, a perceived necessity. The point is, if anyone had emerged triumphant from that embarrassing history in how *not* to make public policy, it would have been a phenomenal accident. And no one did.

Coll's conclusion, from my point of view, is mostly accurate. No one person or organization can be held solely accountable for the breakup of the Bell System. Just as no one person or organization can be held accountable for the difficulty that followed. But in looking, with the clarity of hindsight, at the leadership deci-

---

4. Steve Coll, *The Deal of the Century: The Breakup of AT&T* (New York: Atheneum, 1986).

sions following those events, there seems to be one area in particular for which the AT&T leadership should be held accountable—the failure to achieve a clear, coherent, and compelling vision for the future of the business.

In recent years, many journalists, analysts, and historians have reached similar conclusions. Reviewing the October 2000 decision of Mike Armstrong, then AT&T CEO, to break up the remainder of the once-powerful corporate giant into four companies—sixteen years after divestiture—*USA Today* columnist Kevin Maney noted the following:

> It is so tempting to nail the downfall of AT&T right on the head of leader C. Michael Armstrong. It's tempting because Armstrong has crowed so confidently about his "vision" for AT&T. Tempting because, like a handsome, cocksure quarterback in high school, Armstrong clearly believes his zillion-watt charisma allows him to do anything and get away with it. But it would be wrong. Blaming Armstrong, that is. . . . The tragedy of AT&T goes back to the breakup of the Bell System. It has only a little to do with changing technology, shifting regulation and dumb strategic moves, though none of those helped. It has only a little to do with Armstrong's frantic maneuvers and ping-ponging vision, though those certainly haven't helped either. At its core, the company's troubles have everything to do with people—and the consistent failure of AT&T's leadership to see that. . . . The split [divestiture] shattered AT&T's purpose. In a newly competitive industry, public service was out. What was in? What would AT&T stand for?

For many business-school students and would-be leaders, the words *vision* and *strategy* are confusing. They are often used interchangeably, but for me, they are more like cousins than identical twins. They are related, to be sure, but they are quite distinct. Creating a vision involves deciding where the organization must go, and then, with some passion, communicating (and communicating and communicating) a simple, straightforward, and understandable message describing that destination. It's like an infantry company commander saying, "We're going to take that hill over there on the right. Not the one straight ahead. Not the one on the left. The one there on the right." A strategy, on the other hand, is the plan that will be used to take that hill. Like a trail map, a strategy recognizes that there are many possible roads and many possible diversions on the way to a given destination and makes clear the one that's been chosen.

But unlike in the military, organizational acceptance of a vision and a strategy in the corporate world depends on the leader's ability to build a consensus, to gain buy-in, to articulate the vision with a passion that translates to credibility and believability. Most visions have many fathers. How the ideas are initially formed is not important. But in the end, people must be able to see and believe that their leader is the ultimate father, who truly owns the vision. Lou Gerstner did not craft IBM's turnaround vision and strategy on his own. But in the end, no one questioned whether he owned it down to the last detail. No one questioned that Jack Welch owned G.E.'s. No one questions that Bill Gates owns Microsoft's. I have yet to see a vision successfully implemented unless the leader is seen as having a thorough and passionate conviction and understanding of all the details and nuances of the vision he's chosen.

Fortune magazine summed it up well in an article in the October 1, 2001, issue entitled "Say Goodbye to AT&T":

> The conventional wisdom about AT&T's decline and fall is that the company couldn't bridge the gap from regulated market to free monopoly. Very few companies in history have been able to do so. But that truism is only part of the story. AT&T's tragic flaw has been its failure to find a raison d'être once it had fulfilled its original mission—to put a durable telephone in every house in the country and hook them all into a national network.

Invention or Innovation?

The creation of AT&T's original vision is an interesting story. It is usually the invention of a new product that draws the attention, and that was the case initially with the telephone. But this is really a story about innovation, involving much more than the invention of the telephone itself. Innovation is a central theme in the mythology of American culture. As schoolchildren, we learn to recite the names of the lone inventors—Edison, Pasteur, Tesla, Whitney—or the small teams—Crick and Watson, Hewlett and Packard, even Lennon and McCartney. As we grow up, we learn it's seldom so simple, that even in the stories of the great inventors, there are other people, supporting, assisting, contributing to the eventual success. *Ringo* is a household name for a reason. Even so, when we talk about innovation in the business world, we tend to associate it with the critical invention that begets a new product for the marketplace. But invention is just one part of the innovation process—a critical part, to be sure—but not always the most critical part. Several years ago, I came across a book called *Diffusion of Innovations*. Its author, Everett Rogers, makes this key distinction between invention and innovation. Invention, he says, is "the process by which a new product is discovered or created." In contrast, innovation occurs when "a new idea is adopted in the market."

Take, for example, the telephone, invented by a tinkerer and teacher of the deaf, Alexander Graham Bell, in 1876.[5] Bell's invention was, to state the obvious, the most significant technological development for AT&T in its early history, to say nothing of the invention's profound impact on the world. And while the telephone was certainly the impetus for the formation of the company that AT&T would become, it wasn't the only important innovation in the company's early history, and arguably, it wasn't even the most significant. That distinction, many have said, belongs not to the man who first built the telephone but to the man who first

5. Ironically, that was the same year that Colonel Eli Lilly founded his pharmaceutical company in Indianapolis.

built a business around it, Theodore Vail, AT&T's legendary early leader.

Vail, the company's first real CEO in the modern understanding of the term, built AT&T around a vision of "Universal Service"—to provide every household with a telephone connected to every other telephone in the country, through affordable, reliable, high-quality service. After all, the telephone was an extraordinary breakthrough in communications technology, but without anyone to communicate with, it would become little more than a novelty. True innovation, as I've described it, began with Vail's vision. But what causes innovation to continue? Or, just as important, in the case of AT&T, when (and why) did it end?

To understand how AT&T came to be the world's largest corporation and to understand the later seeds of its undoing, it is first necessary to understand the implications that the company's corporate vision (and eventual lack thereof) has had on its successes and failures.

The advent of AT&T's long-standing vision goes back to the late 1800s, soon after the company was founded. The company's Boston-based investors had hired Vail as chief executive. Soon, however, tensions developed. AT&T owned Alexander Graham Bell's patents, and investors had put up their money on the assumption that it was the technology itself that should be exploited. Vail had a very different vision. In the words of Ed Block, "[Vail's] concept was to invest in building a telephone *system*. In short, he saw the future of the business as the telephone call, not the telephone itself." To the company's investors, this innovative thinker was a bit too radical for their tastes. Vail was fired.

A few years later, the company was making no progress with its growth strategy while spending enormous sums just to defend its investment in the intellectual property rights to the Bell patents. Enter J.P. Morgan. The legendary financial guru put up the money to buy the company, brought Vail back as CEO, and financed his vision for the business. As a result of this change in direction, the company was now on the path that would eventually make it the world's largest corporation. The company's success began with a cogent, clearly defined, companywide strategic vision. Importantly, this vision became more than simply the dictates of the company's CEO—it became the shared raison d'être of the entire company. In his first tenure, Vail gave his company's investors an ultimatum—get behind my vision or get rid of me. So they got rid of him. When he returned a few years later, implicitly at least, the ultimatum was even clearer—sign on to my vision or I'm not coming back.

In my opinion, Vail was the prototype of the quintessential modern leader. He understood that making a vision stick—getting the band to follow the leader down the parade route, so to speak—consists of two very critical components. First, he understood that to be successful, any organization must have a clear and compelling vision—and that ultimately the responsibility for the creation and communication—the selling—of that vision falls to the organization's leader. Universal Service, as Vail defined it, was the path AT&T had chosen to pursue. If you disagreed, you either kept quiet about your objections and got quickly onboard or stepped aside. But Vail understood a second critical nuance as well. You cannot simply order people to believe. For an organizational vision to take hold, it has to be one that is compelling, or it will have no chance. It has to be a vision that the organization *truly* buys into.

Says Block, "Vail's vision was encapsulated in *One system. One policy. Universal Service.* From those six words, generations of operators to chief engineers to the R&D teams could find their places and their sense of fulfillment. We knew where we were going, we knew how we were going to get there, and we could deduce a credo that shaped a culture and defined the terms of our relationships with employees as well as customers. Yes, Vail conceived it and owned it, but he insinuated it into the DNA of the whole organization. As I have said many times, the old Ma Bell was one third business, one third family, and one third religion."

Years before Charlie Brown would make his own historic decision, Theodore Vail's AT&T had developed the resources to support the vision of Universal Service. As Block recounts the history, "Theodore Vail's strategy created an enormous, vertically integrated business. He had sought and welcomed government regulation because he knew the public would not otherwise tolerate a monopoly of the scope and scale he had in mind. His companies were dedicated to quality service at affordable rates. He delegated operating authority to local managers. His research and development organization invented the technologies he needed to grow the business. And grow it did, raising and deploying huge amounts of capital. Ma Bell became America's phone company. Competition was unthinkable. Good service, affordable prices, and government regulation all in one package was enough to keep consumers content—if not always completely satisfied."

Change in the Wind

In the late 1970s, about the time I was moving from Indiana Bell to Illinois Bell, the effort to begin preparing Bell System managers for change had already begun. AT&T senior leaders began a series of weeklong meetings at a conference center just outside Princeton, New Jersey, within helicopter distance of both the company's Manhattan headquarters and its campus in Basking Ridge, New Jersey. Each week, a group of the company's department heads and officers, from all units of the company, gathered there to listen to and discuss the challenges and opportunities that lay ahead. And each week, the company's senior leadership shuttled between Basking Ridge and Princeton to direct those discussions. It was an enormous commitment of resources. Only later would it be widely recognized as the beginning of the work to build a broad-based understanding of the issues the company was facing, and the beginning of the effort to build a consensus around the yet-to-be-determined decisions to resolve the dilemma the company faced.

"In 1977 I attended a corporate policy seminar with a group of AT&T senior leaders entitled 'The Shaping of Tomorrow,'" says AT&T's longtime Senior Executive Vice President for Human Resources, Hal Burlingame, who was then working in the company's Ohio Bell subsidiary. "We knew that a major change was coming; we just didn't know what we were headed for."

In February 1979, John deButts approached retirement age and announced he was stepping down as the company's leader. Insiders postulated that deButts had been so associated with the defense of the company's longtime vision of its role that it would have been impossible for the company to resolve its problems while he was still at the helm. Charlie Brown was named AT&T's Chairman and CEO. Immediately, he began signaling that his company was "ready, without preconceptions, to explore alternative futures."

Historians will likely continue to debate ad nauseam why the decision was finally made and why the terms were shaped as they were. In Brown's own words, "Our decision in January 1982 to accept the Justice Department's divestiture proposal did not reflect a change in philosophy, but a change in circumstances. Our decision to divest was, in reality, a decision to adapt our organization to the changed expectations of the American public. Or rather, I should say to the expectations of the public's representatives in various branches of government."[6]

Ironically, Charlie Brown understood how to strike the balance between making the hard choice himself and building sup-

---

6. From Harry M. Shooshan II, ed., *Disconnecting Bell: The Impact of the AT&T Divestiture* (Elmsford, N.Y.: Pergamon Press, 1984).

port so it would stick. It was his ability to ultimately take owner-ship of a decision, communicate it broadly throughout his organi-zation, and build consensus that led to the dismantling of the empire that his distant predecessor—Theodore Vail—had built a century earlier. "Charlie was a very strong leader," remembers Tan-enbaum. "He was a very, very good listener. He would come around and talk to people individually, and then he would go make up his mind. And when he made up his mind, that is where we marched. Breaking up the company was not an easy decision for him. He came from a telephone family; his mother was an operator in New Jersey. And so it was a difficult decision emotionally as well as intellectually. But when he made the decision, we all got on to it."

Two decades later, there is good reason to believe that might have been the last time the entire leadership of AT&T would march in lockstep toward a shared vision of the future.

"Following divestiture, there were many, many camps within AT&T about what direction the business should follow," says former AT&T Executive Vice President of Public Relations Marilyn Laurie. "And there were many options available to the company in the time there was to act. You could argue, as it turned out, that many of the choices that were made were certainly the right choices—they just maybe didn't always happen at the right times. And as a result, we really missed out on some opportunities. For instance, America Online should never have happened. We really dropped the ball on understanding just how important e-mail would be-come to our customers. But after divestiture, we still had the mind-set of a monopoly. We took the approach that there will always be more time to act because the customer will wait for us. The cul-ture of AT&T was inexorably bureaucratic. Dramatic change was just not in our genes. Powerful and dramatic leadership knows how to grab deep into an employee body and inspire large-scale change. But since divestiture, there have been so many strategic back-and-forths—potential partnerships with Time Warner and

American Express and others—you literally couldn't count them all."

"Whether you bought into the company's post-divestiture direction and the ability of the company leaders to carry it out depended on what side of the strategic vision one happened to be on," says Willcoxon. "If you happened to be with the group that believed our future was in computers, then it would be logical to assume that people who had grown up in the old Bell System and knew those kind of skills and capabilities were out of date. If, on the other hand, you came at it from the standpoint of a services organization going into software and software-defined services, and value-added services, then it was a natural growth and extension of the old culture's skills that could be developed in the new environment. I've often said that any one of a half dozen strategies might have worked if we had had the . . . perseverance to stick with any one."

The original vision of AT&T coming out of the breakup was one of trying to be integrated and monolithic. We were trying to be all things communications to all people communicating. For a time, we operated under what was known as the "Single Enterprise Strategy," meaning our success was thought to be predicated on all of the pieces of the company coming together in some fashion so as to make the whole greater than the sum of its individual parts—much as had been the case in the former Bell System. In reality, in the new environment, the opposite was true. In my view, the interdependence contemplated in our initial vision really meant what most interdependence of that type seems to lead to—the company was positioned to be only as strong as its weakest link. And indeed, some senior officers had the view that the strongest businesses should be required to share the pain of the weakest. It was difficult to see how that could make us more successful in the new competitive world.

Ironically, one of the factors that drove the terms of the 1982 consent decree, the desire of AT&T's leadership to enter the computer business, turned out to be the most elusive of all the post-divestiture objectives. There were some early efforts within Western Electric to leverage the capabilities that existed as a result of the company's massive investment in the design and development of central office switching machines. There were proposals on the table to acquire any number of computer hardware companies, each driven by an alternative view of what the company's vision for the computer business should be. There were efforts to form joint ventures, such as the major investment in Carlo Debenedetti's Italian computer company, Olivetti Corporation. Finally, there was the decision to acquire NCR, in what turned out to be an unexpectedly protracted and acrimonious transaction. But nothing worked.

There are probably as many theories about the reasons for the company's failed efforts to transform itself into a computer company as there are people who were involved. As for the NCR transaction, some would say it was a flawed idea from the start. Says Bob Allen, the CEO who drove the transaction,"[It failed] for two reasons, essentially. One was that the computer business per se and its potential relationship to the telecommunications business changed very dramatically, almost as we made the purchase. The other reason it didn't work was . . . a culture conflict. We made some leadership errors in choosing who was going to run the NCR business. So it was partly our fault and partly a change in technology."

The 1982 decisions regarding which parts of AT&T would be retained in the post-divestiture world were based on the best thinking of the company's leaders at that time. This thinking was based on the prevailing assumptions about the company's inherent capabilities and about the opportunities that would exist to leverage those capabilities. All of this was principally based on Charlie Brown's view that what counted most was a technological integration from research and development, through manufacturing, and on to deployment of that technology in the network. Over time, it became unmistakably clear that we hadn't really understood how the dynamics of our business would operate in competitive markets. As the haze over the new environment began to clear, it became evident that many of our best guesses about the future of our businesses were not working out in their implementation. For a long time, years, in fact, we were reluctant to even revisit the original assumptions—choices which had become almost sacrosanct. But in 1996, more than a decade after the breakup of the company, Bell Laboratories and AT&T's manufacturing assets were spun off into a stand-alone company that today is known to the world as Lucent Technologies. At the same time, AT&T spun off computer maker NCR.

In the early years of its young history, Lucent was a phenomenal success—tripling in market capitalization in less than four years of operating on its own. But the situation changed abruptly, and its outlook now, like that of many telecom industry players, remains uncertain at the time of this book's writing.

With those 1996 decisions, the company had made some choices. It would no longer be in the business of manufacturing and selling computers, nor in the business of designing, developing, manufacturing, and selling telecommunications hardware. It had abandoned the notion that what counted above all else was "technological integration," and it had abandoned the dream of entering the computer business. After all the years of identity crisis, it would appear the company was finally developing a clearer and more focused vision for its business, going forward. What was not clear was whether there would be time enough left for the company to survive and prosper as more than a shadow of its former self. Six years after the 1996 decisions, one of my former colleagues, still working at AT&T, agreed to review part of the manuscript for this book to help confirm the accuracy of certain of my recollections. After that review, I received this note: "What is so sad is that the same 12 years you describe (accurately) as 'filled with uncertainty, confusion, and disagreement' are the good old days when viewed from the perspective of someone who was here then and is still here today—me!"

Many would argue that these decisions should have been made long before. But the man with the responsibility during much of that period thinks not. "From a timing point of view, the spin-off of the Lucent equipment business was a judgment that I had to make," says Allen. "In retrospect, it turned out to be almost precisely the right time [to let it go], because we had come to a critical point where the retention of the business was going to create more difficulty than opportunity."

When it comes to the difficulties for AT&T in the years following divestiture, I'm not particularly interested in whose vision was right and whose was wrong. For the most part, people were doing the best they could in an extraordinarily challenging environment for which many were ill prepared. Nor is it my intention to try to divorce myself from the decisions that were made while I was there. As a member of the senior management team from 1981 until 1993, I accept full responsibility for the decisions that were made—and in some cases were not—including those I found myself joining with less than total enthusiasm. After all, when you're part of the team, if you can't sign on, then you need to sign out.

What's of most interest to me in reflecting on that period is sharing the major lesson I learned from all of this experience:

Without a shared vision that is compelling and truly embraced with passion, it's nearly impossible for any organization to be successful.

Ironically, thanks in large part to the difficult leadership lessons I learned through my AT&T experience, when I accepted the challenge of leading Eli Lilly and Company during another period of massive change, I had something important to offer from that experience. For starters, it had become crystal clear to me that when one is in the midst of enormous change and all of the ground rules are being thrown out the door, it's absolutely essential to ask—and to answer: *What businesses are we really in?*

THREE

The Opposite of Wine

*You can have brilliant ideas, but if you can't get
them across, your ideas won't get you anywhere.*
—Lee Iacocca

Contingency Plans

Of all the unexpected developments during the course of Monday, August 9, 2000, perhaps most surprising was the sense of composure on the face of my successor, Sidney Taurel, Eli Lilly and Company's Chief Executive Officer.

In 1999, a U.S. federal district court had issued a ruling upholding, until the year 2003, patent protection for Lilly's top-selling Prozac, the sixth-best-selling drug in the world. Earlier that afternoon, with an abrupt and unprecedented reversal, the U.S. Court of Appeals in Washington, D.C. overturned the 1999 lower-court decision. This appellate court ruling, if upheld, would mean that Lilly's blockbuster antidepressant would soon be open to competition from generic rivals for the first time ever, and more than two years earlier than most industry observers had anticipated. In essence, on that late-summer afternoon, Eli Lilly and Company was ordered to forfeit to its rivals a significant chunk of its $2.64 billion-a-year bottled-up cash cow.

Lilly Chairman and CEO Sidney Taurel being interviewed on August 9, 2000, on CNBC's Market Wrap by On-Air Stock Editor Joe Kernen just a few hours after the U.S. Court of Appeals effectively ended the company's Prozac patent protection. Video capture.

For many analysts and investors, the court's decision seemed to arrive from just this side of nowhere. A court reversal on patent rulings in the pharmaceutical industry is extremely rare, and even the most sedulous observers could not recall a case of this magnitude having occurred, well, ever. One stock analyst called it "the mother of all patent challenges" and went on to say, "I can't even think of anything" comparable in the drug business.

Just hours after news of the decision hit Wall Street, Lilly's stock price had lost nearly a third of its value, reversing a recent run-up in the value which had brought the price per share to an all-time high. Trading was so heavy that curbs were set in motion, momentarily freezing the stock's rapid descent like plane-crash footage on pause.

Within twenty minutes of the trading day's final bell, as broad-cast commentators began sifting through the carnage and making the inevitable, if obvious, speculation about how the company was going to need a good dose of its own patent-expiring medicine, there on CNBC's *Market Wrap* was none other than the company's leader himself, live via satellite from Lilly's Indianapolis headquarters.

Clad in a gray double-breasted suit and silver tie, Taurel seemed unfazed by the surprising news; it was almost as if he had antici-pated it. In short order, he systematically defused a series of rapid-fire queries from the show's on-air personalities, outlining the posi-tive outlook for a group of promising new drugs in Lilly's pipeline. But perhaps most impressive was the way Taurel candidly turned a dire public-relations nightmare into a platform to delineate the ways Lilly planned to weather the storm. He offered updated earn-ings projections for the next three years; he detailed the company's commitment to innovation; he rattled off the names of eight new drugs in phase III clinical trials. In short, he provided evidence that while the loss of patent protection for Prozac was a short-term setback for the company, it was clearly not the end of the world, and more specifically, not the end of Lilly's success.

On-Air Stock Editor Joe Kernen seemed taken aback by Taurel's obvious preparation for the unlikely news. "How come you were so ready for this?" he asked. "Was it clear to you that this decision was going to be handed down today and going to go against you?

Answered Taurel, "No, not at all. This is called contingency planning. We are ready with strategies and communication plans for the various scenarios, and while this was one of the worst we could expect, we are ready for it."

What thousands of cable viewers probably didn't realize that afternoon was that for several months prior to the announcement of the unlikely court decision, Lilly had been working on a variety of planning assumptions, each including an appropriate commu-nication plan, to address all manner of outcomes for the patent appeal. Says Taurel, "We were extremely prepared with contingency plans, thanks to the 'year X' team we had formed in 1997.[1] That planning involved looking at a variety of different scenarios, including the bad one that came to be on August 9, 2000."

The company's leaders and their legal advisors had pegged the likelihood of a court reversal at something like 10 percent at most. Nonetheless, three different press releases covering at least three different outcomes of the decision were written and approved several weeks prior. Plans for a conference call with media and analysts were set. Statistics were ready. A voice-mail announcement from Taurel to employees was recorded. A worldwide internal television transmission to employees was prepared. The communications department even conducted drills in advance of the announcement, outlining the company's updated growth projections and detailing its robust pipeline. Says Ed West, Lilly's Director of Media Relations, "In recent years at Lilly, we had begun to take the approach of not leaving much to chance when it comes to communications. When the decision from the courts came down, we were ready to move on a dime." In fact, that court decision did not "come down"; rather, it was "put up" on the court's web site, says West. "We found out about the news that was going to cause our business to lose something like thirty-eight billion dollars in market capitalization in one day at the exact same time that the world found out," says West. "People wanted answers, and thanks to a good deal of planning and preparation, we were in a position to provide them."

After Taurel's television appearance that afternoon, even the most jaded observer could not help but feel that perhaps reports

---

1. Soon after it was launched, the focus of this planning effort became known as the "year X" project. The planning team was charged with developing contingencies for all possible outcomes. But the exact year in which intellectual property protection for Prozac would expire would not be clear until the ultimate resolution of the legal questions surrounding the Prozac patents—thus, year X.

of the demise of the pharmaceutical giant were slightly exaggerated. And the following morning, many Wall Street analysts reiterated their opinion that the long-term prospects for ownership of Lilly stock continued to look positive. "I think there is a correlation between the messages we got out immediately and the recovery that we saw in the days and weeks that followed," says Taurel. "Just as importantly, I think our communications efforts gave a basic notion of openness, professionalism, preparation, and competence of management that created a lot of goodwill with the financial community. If you talk to security analysts today, I believe that most would tell you that Lilly is the very best company in dealing with them in an open, transparent fashion."

Watching these historic events unfold from my own office on Indianapolis's north side, several miles from the Lilly Corporate Center, I felt a sense of pride in what Sidney and his team had accomplished, not unlike the feelings of job-induced joy I experienced from time to time during my own tenure as Lilly's CEO. But this time, those feelings were more like those of a proud parent, for in the current CEO's careful and precise actions, I saw the demonstration of his superb leadership, taking charge of a situation and leading by example, being prepared for the unexpected, building consensus with the management team, and moving quickly to articulate the decision. But underneath it all, I saw in Sidney's "televisual" aplomb the masterful execution of an approach that had been at the top of my own change agenda, the need to communicate deliberately and openly with all of the people the company touches.

During my time at AT&T, I learned from Ed Block, Hal Burlingame, Marilyn Laurie, and others that not all audiences hear a particular message in the same way. So, through experience, I learned to be very sensitive in trying to understand and anticipate what would be *heard,* not just what was being *said.* Before making significant announcements impacting employees at AT&T, I fell into the habit of letting at least a small sample of people I trusted at various levels in the business have an opportunity to react to the words, to feed back their interpretation to determine whether it was communicating exactly what we wanted to communicate. It was more than just saying X is going to do Y and Z is going to do A—it was how it was said or what was not said that people focused on. I learned that messages must be timely and must communicate as much as they possibly can to produce the most desired results.

Leaving an *information void* is always a terrible mistake. It has been my experience that whenever the media or employees or analysts or others have to fill such a void, they are most likely to fill it with the worst-case scenario. Years ago, I read the book *An American Life: One Man's Road to Watergate* by former Nixon presidential assistant Jeb Stuart Magruder. The author was one of the "Watergate 8" sentenced to jail for a brief time for his role in attempting to cover up the scandal. When summarizing the lessons he had taken away from the Watergate experience, the author used a line I have quoted many times over the years, for I believe it to be pretty effective shorthand for my take on organizational communications. What had Magruder learned about the scandal after endless hours of jailhouse reflection? "Bad news does not improve with age."

Magruder was simply reiterating what Washington pundits have long known—that political leaders don't get into as much trouble for their problems as they do for trying to cover them up. The same holds true in the rest of the world. More recently, we saw that play out in the handling of the Enron situation by Arthur Andersen. Now, it goes without saying that organizations that are run on shaky ethics and questionable practices are destined to find themselves in hot water. There is no way they can "communicate" themselves out of trouble. It just doesn't work that way. But what many leaders fail to realize is that without proper attention to the management of communications, foibles, day-to-day snafus, or unanticipated bumps in the road can also grow into the stuff of which my-side-of-the-story memoirs are written. Corporate communication is very much about filling information voids.

Eli Lilly and Company speechwriter Terry Busch knows a thing or two about the power of persuasive words. Busch holds a doctorate in rhetoric from the University of California, Berkeley. He says it's not necessarily the words themselves that cause a message to take hold with an audience. Rather, it's how those words are managed by the individual communicating them. "I believe that the hardest part and the most important part of communicating is the way a message is structured," says Busch. "And structure is the way you arrange the thoughts to best achieve a desired effect. It's figuring out what your intentions are and what you want the audience to do when you are done. When the talking stops, what's the end effect? The structure and design part of business communications is the least studied and the least attended to, yet in my view it is hands down the most important aspect. Many business communicators deserve the title of wordsmith because they actually come at communicating their messages from the level of building single statements into a sort of mesh that may be great on paper—but doesn't necessarily persuade and move and change attitudes."

For some corporate managers, *communications* is defined as a set of writing and speaking functions—a collection of specialized events. As I define it, *communications* is that—but much more. It is the sum of all the activities that demonstrate, through words and actions, what a leader—indeed, what a *business*—really is about. If it's an airline, for example, then it's the media releases, the employee publications, and the advertising. But it's also the quality of the experience in dealing with the ticketing process, the way baggage is handled at check-in and arrival, the size of your seat on the plane, and the attitudes of the flight crew. For a business like Singapore Airlines, with its unprecedented attention to these areas and others, communicating doesn't mean talking as they would like to walk. It means both talking the walk *and* walking the talk. It's the old saying that "your actions speak so loudly, I can't hear what you are saying."

Even before I took over as CEO at Lilly in late June 1993, Wall Street was clamoring for information. The analysts who followed the company, as well as the investment professionals who managed funds and portfolios invested in Lilly stock, had received little or no direct input from the senior leadership of the business in a long time. They were concerned about the company's prospects, and they were receiving little information. Rumors were swirling that the dividend might even be cut. The arrival of a new and unknown CEO simply exacerbated their appetite for information. One of my first decisions was to fill that void.

With the strong encouragement—in fact, urging—of Jim Cornelius, then Chief Financial Officer, we promptly announced a meeting in New York with the investment community. On July 20, I stood before some three hundred Wall Street professionals to say, "This is the first of what I expect will be frequent and regular meetings between this management team and the investment community. This is my sixteenth day on the job at Lilly—and so today I obviously don't intend to lay out a set of thoroughly considered answers to all the issues we face. But I *do* plan to focus on the questions before us. Arranging this meeting was one of my first decisions after accepting this job. I thought it was imperative to establish a baseline from which we'll *all* be better able to measure the progress at Lilly in the months and years ahead."

I then laid out the major issues as I saw them and provided some direction regarding my initial thinking about what must be accomplished in the days and weeks ahead. My remarks were followed by presentations from Sidney Taurel, then the head of the pharmaceutical division; Gus Watanabe, then responsible for the company's discovery research activities; and Richard DiMarchi, Steven Paul, and John Termine, three of the senior leaders in Gus's organization, each responsible for major products in the pipeline. At the end of these presentations, I provided some concluding thoughts, then introduced Ron Dollens, the head of the medical devices division; Jim Cornelius, the CFO; and Bob Graper, the head of investor relations, who joined the rest to answer questions from the audience. It would be a long road, but we had begun the process of building bridges to this very important group of stakeholders. And we'd bought some time.

The real message was not just in the words that were delivered. It was far more. It was the fact that I was there at all, that I was there on my sixteenth day on the job, that I was committing to regular meetings with the investment community, and that I was exhibiting a first-class team, largely unknown to the audience. Clearly, I was in charge, and change was in store at Eli Lilly and Company. But equally clearly, I was not a one-man band.

The real challenge for many leaders is not only communicating per se; it's also integrating what they speak and write with the way they behave. It's shared behavior that is single-mindedly focused on customers and their needs, as well as on the needs of each of the other stakeholders of the corporation.[2] In my view, the activities of organizational communicators are simply the means to other ends and not ends unto themselves. For me, *communications* must be defined as including all forms of a corporation's behaviors toward all of its stakeholders. When it comes down to it, corporate communications is just another form of cross-functional

---

2. Brice Dunshee, currently the Director of Eli Lilly's Elanco cattle business unit, worked for me as an executive assistant. He has an additional observation about communicating: "What business school teaches you to do is to create a logical argument out of the facts that you have, and defend it. But what I learned from Randy is the next step. You have to be able to communicate your argument in a way that is credible, defendable, and persuasive, regardless of the size of your audience. It may only be one person. I learned at Harvard that you have to have the facts and structure for that argument. But I learned from Randy that you also have to be a good storyteller."

teamwork. It's silo-busting—doing away with fiefdoms, doing away with turf. Put another way, communicating effectively is another way for an organization and its leaders to do the right things right. Communicating effectively is another way to lead by example. If *bad* news does not improve with age, then a *lack* of news, to those who need news most, is flat out the opposite of wine.

From *No* to Knowing Comments

Sometime in the early 1980s, a meeting between Indianapolis journalists and the communications department of Eli Lilly and Company was convened at the company's McCarty Street headquarters. The specific date of this event has been rusted away by time in the minds of many who attended, if indeed it can be remembered at all. Which is to say not much of note was said to impart a lasting impression to the press that day. In fact, not much of *anything* was said. The very reason the meeting was called was that Eli Lilly and Company, thanks to repeated badgering from the local media, was about to articulate its new corporate communications policy.

A young reporter named Clyde Lee, then the on-air health-beat correspondent for the Indianapolis-based ABC affiliate, WRTV, was there that afternoon. Lee recalls that long before the days of PowerPoint presentations and cyber-enhanced graphics, Lilly officials had organized an elaborate slide-show presentation to illustrate its well-considered communications policy. Recalls Lee, "Basically, the message they were communicating was this: If you had a question about Lilly, you were to submit that question to the corporate communications department in writing. Then that question, or series of questions, would be submitted to the proper department heads. Those department heads would then formulate an answer, we were told, and would get back to us in due course. However, we were informed that it was highly unlikely we would receive an answer on the same day." Additional caveats soon followed. Lee and the other dozen or so reporters were told that the company would not comment on Eli Lilly stock and its performance. "Mum was also going to be the word for Lilly products, Lilly employees, and, for that matter, a number of other matters."

Says Lee, "After listening to some minutes of this, I raised my hand and said, 'Basically what you are telling us is, don't call you.'"

"Interpret it any way you like," went the response.

For Lee, interpreting the new corporate communications policy was easy, as it bore more than a passing resemblance to the words he had grown accustomed to hearing from company officials in his repeated attempts to verify facts for broadcast. "No comment" was, and appeared to remain, the company's overriding communications sentiment.

Ed West, Lilly's head of corporate communications since 1985, recalls Lilly's tight-lipped ways when he first assumed the role. "When I took over this job, the *Indianapolis Star* and the *Indianapolis Business Journal* would run stories about us but wouldn't call me for a quote or even to confirm a fact. So I called the editor at the *Star* and asked, 'Why would you do that?' He said, 'Ed, why would we call? You guys won't even confirm how many *L*'s there are in *Lilly*.'"

Many of Lilly's cultural initiatives and policies can be traced back, in one way or another, to the philosophies of its founder and his family. The way they comported themselves, their beliefs, and their ideals were and are reflected in the company's culture, values, and traditions. The company's first four leaders—"Colonel Eli," his son J.K., and J.K.'s two sons, J.K. Jr. and "Mr. Eli"—all believed it was unseemly for the company and its leaders to brag about Lilly's achievements. The company's slogan "Let the Red Lilly Speak for Itself" was at least to some degree a reflection of that philosophy. The Lillys and their successors believed that the company's results could and should largely speak for themselves.

And for years, indeed, the results of Eli Lilly and Company spoke volumes. The family was open with the media when discussing business matters, and equally adamant about not discussing personal or family matters. But "Mr. Eli" in particular was well known for his frequent conversations with employees at all levels throughout the company.

In more recent times, the company management had been irritated on a number of occasions by what it believed had been unfair and inaccurate media coverage. To correct the situation, management had reduced media access to information about Lilly and its activities. That approach had once made little real difference. But as times changed and the communications policies did not, the company was really punishing no one but itself. As new technologies began to appear in the 1980s and early 1990s and a media-saturated engine of print, broadcast, and cyber-channels required constant fuel, the words *no comment* were becoming tantamount to *no interest*, or maybe even *no future*. The fact was that by the early 1990s, lacking an effective communications capability in corporate America had a very real impact on a company's financial success.

Clearly, information was needed. At the time of my arrival, terms like *coup*, *layoffs*, *merger*, *hatchet man*, *uncertainty*, *downsizing*, and—arguably the most unsettling of all—*no comment* were being written in the local and national press and spoken on the airwaves of Indianapolis newscasts. And this was just day 1.

My initial meeting with the company's senior leadership concerning the FIAU crisis had served as a strong foundation on which to begin a new policy of open and honest dialogue. But there were more than 30,000 employees, to say nothing of the thousands of shareholders, analysts, local citizens, journalists, and others who also wanted to know just what the heck was going on behind the closed doors of the twelfth-floor executive conference room. So we began to look outside the box for ways to reach them all.

Because Lilly is Indianapolis's largest corporation and one of four area Fortune 500 companies,[3] it has often been said that whenever Lilly sneezes, the entire state of Indiana catches a cold. In June 1993, the Hoosier state was suffering from a bad bout of a Lilly-induced fever. People wanted answers. And in the early hours of my tenure, in the absence of quality information, the press was making do with what it could get. There was a certain desperation evident in what it was willing to consider newsworthy. Take, for example, this snippet from a story that ran in a major Indianapolis publication the weekend before my first full day on the job:

> Tobias could not be reached for comment on this story, but sources say he is neither a tennis player nor a golfer. He likes to watch college basketball. "He is probably a 'basketball freak," says his older brother Roger Tobias.

While the local press was making due with the morsels of information it could squeeze out of its sources, ironically, I was hard at work putting together a plan on how best to get information to the media and others as quickly as possible. Consistent with the new communications philosophy I was trying to espouse during my first meeting with my new leadership team—filling information voids before others did the job for us—I quickly decided that my *second* major responsibility as CEO (the FIAU crisis being the first) was to begin closing those gaps by providing information. So we called the company's old friend, Clyde Lee, by then a nightly news anchor at the ABC affiliate and one of Indy's most recognizable faces.

When Ed West asked if Lee would be interested in having an exclusive, cameras-rolling chat with me about Lilly's future, Lee says he "just about fell out of" his chair. This was the same reporter who, more than a decade earlier, had been told rather bluntly not

---

3. The four are Eli Lilly and Company, Anthem, Inc., Conseco, and Cummins Inc.

My interview in a company cafeteria by anchor Clyde Lee on Indianapolis television station WRTV a few days after I became Chairman and CEO of Eli Lilly and Company. Video capture.

to bother calling Lilly for information. "I was surprised when I got that call, to say the least," says Lee. "So much of what you expect to happen in the news business is based on what has happened in the past. I was skeptical. I was thinking I was going to go sit in a boardroom or in the CEO's office and do a quick little interview where most of the questions I wanted to ask would be off limits. I was pleasantly surprised when that turned out to be not the case."

In fact, quite creatively and with my complete endorsement, Ed arranged for the interview to be held in one of the Lilly cafeterias . . . during the lunch hour. "We set it up like *Oprah*," recalls West, a setting that provided a far more informal atmosphere for the occasion than Lilly employees were used to seeing. I was so new to the company that I'm certain few of the hundred or so people at tables around me had any clue what their new CEO looked like. Were it not for the lights, monitors, and cameras and the presence of a trusted nightly news anchor, I might well have remained somewhat anonymous a little longer. But remaining anonymous was not my intention.

Organizational communication is much like a blank sheet of paper. The longer people have to wait to get information, the more they begin to add words and pictures of their own creation to that sheet. When that happens, communicators have the doubly difficult task of first trying to remove what's already been put on that paper before they can communicate their own version of the story. As the camera began taping and Lee asked his first question, I was well aware that a paragraph or two had already been written on my sheet of paper by some of the employees who now surrounded us. It was my job to keep them from adding any more on their own.

It has always been somewhat amusing to me to watch how, over time, certain actions, behaviors, and objects in corporate cultures become imbued with a symbolic significance in ways that in other company cultures would seem utterly bizarre. When I arrived at Lilly, suit coats were such icons. They were seen as a kind of symbol for leadership inaccessibility. The officers working on the executive floor were assumed to never take theirs off. That's the way they were seen by employees, and that's the way it was assumed they worked. This formality was merely a reflection of Lilly's long-standing corporate culture, which was seen by many employees in the context of the corporate norms of the 1990s as quite, well, . . . stuffy. Vaughn Bryson had begun to change that. He was often seen without a suit coat, and employees had interpreted this as more than a sign that they, too, could do the same. They had interpreted it as a clear signal that the culture was beginning to change in dramatic ways. Only I didn't yet know any of that.

When I sat down for the interview with Lee, the first thing I did was remove my jacket, and as I did, there were glances and smiles among the employees who surrounded us. Because I was an outsider to the company, the significance of this was lost on me, until it was explained. But from that day forward, whenever I was eating lunch in the cafeteria, which I liked to do often, I left my suit coat hanging on a chair in my office. The lesson? Again, communication is much more than simply a collection of words. It's the sum total of how attitudes and behaviors are articulated. Even the fact that I ate lunch in the cafeteria as often as I could turned out to be a major component to my initial communications plan. "The word spreads," says Ed West. "That was the case with Randy's cafeteria visits. [Not only would] employees see him there in his shirtsleeves, often sitting with other employees who just happened to be having lunch at the same time, [but] the visits created a kind of buzz throughout the corporation. It seems sort of silly today that these cafeteria visits created so much goodwill with employees, as executives are now frequently found out and about talking to our people. But back then, that just wasn't the case."

In watching the tape of my interview with Lee that day, as I did recently, it's clear that most of what I said was pretty straightforward CEO boilerplate. ("What I do see is a need for continuing change. We must not fear failure. I'd rather work with people who are willing to try one hundred things and ninety of them are very good than to work with people who only try three things and all three of them are successful.") But it's not necessarily the actual words I chose to respond to Lee's questions that had the greatest impact—it was just as much the fact that I was communicating, whatever I was saying. In this particular case, when all the talking stopped, the most immediate effect far exceeded my expectations—there was a standing ovation. I would like to think my words were so profound and thought-provoking and employees were so overcome with emotion that they could simply not contain themselves—that they just had to applaud their new leader. But I know

One of my numerous trips in the United States and around the world to communicate with Lilly employees, customers, government officials, and shareholders. This visit was with the Lilly sales force in Ho Chi Minh City, Vietnam, in 1996.

better. It was apparent their applause wasn't really directed at me. As West recalls, "At the conclusion of the interview, Lee asked the employees if there were any questions they wanted to ask, and that was initially met with silence. Until a longtime employee stepped forward and offered the following: "I knew Mr. [Eli] Lilly. I worked here when Mr. Lilly was in the company and watched him as he would make his way around to talk to employees. I want to say that the things I just heard are exactly the things I think Mr. Lilly would have said. Welcome aboard, Randy."

I was visibly moved.

These Lilly employees were buying into a belief that from that point forward, when it came to addressing the concerns of our employees and other stakeholders by providing needed information, even if that meant providing information that some weren't going to be so crazy about hearing, they could count on getting the full story, at least to the best of my ability. And they could count on hearing it quickly.

Effective communication is more than simply delivering a collection of well-considered statements—it's also *where* and *how* and above all, *when* these words are delivered that truly cause messages to take hold and behaviors to change. It's all about meeting expectations. It's also what makes these well-considered statements credible.

I uttered the following, in response to Lee's last question: "If I had to find one thing that characterizes my management style, [I'd say] it is the recognition that we are, in this company more than others, a people business. We own a lot of physical assets—this building, the factories, and the laboratories. But the most important assets we have are the people in this business because they are the people who discover it, make it, sell it, and everything in between. And if we don't nurture that asset, then we will not be competitive. I think that the people I've already met here know that I want to be a very open and accessible leader." It was clear from the reaction that no one disagreed.

Unimaginable Grief

On May 16, 1994, Marilyn Tobias, my wife of twenty-eight years and the mother of my two children, took her own life.

I had been Chairman and CEO of Eli Lilly and Company for almost eleven months when Marilyn died. About eight months prior, after several years of discomfort and uncertainty and numerous visits to various physicians, we had finally learned what was wrong: She was suffering from clinical depression.[4] Had I not agreed to join Lilly when I did, I am convinced that this diagnosis might never have been made. Tragically, it was made too late.

Lilly was, and is, home to one of the world's most significant assemblages of expertise on diseases of the brain, starting with Dr. Steven Paul, former head of the National Institute of Mental Health at the NIH and now head of neuroscience research at the company. Were it not for my Lilly relationships, I'm afraid we would not have received the help we needed. That help eventually led us down the right path through America's horribly disconnected and overly complicated health-care system, which is particularly so when it comes to the treatment of mental health. At the time, Marilyn and I both knew from her nagging symptoms that something was terribly wrong. Clinical depression, however, was not on our radar screen. Prior to our moving to Indianapolis from New Jersey, her illness had been variously diagnosed by some fine primary-care physicians and specialists in other fields as possibly Lyme disease, chronic fatigue syndrome, sleep disorders that were suggested to have various causes, reactions to unknown environmental causes in our home, a liver disorder of unknown origin, and possibly even lupus.

4. Nearly everyone has occasional feelings of sadness or gloominess. That's perfectly normal. Clinical depression, however, is more than a period of sadness. Clinical depression occurs when these feelings endure for long periods of time, from several weeks to several years. It is a serious medical illness that affects the body as well as moods and thoughts. And it requires treatment, just like diabetes, asthma, or heart disease. Depression can be caused by an imbalance of certain chemicals in the brain that allow brain cells to communicate with one another. It can also be triggered by stress or other factors. Certain personality traits and genetic factors can also contribute to depression. If someone has had at least five of the following symptoms for most of the day, nearly every day for more than two weeks, depression may be present and treatment should be sought: feelings of sadness, depressed mood, and/or irritability; loss of interest or pleasure in activities, such as hobbies or spending time with family/friends; changes in weight or appetite; changes in sleeping pattern—sleeping too much or not at all; feelings of guilt, hopelessness, or worthlessness; inability to concentrate, remember things, or make decisions; constant fatigue or loss of energy; restlessness or decreased activity; or recurrent thoughts of suicide or death.

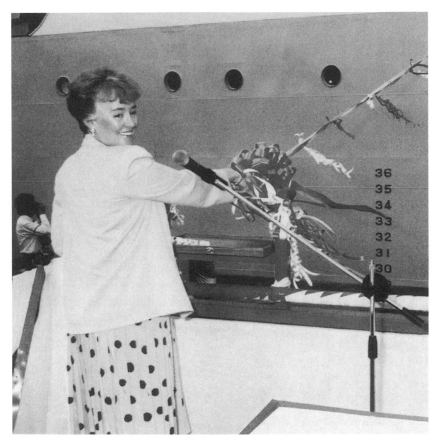

Marilyn Tobias preparing to christen the AT&T cable ship CS Global Link *in the Fells Ship Yard in Singapore, where the ship was built.*

We simply did not know enough to be able connect the dots in a way that disclosed the true cause of Marilyn's illness. Nor did we know that unless, on our own initiative, we went through the door to this nation's health-care system marked MENTAL HEALTH, it was not likely that we would be led there by physicians outside the field of mental health. In most other specialties, it would seem, many physicians are simply not sufficiently focused on mental illness as a possibility when they are seeking the causes of complex symptoms.

As the true cause of Marilyn's discomfort was identified and our knowledge increased, the perceived stigma associated with mental illness took hold. Marilyn joined the ranks of the many patients who know they are depressed and are desperately trying to disguise the pain of their disease so that those around them will not even know they are sick, let alone know they are mentally ill. Removing the stigma of mental illness from the culture of our society needs to become a much higher priority of our health-care system. If you are suffering from the flu and you ache all over and feel awful, you can tell the world that you're going to stay in bed, and everyone understands. Imagine feeling ten times worse, as those who are suffering from depression clearly must, but feeling compelled to go on with your life, trying to convince the world that you're feeling just fine. It's an additional burden that is so unfair.

Once the diagnosis was made, Marilyn made me promise that I would not tell Paige and Todd what was wrong. For a time, I did my best to keep that promise. But as her condition worsened and the periods of despair became more frequent and more debilitating, I felt I had no choice. While we were all together at our vacation home in Florida during the 1993 Christmas holidays, I took them aside, and with a feeling of guilt at betraying the pledge of silence I had made to Marilyn, I explained what their mother was enduring. I suspect part of the source of my guilt was that I knew I needed their support myself.

While neither Paige nor Todd knew much about depression at that time, the news that *something* was wrong certainly came as no shock to either of them. It had become abundantly clear that their mother was not herself. In the months that followed, the three of us did the best we could to help her cope, with the children carrying the additional burden of being unable to let on to her that they knew what she was trying so valiantly to hide from them and from the world. Just before the holidays, Todd had completed his undergraduate degree at the University of West Virginia. He soon announced that he would move to Indianapolis, get a job, and take some time off before starting graduate school. Paige was beginning her final semester in law school and was planning her wedding for the following August. She began to come home more frequently on weekends to consult with her mother about the details of the wedding. But even that was difficult. On one particularly stressful weekend, when Paige showed her mother the newly arrived wedding invitations, Marilyn's mood was such that she was barely able to show any interest. This was an enormous departure for the mother who over the years had spent hundreds of hours at the kitchen table helping to complete countless class projects, and who had stayed up half the night decorating bicycles or Big Wheels for neighborhood Fourth of July parades.

As the months wore on, Marilyn saw her psychiatrist regularly, submitted to the treatments that were recommended, and above all, tried to put up a brave front.

Now I could tell you a good deal more about what occurred in late 1993 and early 1994, obviously a personally painful time for me and for my family. I could tell you about the heroic efforts of Drs. Peg and Gus Watanabe in finally determining the proper diagnosis and then discreetly organizing the best treatment available. I could tell you about all the steps that were pursued, and all the efforts that were undertaken on her behalf by the caregivers who were trying so hard to help. But the hard reality is that my wife is dead. In spite of her best efforts and mine, the help that she needed to identify her illness and treat it in a timely way had simply not been there. This nation's health-care system, coupled with our own lack of knowledge about the symptoms of clinical depression, did not provide an easy enough path to the treatment of her illness in time to save her life.

When treatment finally came, I believe she was convinced that she was receiving the best care available, and that everyone was doing their best to try to help. It just wasn't good enough. As the weeks wore on, her frustration and anger with everything around her continued to increase. She told me repeatedly that no one could possibly understand how she felt. Beyond that, I know she anguished that she was becoming an enormous burden to all of us who loved her so much. Nothing I could say or do seemed to relieve that anxiety.

Through all of this, prior to the diagnosis of her depression and after, she gave no hint to me or to her physicians that she was in any way contemplating suicide. In fact, when her psychiatrist received an urgent crisis signal on his pager on that horrible day when she was taken to the emergency room of the hospital, from experience he feared the worst. He told me later that while he was placing the call to respond to the page, he found himself mentally going through the list of his patients, speculating about which one might be the reason for the summons. Marilyn, he said, was the one he'd placed last on his list. But it is clear now that she had been planning to end her life—and probably for some time.

The last family photograph was taken just a week before her death, on May 8, the day Paige graduated from the Duke University School of Law. It had seemed a very happy occasion for everyone. But in retrospect, maybe it was also a day she saw as a symbolic end to her duties as a mother. With Todd having completed his undergraduate degree and Paige now having received her law degree, perhaps she felt that those commencement ceremonies provided permission to let go. Perhaps she felt that she no longer had to cope. That's pure speculation, because we'll never know her reasons with total certainty. But it's my own conclusion that, at least in part, she did not really believe that she would ever feel better, and she was simply unwilling to continue with the quality of life she had come to know.

Not only was this her first attempt at suicide, she clearly intended it to be the only one. On that May morning, she put her plan in motion fully expecting that no one else would be in the

The last photo taken of the Tobias family prior to Marilyn's death. The occasion was Paige's graduation from Duke University School of Law on May 8, 1994. I participated in the ceremony as a member of the Duke board of trustees.

house for several hours. Paige was in school at Duke. I had left for the office about 7:30 that morning and was not expected back until 6:00 or 6:30 that evening. Nor did she expect Todd to stop by. When he came through the front door in the early afternoon, his mission that day was ostensibly to raid his mother's refrigerator, but in reality it was just to check in on her. As a result, it was Todd who found her. Three years later, he wrote an essay about this experience that sums up how we all were feeling. It begins,

> You could set your watch by her Buick. Not once in my mother's decorated tenure as family chauffeur had she ever failed to arrive on schedule. Not in grade school, when her idea of free time was the on-the-road calm between Little League drop-offs and piano lesson pick-ups. Not in junior high when, in addition to me, more likely than not she was carting around the rest of my testosterone-addled brood. And

not even in high school, after I had missed a ride for some ignominious reason like an after-school detention or for girls with names like Alexis.

Maybe that's why of all the infinite number of things that could have come as a shock that afternoon: the roar of the engine, the intoxicating smell of exhaust fumes, the frantic pace of rescue personnel, most surprising of all was the incongruity. For the first time in her fifty-five years, at least the portion that I had witnessed, my mother had placed her own needs ahead of those of her family. I know best, because she staged it that way. Fact or fiction, in the deep of the night when I spring such thoughts from their bell jars, that's the way I spin it: that she knew it would be me; that she recognized that I, better than anyone, would understand. But the moment my eyes fixed on her lifeless body, her legs as long and frozen as ski poles, I died too. Or, more precisely, the selfish me was born. That was three years ago. Or maybe it was a hundred. These days, sometimes it's hard to tell. What I can say for sure is that afternoon, the cries of sirens still tiny in the distance, all time stood still. . . .

Sometimes families disintegrate in the wake of tragedies like this one. Ours, always close, pulled together even more tightly than before. In the weeks that followed, night after night Paige and Todd and I sat quietly together until the wee hours of the morning, talking, speculating, weeping, sharing our reflections and our recollections, and always wondering what more we could have done.

Paige and her fiancé, Tim Button, decided to carry on with their plans for an August wedding. I quickly announced that since the father of the bride was not overwhelmed with wedding planning assignments, I was available for duty. I would also become the mother of the bride. I soon found myself immersed in guest lists, seating plans, and floral arrangements. And it was the best thing that could have happened to me. It meant that even though I was more than fully occupied at Lilly, in those private hours away from the office I was also fully occupied with the wedding.

On the day of the wedding, when Paige and I began the long walk down the aisle of the same church that three months earlier had been the site of Marilyn's funeral, I knew that everyone there must be thinking of her. So was I. When it came time to respond to the question "Who gives this woman in holy matrimony?" without hesitation but in a quavering voice I said, "Her mother and I do." I'm sure there was not a dry eye in the sanctuary—certainly not my own.

Following Marilyn's death, some observed that the circumstances were indeed fraught with irony. She had succumbed to the disease her husband's company was most associated with treating successfully. Tragically, the Lilly drug that had helped so many did not help her.

The Table Moose

"If you step back and kind of reflect on that period of time, it is really pretty amazing," says Dr. August M. Watanabe, Executive Vice President of Eli Lilly and Company and the head of the company's Lilly Research Laboratories. "It's amazing that Randy was able to not fall apart, because most people would not have been able to get through all that. In addition to what was happening at the company during that time, he lost both of his parents. His diabetes was becoming more clear-cut. He was diagnosed with a melanoma which was surgically removed, which many people probably don't know about. And also during this period, he was trying to help Marilyn cope the best she could. I was with him a number of times when he would say, 'I got a call from Marilyn, and I have to go home,' or 'I am going to be late for a meeting this morning.' I think perhaps one of the things that helped him cope so effectively was his ability to confide in people. I think his openness afterwards about her battle with depression, with the press, and with the company set an example of what he meant by 'getting the moose on the table.'"

"Get the moose on the table." It's one of my favorite sayings. Like most good ideas, it was one I had borrowed—from my friend

Dr. David Nadler.[5] In my five-plus years as Lilly's CEO, I uttered these words with great frequency. In retrospect, I suppose I first began to articulate this concept to Lilly employees well before Marilyn's death. I spent a good deal of time talking to Lilly employees about our core values—people, integrity, and excellence—and the relationship those values had to our business success. To me, the accepted definition of the second word in our values statement—*integrity*—was far too limited. As such, it was hampering our ability to communicate effectively and to make timely and effective decisions.

A strong case can be made that integrity has been and continues to be an enormously important part of the culture of Eli Lilly and Company. The company does not tolerate those who lie, cheat, steal, or break the rules. However, that, to me, was a very limited definition of *integrity*. For example, if you were a Lilly employee in 1993 sitting in a conference room talking about alternative ways to deal with a particular problem, and you had a strong point of view but not necessarily one that was going to be popular with the group or with your boss, well, chances are you probably did not offer that opinion for fear of career reprisals or worse. And you also didn't want to hurt someone's feelings.

"We had a tendency [at Lilly] to sometimes not say things as they really were in order not to offend one another," says Lilly CEO Sidney Taurel. "That can be very counterproductive. So we adopted Randy's phrase 'get the moose on the table' as a light-hearted way to signal that we needed to speak openly and transparently about an issue at hand."

In the weeks following Marilyn's death, I received several inquiries from the national and local press to gauge my willingness to talk about Marilyn's death and my thoughts on the treatment of

5. David Nadler, in turn, credits his friend and colleague Dr. Dennis Perkins with originating this concept. Dr. Perkins describes his first use of the concept in his book *Leading at the Edge.*

clinical depression in this country. I'm sure I offended the *Wall Street Journal* reporter covering the company with my repeated resistance to his efforts to do a feature story on the subject. He was a reporter I'd come to respect, and even though I had complete confidence in his understanding of Marilyn's illness, and in his motivation, from experience I was less certain how sensitive his editors would be. I was not about to have this story used as a vehicle to sell papers. Clearly, however, it was a moose we needed to get on the table.

At the time, son Todd was working for *Indianapolis Monthly* magazine and had a great relationship with another writer there, his wonderful friend Donna Heimansohn. The editors there indicated that Donna would be the one assigned to do the story, and we were convinced that she would cover it fairly and thoughtfully and would be given the necessary latitude by her editors to do so. Therefore, we agreed to let her tell it.

"To be perfectly candid, we had a business reason to do it too," says Ed West. "It was part of our newly endorsed philosophy here that when there is no communication going on, when there is a lack of facts and information on a given topic, all kinds of things spring up. Randy and I both agreed that it was important that the story be told accurately, somewhere, somehow. Our employees deserved to know more, and the community was certainly not going to leave the topic alone until it was properly addressed."

When that story was published in February 1995, an unexpected thing occurred: My office was flooded with thank-you notes from families who had gone through circumstances similar to ours. One of these letters reads as follows:

> I'm clinically depressed. Today if in some small way I can ease your pain and help you have a better understanding of depressed people, then maybe it will be a little easier for you. It seems to me that rational thinking people have very little conception of the true feelings

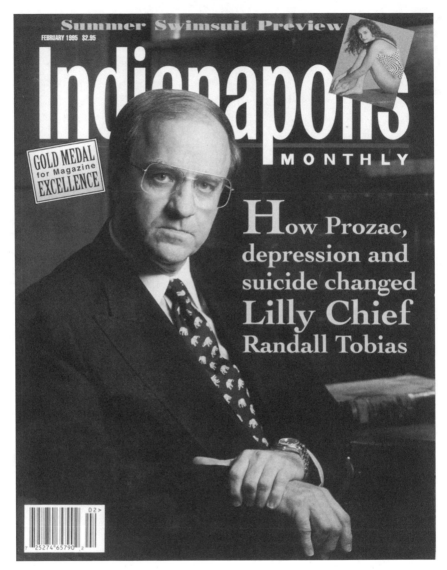

The February 1995 cover of Indianapolis Monthly. *The magazine's cover story described Marilyn's losing battle with clinical depression and our family's efforts to come to grips with her decision to take her own life. Photo courtesy of* Indianapolis Monthly.

that go on inside the mind of someone like myself who suffer from extreme bouts of depression. But I feel the pain of your own family and I'd like to help.

The writer went on to describe a bit about her own situation and concluded with a poem she had written, which read in part:

> I walk around with a painted-on smile
> Camouflaged by a twinkle that shows in my eyes.
> I greet everyone, hang around for a while
> So the world doesn't know how my insides cry.
> Through the eyes of my children I see that they care.
> But they just don't understand my panic and despair.
> I can't understand why the rage is there,
> But at this point in my life I just really don't care.

This woman's words were important to me because from those thoughts, I gained a better insight into how Marilyn must have felt. I think I began to understand why—through her lens on the world —she felt the hopelessness that caused her to do what she did.

Over the years, as a result of my role at Lilly and my personal experience in this area, I've become aware of many patients who have overcome great odds to get well, but also many who have not. I've heard and read stories like this one, from Elizabeth Wurtzel's 1994 memoir, *Prozac Nation*:

> It seems entirely possible to me now, given the tone of so many of the articles about Prozac, that people will forget how severe, crippling, and awful depression really is. And I'm not the only one who is concerned. Eli Lilly and Company, the manufacturer that has profited bountifully from the excesses of Prozac, recently launched an advertising campaign in medical trade journals that begins with the headline "Trivializing a Serious Illness." The ad first appeared in *Psychiatric News*, with copy that derides Prozac's "unprecedented media attention in recent weeks" and declares that "much of this attention has trivialized the very serious nature of the disease Prozac was specifically developed to treat—clinical depression." In an article in the *Wall Street Journal*, Steven Paul, M.D., the head of central nervous system re-

search at Eli Lilly, explains that the point of this ad is simply to help Prozac reach those who need it most.

. . . While many of the people commenting in the *Journal* article suggested that the advertisement was the result of Eli Lilly's fear of liability suits as Prozac is overprescribed, or even because the corporation is concerned that the drug will be excluded from a national health care plan because it is seen as too frivolous, I'd like to believe that its aim might be honest. . . . I wouldn't mind believing that they're doing a little bit of public service.

Elizabeth Wurtzel powerfully and bravely chronicles her battle with clinical depression. Today, thanks to drugs like Prozac, she continues to thrive in life and in a career as a best-selling author. In the epilogue to that book, Ms. Wurtzel ponders whether Lilly's "aim is true" when it comes to its customers' needs. I can assure her that no people on earth could possibly care more than the men and women of the company.

Not a day goes by that I don't think about Marilyn, and people like her, and wonder whether if perhaps our society were more willing to address mental illness openly and candidly, to put the moose on the table, perhaps my beloved wife would still be alive today. My aim could not be any truer.

The First September 11

It was a pleasant early fall afternoon—September 11, 1992. Marianne Williams McKinney was at her desk in her Indianapolis residence, putting the final touches on a program note for an upcoming concert of the Indianapolis Symphony Orchestra. A graduate of Radcliffe College and the Longy School of Music, with a doctorate in musicology and piano performance from the University of Minnesota, Marianne was enjoying her work for the symphony, her occasional piano concerts, and life in general. Her thoughts were interrupted by the ringing of the telephone on her desk. It was a friend calling, asking if she had her television set turned on. A local station had just broken into its regular programming with a bulletin that two small planes had apparently collided in midair over the south side of Indianapolis and that the flaming wreckage from both was reported to have plunged to the ground. Further details were not yet known.

Marianne was immediately struck with a sense of deep foreboding. Her husband, Frank McKinney Jr., former Olympic swimmer and now Chairman of Bank One, Indiana, was departing that afternoon from a small airport in the same area. He and three other well-known Indianapolis civic leaders had agreed to make a quick trip to Columbus, Ohio, to inspect a community development effort thought to have potential application in Indianapolis.

As she turned on her own television, almost immediately her worst fears were confirmed. The identities of some of those involved had just been provided to the authorities by people at the airport who had seen them board the plane. Before anyone could keep it from happening, Marianne became one of several thousand viewers informed, by an overeager reporter, that her husband had indeed been involved. In the hours ahead, it would be confirmed that the pilot and all four passengers on Frank's plane had perished. So, too, had the pilot of the other plane involved. Two passengers on the second plane were gravely injured.

This was not the first aviation tragedy in Marianne's life. When she was sixteen, her own father lost his life when the small corporate plane in which he was a passenger struck an unlighted commercial broadcasting tower while approaching a New York–area airport on a flight from Indianapolis. And there had been other crises along the way. But Marianne had demonstrated time and time again that she was one of life's survivors. She had picked up the pieces of her life and gone on before. She would do it again.

Soon after returning to Indianapolis in 1993, Marilyn and I began to cross paths with Marianne at various community functions. Almost immediately, we both saw her as a new friend. In fact, Marilyn had enjoyed a small luncheon in Marianne's home not long before her death and had come home somewhat uplifted. She had remarked to me how she looked forward to getting better acquainted.

Knowing what Marianne had been through, it was comforting when I saw her come through the door of the funeral home to pay her respects to our family. She'd brought with her two copies of a book, not for me but for Paige and Todd. It was the 1927 Pulitzer Prize–winning novel by Thornton Wilder, *The Bridge of San Luis Rey*. In the story, a foot bridge over a deep gorge in eighteenth-century Peru suddenly and inexplicably collapses, hurtling to their deaths the five people who at that particular moment happen to be crossing. Over the years, thousands had passed safely over the bridge. So why those five? The book recounts the efforts of a monk who witnessed the collapse to try to discover the answers. Marianne explained that the book had given her some comfort in trying to come to grips with the unexplainable following Frank's death, and she hoped it might do the same for Paige and Todd.

I did not run into Marianne again for several months, when we found ourselves together at the annual dinner for an organization on whose board we both served. In the weeks preceding that evening, I had begun to receive a few well-intended dinner invitations from friends and acquaintances, mostly acquaintances, who had someone in mind they thought I should meet. It was clear there were agendas afoot, and I found the whole idea upsetting. That evening, I think it occurred to each of us that we'd found a dinner partner we could trust. We had both suffered a deep loss and could relate to the other's feelings of grief. In the short term, that was something important we shared. Beyond that, there wasn't any long term in sight. Neither of us needed or wanted anything from the other, and we both knew it. That, too, was comforting.

As time passed, we began to discover that we had more in common than simply our grief, and we began to see more of each

Marianne and me at the family's Twelve Springs Ranch near the small town of McLeod, not far from Livingston, Montana. Many of the scenes in the Robert Redford motion picture The Horse Whisperer *were filmed on the ranch, including an important scene with Redford and Kristen Scott Thomas seated in the location pictured here.*

other. In July 1995, we were married by our good friend Dr. Bill Enright at the Second Presbyterian Church in Indianapolis. In the years that have followed, we've enjoyed many wonderful experiences together—on business trips across the United States and around the world, at our Twelve Springs Ranch in Montana, at our Casa de Sueños in Florida, and at the places we enjoy in Indiana. As our marriage has grown, without a doubt the highlight of it all is that "her" children and "his" children have produced "their" grandchildren—five as this book goes to press, with three more on the way!

Both of us treasure the memories that came before the terrible storms of September 11, 1992, and May 16, 1994. In the Spanish language, the term for "rainbow" is *arco iris*—*arco*, meaning "an arc," and *iris*, meaning "multicolored." That's why we named the home we now occupy in Indianapolis Arcoiris House. For us, it represents the sunshine and the sense of renewal that often comes after the storm—the chance for a bright new day.

FOUR

Small Town, Big Lessons

*Life is what's happening to you while you're busy
making other plans.*
                        —John Lennon

Remington, Indiana 47977

I was born in a small town. Remington, Indiana, in the 1940s
and 1950s was the kind of place where Dr. Marcus Welby could
well have lived down the street, and Ozzie and Harriet, next door.
I grew up in a wonderful old brick house, right on the edge of
town. We had one foot in each of the two worlds that comprised
the Remington community. The front of our property was "in town,"
right on Brown Street. The rear, however, was "in the country." A
neighboring farmer's field bordered our property on the south. We
had a big lawn, two acres or so, and several acres of pasture to the
west of the lawn. There were great places for everything from hide-
outs to a dirt basketball court. We usually had a few sheep to keep
the grass down in the pasture, and I'm sure they also provided a
little extra income for my parents.

It was in Remington that I learned some of the very basic things
that have been important to me all of my life. I learned that when
you make a commitment, you keep it. I learned that life's respon-

The house on the edge of town where I lived while growing up in Remington, Indiana.

sibilities include always trying to make things better as the world around you changes. As near as I could tell, the people in Remington operated with integrity, and I was taught that nothing in life was more important. They took their obligations seriously, they cared for their families and their community, and they worked to improve the quality of life for themselves and for those around them. What I observed growing up was very consistent with what I later learned to be the philosophy of the founder of the Indiana company I was privileged to lead. Nearly 120 years ago, when Colonel Eli Lilly turned over responsibility for what was then a very small and very young family business, he said to his own son, "Take what you find here and make it better. . . ." I suspect my parents never heard those words, but that's the same philosophy they practiced every day while I was growing up. And it's the same philosophy I learned from watching others who influenced my early life.

"Randy and I were lucky to have had some extraordinary mentors growing up in Remington, beginning with our parents, who were lifelong friends," says Bill Biddle, my friend from boyhood and now my operating partner in a grain farm I own near Remington. "One of the things we both learned early on, I think, was how to relate to people, how to get the best out of people, in an unobtrusive way. In other words, some people lead with an iron fist, but the mentors we had in Remington taught us there is a way to treat people decently and with respect, and if you learn how to do that, they will go the extra mile for you."[1]

The Mother of All Examples

Leadership is a mysterious quality, hard to define, but maybe we always know it when we see it . . . even as kids.

I had the great good fortune to study at the feet of some exceptional mentors over the course of my lifetime. But no individual has had a more lasting influence on my personal and professional life than my own mother. In fact, perhaps one of the most effective leadership strengths I possess I owe to her influence.

1. John D. Zeglis, Chairman and CEO of AT&T Wireless and formerly AT&T's General Counsel, remembers an occasion when he needed a little reinforcement. "Maybe the single best thing Randy ever did for me, he probably doesn't even know he did. I'm certain he doesn't know the impact it had on me then, and on my thoughts on leadership since. The top fifteen or twenty people in the company had a meeting somewhere, right after [longtime AT&T General Council] Howard Trienens retired in 1986. I had just taken over as General Counsel and I had no idea how I was supposed to behave at these meetings. I was the guy people were looking to for insightful legal advice. I was getting paid to say 'yes' or 'no' or 'smart' or 'dumb' at the appropriate times. But I had no idea whether I was to participate in the debate or just react. I had no idea what the expectations were for this job. So for three days, I did what I felt was right, speaking up when I thought it was appropriate, but on the edge of uncertainty every moment. When the meetings were over, we all flew back to New Jersey. I'm carrying my bags to my car as another car leaving the hangar begins to slow down next to me and stops. It was Randy. He simply said, 'John, I just wanted to tell you it was like Howard never left.' And then he drove off. He couldn't have done anything better for me at that moment. At thirty-eight years of age, I didn't know whether I could do this job or not. And that was the most important thing for me to hear. I have always remembered that gesture, and ever since, I have always tried to make an effort to recognize when people may need that kind of encouragement."

She was born Fern Beatrice Harwood in 1904 on her family's small farm in southeastern Kansas, near the town of Leon. While a Kansan by birth, Fern Hardwood was raised among chickens and cows and hogs on several sprawling acres in northern Illinois, near Gilman. In 1922, her family moved to Gilboa Township in Benton County, Indiana, near Remington. It was there, as a high school junior, that the new girl in school caught the eye of Roy Tobias, two years her junior. Retired farmer Harold Hackley recalls his classmate's immediate infatuation. "Being that our school was so small, not many of us were interested in dating the girls in our own classes. We were more interested in going into town and getting acquainted with the girls there. But Roy was different. He had his eye on Fern from the very beginning." Aunt Helen Butcher, my father's younger sister, describes a little more poetically this relationship which would eventually form a union lasting some sixty years. "Roy and Fern were like two halves coming together to make a whole," she remembers.

While these two "halves" seemed like soul mates from the very start, my mother had far more in mind for herself than becoming simply a wife and mother. When she graduated from high school in 1922, she took an examination that enabled her to become an elementary-school teacher, a career she pursued full time in the public school in Gilman. When her own school was not in session, this grade-school teacher became a college student. And after a long stretch of summers of self-financed learning, along with a year away from teaching as a full-time student, she accumulated the credits required for a college degree in education—something most women just didn't do in those days. Mom was the first in her family to accomplish this. But she never forgot Roy Tobias, and he never forgot about her. They began a long-distance romance in the early 1930s and were married in 1934. It was a modest ceremony. In fact, it was so modest that they kept it a secret for a while. You see, my mother was ahead of her time. She was a married career

My parents, Roy and Fern Tobias, on their wedding day in 1934.

woman in an era when those three words, placed side by side, created something of an oxymoron. It was thought to be particularly unseemly for a teacher to be a married woman. And it was the heart of the Depression, when jobs were hard to come by, so she kept her marriage a secret. During the late 1940s and the 1950s when I was growing up, my mother taught sixth grade in the Remington elementary school—that is, until my own class was ready to enter sixth grade. For that year, she exchanged classrooms with William Casey, the longtime fifth-grade teacher, so as to avoid any appearances of nepotism with her own child in her classroom. I suspect that was one of my earliest lessons in the importance of avoiding the slightest appearance of any conflict of interest—even when it meant a good deal of personal inconvenience. I'm quite positive that I gained my first respect and appreciation for work-

Roy and Fern Tobias on their fiftieth wedding anniversary in 1984.

ing women from watching the sacrifices my mother made to balance her home and work lives. But the way my mother affected my leadership style had less to do with her chosen profession of teaching and everything to do with her profession's stated purpose—learning.

Fern Tobias was a lifelong learner, and nowhere was this more evident than in the attitude she instilled in my brother and me at a young age. "Everyone has something to teach," she often said, "so keep your ears open." She never met a stranger, and she didn't think I should, either. She stressed the importance of being sensitive to other people, whether it was your neighbor, your friend, your coworker, or a stranger. She believed that everyone, no matter their station in life, deserved to be treated with respect.

Leadership is as much about listening, about building relationships, about providing encouragement when it's needed as it is about communicating one's own ideas. I'm sure that growing up, I didn't realize just how significant her influence would be on my approach to my jobs over the years. I credit my mother's early influence for any particular skills I might have for listening to, learning from, and encouraging and respecting others. When she died in February 1994, shortly before her ninetieth birthday, she was respected by all whose lives she had touched. I miss her every day.

Horse Sense

You know the stories grandfathers often tell that begin with the phrase "in my day" and then proceed with a litany about having to walk countless miles to and from school through freezing gusts of ice and snow? My father frequently told a version of that story to his grandchildren. Only, as with most things unique to my dad, his version was not delivered with the intent of soliciting sympathy or eulogizing the past. His version was told for the purpose of celebrating his experiences. And his version involved a horse.

Dad lived through the Great Depression at a relatively young age, and as a result, he was a careful and conservative man. Despite the hardship he had seen, which formed his lifelong aversion to risk and change, he was the most affable and well-liked man I have ever known. When I think about the traits I've learned that are required for effective leadership, I think often of him.

According to family lore, young Roy Gordon Tobias did not begin his education until the age of seven because the distance to the one-room schoolhouse serving the rural Indiana farm where he was raised was deemed too great for a boy of small stature to travel by foot. But by age seven, dad was considered man enough to handle the responsibility of making the several-mile round trip to and from the Gilboa Township schoolhouse the way most folks covered long distances in those days. He arrived via Chester. His horse.

Roy's former classmate, Harold Hackley, remembers those days well. "Behind the original school building there were several horse stalls, so any kid that was old enough to ride a horse to school, or drive a horse and buggy and bring his younger brothers and sisters to school, would put the horse in the barn there while they attended classes."

While it was typical for most young men growing up in that part of the country to begin planning for a career as a farmer at an early age, Hackley recalls that his former classmate seemed destined for other things. "It was rare that anyone would attend college after high school graduation back then. Occasionally, you would hear of some girl that was headed to a teacher's college, but in those days a college education was just not an option for most folks. But Roy was pretty much his own person. He did what he set his mind on."

In 1925, having made the sojourn to school atop his trusty steed so many times that he could do it in his sleep (and according to family legend, occasionally doing just that), Roy Tobias completed his high school education. Under more conventional circumstances, this diligent and gifted student might very well have been recognized as the valedictorian of his class. However, in a graduating class of ten, the academic standing of the outgoing scholars was left untallied.

For his peers, high school was as high as higher education would ever get. Farming was more than a vocation in Remington at the time; it was the way of life. And it most likely would have been the way of Dad's life, too—a member of the fourth generation of a Hoosier family, expected to devote his adulthood to working the heartland like those before him—were it not for the encouragement of an inspired teacher who urged him to fill out the applications for financial aid and admission to DePauw University in nearby Greencastle, Indiana.

In part to afford himself the peace of mind for having tried, in part to silence the persistent urgings of his teacher, and in part with the real hope that something might actually come of it, my father mailed those forms. To the surprise of no one, save perhaps himself, he was awarded DePauw University's coveted Rector Scholarship. Four years later, he graduated with a degree in economics, ironically only a few weeks before the 1929 stock-market crash. Following a series of increasingly scarce employment experiences, the would-be businessman found himself back in Remington, doing farm work for an uncle.

But when he retired in 1976, at the age of seventy, it was not as a farmer, as some might have predicted, but as the Chairman of the Board of the State Bank of Remington. One day in 1934, two members of the board of directors of the local bank had come to visit with him as he was plowing a field. They asked if he might be interested in a job. It was always my impression that in the beginning, he did not expect to remain in Remington all of his life. But in the depths of the Depression, his view of the bank job looked much more appealing to him than his view of the horses that were pulling his plow. With no hesitation, he signed on immediately for what would be a career of more than forty-four years as a small-town banker.

From my father I learned an essential recipe for personal and professional success: "Take the job seriously, but never yourself. And at the end of the day, always make time to separate the two."

My high school English teacher and my parents' longtime friend Mary May, now well into her nineties but totally engaged in life as she has always been, recalled for Todd the business-related opportunities my dad gave me at a young age. "In his spare time away from the bank, Roy sold insurance. One time, he took Randy with him on a sales call, and he said he came out of that meeting feeling like he had done a pretty good job until they got out to the car and his seven-year-old boy looked up at him with wide eyes and said, 'Dad, don't you think you overdid it just a little?' I think it was clear," she said, "that Randy had a strong business sense from a very early age!"

Like most banks in those days, the State Bank of Remington operated under what were referred to as bankers' hours, opening at 9:00 in the morning and closing at 3:00 in the afternoon, Monday through Saturday, except Thursday, when it closed at noon. That was the afternoon that my dad sold life insurance. It took me years to really become fully aware of the bank's hours of operation, because Dad was at his desk at 7:30 every morning. When he returned home at 5:00 or 5:30 in the evening, it was to have dinner and spend some quality time with his family, after which, on more than an occasional evening, he would resume work. But instead of going to a study or poring over papers and books in front of the radio, my father's typical evening work sessions were conducted, weather permitting, on our back porch.

One of the most enduring memories I have is watching him on those evenings, sitting on the top step, a cup of coffee in one hand, a notebook in the other. What made the image so memorable was not so much *how* he looked. That more or less remained the same— a pressed white shirt, dark slacks, and a tie. Rather, the memory endures of how comfortable he looked seated next to the worn flannel and denim of one or another of the farmers who would be visiting with him. You see, my father, for all of his success in that small town, never thought of himself as a big shot bank president. He thought of himself as a farmer in banker's clothing. And as the son of a son of a farmer, he knew that at certain times of the year, it was next to impossible to leave one's crops in the middle of the afternoon to make it into the bank before its 3:00 P.M. closing. So as the president of the bank, my dad in effect extended those hours in a very natural and informal way. He made himself available on our back porch whenever someone needed his help or attention.

Clearly, there is a lesson here about customer service, about trying to do whatever a customer needs. But for me, an even more significant lesson was that he never let his success define how he related to people. That, I believe, was a large measure of why he was successful.

That's not to say that he wasn't comfortable with his professional identity. Dad was a banker through and through. In fact, he loved his job so much that he went to great lengths to uphold his professional image. He did not drink much, but he would occasionally enjoy one small glass of Kentucky bourbon before dinner. Never once did I know him to have a drink in public in the Remington community. This was a rule he maintained even after he retired. He wasn't trying to hide anything. He simply understood the culture and expectations of our town, and he felt that having a cocktail in public would be an unbecoming reflection on the bank and his position there.

Yet for all the pains he took to maintain his professional image, he never let his career define who he was as a human being. He never let his professional success define how he related to other people. While his position in our small town carried some degree of prestige, when he left his office for home each evening, he made every effort to leave any trappings of his professional role right where they belonged—on his desk.

After my brother Roger and I were grown and gone and his career had ended, Dad continued to begin his days in the local coffee shop in much the same way they had so frequently ended on our back porch while he was working, enjoying a cup of coffee and bit of good conversation with his friends, many of them Remington-area farmers.

Shortly before his retirement, he orchestrated a merger of the bank for which he had worked his entire life and two other similarly situated small-town banks. A short time later, the combined bank was purchased by Bank One. Even small Midwestern towns, it would seem, are not immune to corporate change.

He passed away in 1996, shortly before his ninetieth birthday. He was among the most respected people in his community, successful in life in every possible way. Roy Tobias largely made his own luck, and as a result, he dictated the course of his own personal and professional fate. My dad, like all great leaders, took his career quite seriously. But never himself. And at the end of the day, he always took time to separate the two.

Tomatoes, Yards, Chickens, Corn, Pork Chops, and Campfires

For as long as I can remember, I wanted to have some kind of job. As a child, I suppose that was at least in part because I thought it would be evidence that I was growing up. After all, nearly everyone I looked up to had one, starting with my parents and my older brother and his friends.

One of my earliest jobs was loading vegetables from our family garden into my wagon—tomatoes, sweet corn, and the like—and pulling them down the hill of our long gravel driveway, where I would attempt to sell them to people driving by. I must not have been more than six or seven. Most families in Remington had their own vegetable garden, and not very many cars drove past our house, so I can't imagine that I sold very much. But I'm sure that didn't matter. What did matter was that I had a job. And I had the complete support and encouragement of my parents.

My first job involving real money was mowing lawns in the summer. I suppose I was about ten years old when I was permitted to knock on the door of a likely candidate, seeking the assignment to cut her grass during the following summer, often a "widow lady" who had just moved to town from a farm and didn't already have an arrangement with someone. This was my first experience with business development. If the mowing job was available, there usually followed the query I've gotten from older people in Remington over most of my life: "Are you Roger or Randall?"

Then there were always instructions about what was expected, but when it came to compensation, I was usually just told what the job was worth. I still had a few things to learn about business development! But I was just pleased to have an opportunity to earn a wage, even though I knew I would be expected to come in with my passbook and deposit at least half of what I made into my savings account at the State Bank of Remington. At that age, I was certain I would never see that money again.

With the support and encouragement of my parents, there were some useful lessons from my mowing experience. Most notably, I learned that when you have the responsibility to do something, you do it. Period. What I did not learn until much later, however, was the difference between revenue and profit. I thought they were the same thing. I was well aware, although probably not appropriately appreciative, that it was my father's mower I was using and that he provided the money to keep the gasoline can filled. But the economic implications associated with the capital and expenses involved completely escaped me. As far as I knew, everything I took in was profit. I've subsequently concluded that I was not alone in that early misinformation—in fact, too many U.S. consumers never come to understand the difference between revenue and profit.

As I got older, I occasionally supplemented my grass-cutting income with other odd jobs that were available in our town. The Nussbaum family operated a large chicken business, Fairview Hatchery, just south of town. Occasionally they would put out the word that they needed chicken catchers. If you hadn't done it before, it was a bit scary, but it wasn't rocket science. Those hired for the day would walk into a large chicken coop, a long, narrow building filled with hundreds, maybe thousands, of chickens, and begin gathering up the squawking, scratching chickens by their feet and handing them to one of the regular employees of the hatchery, who would perform whatever activity was scheduled, such as inoculating the birds. When we completed one building, we'd move on to the next, and so it would go. It wasn't one of my favorite jobs, and I don't recall that I did it very often, but years later, I would be glad I had. I flew to Arkansas one day with Dr. Brendan Fox, then the President of Elanco Animal Health, a wholly owned Lilly subsidiary.[2] The purpose of our trip was to visit the headquarters and facilities of Tyson Foods, one of the largest producers and processors of chickens in the world, and at the time one of Elanco's most important customers. As we toured their very modern and highly automated processing operations that day, you can imagine the surprise of the Tyson CEO when the Lilly CEO described his own experiences as a chicken catcher.

I also logged some time detasseling corn for Biddle Farms, a producer of hybrid seed near Remington operated at the time by Chester Biddle, one of my dad's best friends, and now by his son Bill.

Detasseling corn means exactly what it sounds like—removing the tassel from the top of a cornstalk—so that it cannot pollinate itself and will be pollinated by a second variety with different characteristics, planted in the same field. Depending on the level of moisture in the ground and other factors, the detasseling operation may be done on foot, which I recall as backbreaking work. If conditions are right, the work is done from a detasseling machine, a tall tractorlike piece of equipment, driven along over several rows of corn at a time, with narrow wooden platforms suspended between the rows. Those doing the detasseling stand on the plat-

---

2. I've often been asked about the origin of the name *Elanco*. Apparently unknown to many, even inside Lilly, the company's animal-health business quite simply takes its name from the first letters in the words in the name of the parent—*E* from *Eli*, *l* from *Lilly*, *an* from *and*, and *co* from *Company*.

forms and pull out the tassels as they go past, in an almost assembly line–like operation. Even to this day, I can close my eyes and bring up a vision of tassels going by, millions and millions of tassels. Detasseling was an experience that over the years has helped me appreciate some of the challenges that employees face in repetitious manufacturing operations.

When I was fourteen years old, I traded my free Saturdays during the school year for a cash register and a white butcher's apron. My first "real" job was working as a clerk at Peck's Grocery in Remington. For two years, I reported to work every Saturday at 8:00 in the morning and worked right up until closing time at 9:00 P.M. I was paid $5 each Saturday for the first year, and then I was given a quite unexpected raise to $5.50.

Alice Medley was seven years older and had worked at Peck's as a full-time clerk from the day she graduated from high school. She was a welcoming, friendly, and caring mentor, I suspect without really realizing it. I learned a great deal about life in the workplace from what she told me and from simply watching how she did things. As Alice recalls the times, "We didn't have a whole lot to do in town back then. We had a movie theater, and the high school events were always popular, but the grocery store was kind of the social center for the community, the place everyone came when they were in town. For those of us who worked there, we knew just about everyone in town and they all knew us."

Her future husband, Bill, came by every Saturday evening at closing to pick up Alice, and we became well acquainted. When Alice and Bill announced that they were getting married, I was honored by their invitation to sing at the wedding. And when their first child was born, a son, I was overwhelmed when they named him Randy.

My first real boss was the man who ran Peck's Grocery, Doc Milner. Doc was the kind of small-town archetype one doesn't find all that easily anymore. He was more than simply a town fixture;

he was a town elder, who, among other things, served as president of the town board. You couldn't live in Remington in the 1950s and not be on a first-name basis with Doc. He worked long, tedious hours, longer than anyone else in the store, but never really seemed to mind. He had high expectations of everyone but set the example through his own work habits. He also made it a fun place to work. He had no reservations about taking corrective action with his employees if things got too relaxed, but he just assumed everyone would work hard and have fun doing it. For the most part, that's just what we did.

Peck's predated today's supermarkets in a number of ways. Rather than pushing a cart around the store (for which there would not have been room anyway), each customer was waited on by a clerk who assisted with their shopping list, picking items off the shelves as instructed by the customer and placing them on one of the store's two counters.

There was an ancient cash register in the center of the store where the order was rung up by entering the correct amount of the sale with the proper keys and then turning the large crank handle on the side. There was a prescribed way, Doc's way, to do virtually everything in the store. To this day, the bills in my money clip are always aligned so that the presidential heads are all facing up, the tops of their heads to the left in ascending order of value, just the way they were to be placed in Doc's cash register.

It was at Peck's that I was first exposed to some of the aspects of running a business—inventory control, marketing, and customer relations, to name but a few. Doc taught me how to run the cash register and cut deli meats. He taught me how to record receivables and unload a shipment of produce. He taught me how to handle bad checks with discretion and disgruntled customers with finesse. It was my first experience in dealing directly with customers, and I learned there were all kinds of attitudes. Most were very kind and friendly, but some were very demanding and came with the attitude that you were most certainly going to try to take advantage of them in some way. I remember in particular one lady who always told me, unnecessarily but without fail, to weigh the pork chops before they were wrapped in butcher paper because she didn't want to pay the price per pound of pork chops to buy the paper, too.

All in all, working there was a wonderful experience that I've thought of often over the years. In many ways, I've come to recognize that Doc Milner's management style probably had a great deal to do with shaping my own.

Like most young people, I viewed my various part-time and summer jobs as simply a way to earn some spending money and pass the time. But when I look back on all the jobs I held over the years, I can honestly say that I learned something lasting and useful from each experience. But I would have to say that the summers I spent at Camp Pottawattomie[3] probably provided the experiences that made the most significant contributions to my career and life, far beyond merely filling the time. I didn't realize just how significant those experiences would be while I was immersed in them. But today, I can trace a connection to many of the values I have come to embrace.

Camp Pottawattomie is located in Indiana's Tippecanoe River State Park, a few miles north of the town of Winamac. During the Depression, federal government employees of the Works Progress

---

3. Those who worked there or camped there during the same period may recall that it was always spelled "Pottawattomie." The Indiana Department of Natural Resources, however, now refers to the camp as "Potawatomi." It seems likely that the camp was originally named for the Potawatomi Indians, who beginning in the late 1700s lived for a time in northern Indiana in the area where the camp is located. It was not until some years later that I became aware that the name of the camp was spelled differently from the Indian name, and I can only guess why. The sign at the entrance to the camp—I'm sure a relic of Works Progress Administration days when some sign maker gave it his best guess—spelled the name, in letters burned into the wood, "Pottawattomie." Over the years, and I suspect only because of that sign, it became the accepted spelling and found its way to camp sweatshirts, postcards, and the like. Here, I have used the spelling I knew when I worked at the camp. It would not look right to me if I did otherwise!

Administration (WPA), a Depression-era jobs program, constructed all of the park roads and other recreational facilities, including the camp.

The camp itself occupied approximately six hundred acres. The main part included a large dining hall and kitchen, rough log cabins for the staff, a four-bed infirmary that included a bedroom for the camp nurse, and a central shower facility, where the water was heated by a coal-fired furnace. One of the responsibilities I shared was to keep the fire burning and the water hot. On those few occasions when I let the fire go out, I was very unpopular!

My brother, Roger, had worked at the camp for several summers before me, and for two or three summers I had helped fill in when extra help was needed—my introduction to working at the camp. In 1956, my first summer there full time, was also the first summer for a new camp manager, Channing Vosloh, or Chink, as he has been known since childhood. After graduation from Butler University and three years in the Army Air Corps, he returned to Indiana and became one of the state's outstanding high school basketball coaches, before ultimately becoming a high school principal. Other than my parents, Chink probably had as much impact on my life as anyone I can name. He was my role model during a very formative period in my life, and a good one. This was essentially a 24/7 job for twelve weeks each summer, so the only adult influence I received during those periods came from Chink and his wife Rowena, whom I respected and also liked very much. Over the years, my parents and the Voslohs became very close friends, and it was always clear to me that they stood for the same things in life.

Beginning with the summer preceding my freshman year in high school and continuing through the summer following my junior year in college, I spent twelve weeks each year—the months of June, July, and August—doing everything from peeling potatoes for 150 people to teaching swimming lessons to fixing broken bedsprings to making pancakes to performing minor plumbing repairs to entertaining by playing my ukulele and singing by a campfire. While these tasks might seem far removed from the day-to-day activities of a corporate CEO, for me, these and other duties added up to nothing less than a crash course in life. It was my first experience with broad and ambiguous responsibilities, with understanding that if something needed to be done, job descriptions didn't count for much. We just did whatever was needed. Often we were called on to solve a problem despite having no prior experience, or to repair some piece of equipment when there was no solution other than to improvise. The lessons about people, their reactions and behavior under stress, the willingness of some to step up and others not—these were also valuable experiences.

My two principal duties involved the dining hall and the swimming pool. "Overseeing the dinning hall might not sound like a huge responsibility, but believe me, it was," remembers Chink's daughter, Channa Beth Vosloh Butcher, who was nine years old when her father became the assistant manager and returned every summer until she was seventeen. "Thirty minutes before each meal—three times a day—fifteen ten-to-twelve-year-old girls would show up for duty. Randy had to teach them how to set the tables and get everything ready by the time the entire camp showed up to eat. Then during the meal, he would oversee the mess hall and direct traffic through the serving line, and when it was done, he would supervise the same helpers and make sure everything was cleaned up and ready for the next meal. Randy also was responsible to make all the camp announcements to the entire group. When I was about twelve years old, I became his assistant. He taught me all the procedures he had developed to get it all done and gradually gave me more responsibility. Then one day toward the end of his time there, he told me, 'Okay, you are in charge now.' That scared me to death—especially having to get up in front of the group and make the announcements. But after a while, I

My good friend Mike Merkel (left) and me at Camp Pottawattomie during the early 1960s. Photo courtesy of Channa Beth Vosloh Butcher.

grew more confident. Randy and I became a great team, and I've always been grateful for what he taught me."

Each summer, there were jobs for two teenaged boys on the staff. During my third summer at camp, I was asked to find someone new to work with me. I immediately settled on my classmate and good friend Mike Merkel. I had known Mike all of my life. His grandfather and my father were lifelong friends and fishing buddies. On more than one occasion, we had been together on fishing trips to northern Wisconsin, and once to South Dakota and Wyoming. In addition, we played basketball together and sat next to each other in the Remington High School band. Without a doubt, our camp summers together represented one of the closest working relationships I've ever had with another human being—essentially twenty-four hours a day, seven days a week. We worked side by side all day and then shared a cabin, where we slept on folding metal camp cots with mattresses about three inches thick. Whatever we did in our time off, we also did together. Through all of that, I do not remember having one major disagreement with Mike. He was a great partner through all of those summers.

On any number of occasions over the years, my children have asked me where I learned to do something—related to cooking or plumbing or dealing with people. My answer has often been "I learned it at summer camp."

Postscript

When I'm in Remington, or passing through on the nearby interstate on my way to or from Chicago, I always stop at the Remington Cemetery on the edge of town. It's a peaceful place, and in some ways it's one of my principal connections to the place where I grew up—to many of the people I knew then and to whom I owe so much. It reminds me of my roots. My great-grandparents are buried there. So are my grandparents. And so are my parents, my real reason for always stopping for a few minutes.

Whenever I'm there, I'm always drawn to two other grave sites, ironically, each within a few steps of the graves of my parents. One is the burial place of Randy Medley, my namesake, who was killed in 1967 when he was ten years old. It was a tragic automobile accident that also took the lives of his grandparents and the driver of the other car, who was at fault. The other spot I visit is the final resting place of my childhood friend and Camp Pottawattomie partner, Mike Merkel—Lieutenant Mike Merkel—who, like too many others of my generation, was killed in action in Vietnam.

Life indeed has many twists and turns, not all with happy endings.

FIVE

A Complete Education

*Education is one of the few things a person is
willing to pay for and not get.*
—William Lowe Bryan

Life on the River Jordan

It was the beginning of the end of an era, only none of us really knew it. We were too young and having too much fun to notice. The final battles of World War II were less than fifteen years in the past. The post-war boom was virtually all we had ever known, and life was good. But it was now the early 1960s, and soon enough things would change. In the wake of the civil rights movement and Vietnam and Watergate, American universities would undergo a radical transformation. They would soon become the cultural centers of protest and the playgrounds of youthful transgression. But not yet. At least not on the Bloomington campus of Indiana University, my home from the fall of 1960 to the spring of 1964.

Some forty years removed from it all, I look back on those years with a feeling that can only be described as longing. My friend since those days, Jim Morris, describes it this way: "It was a wonderful time. We had a grand group of friends who were extremely active in campus leadership and student government. We graduated before Vietnam, at a time when we were all so positive about the university and our experiences there."

It was still a time of relative innocence. Certain university policies, when examined from today's perspective, might seem antiquated and, in some cases, blatantly sexist.

Indiana University's central campus was idyllic, with broad expanses of grass and trees, interrupted only by the meandering Jordan River, a stream about four feet wide. There were plenty of traditions. Girls (as they were known then) had "hours," 11:00 P.M. on weeknights and 1:00 A.M. on weekends, as I recall. The theory was that if the girls were locked up in their housing units at night, then the boys would go home. Generally, that worked. But occasionally, the boys drank too much beer, got too little sleep, and looked for ways to test the limits of their newfound freedom. Each December, there was a campus black-tie dance known as the "Opening of the Formal Season." After that, and only after that, could the fraternities hold their own winter formal dances. It was a time when the Fall Carnival, the IU Sing, and the Little 500 were all can't-miss events of the year, and protests were directed mostly at unsympathetic basketball referees. Crooners filled the radio waves, Bob Hope and Pat Boone filled the auditorium, and madras shirts filled our closets. With the changes that were to come only a short time later, it seems almost unbelievable that the only drugs I ever saw on campus were those prescribed by a family doctor. Indeed, if someone had asked for directions to the local source for marijuana, I would have been clueless.

For many of my classmates, Indiana University was an assumed destination, the only college choice they had ever seriously considered. "I turned down an invitation to go to Harvard and join the wrestling team because all things considered, it just wasn't as appealing to me as attending IU," says my longtime friend, furniture retailing executive Jim Kittle. He was not the only one. Dr. Tom Hayhurst, my fraternity brother and now a cardiologist in

Fort Wayne, Indiana, bailed out on an academic scholarship to the University of Chicago "because I went to visit and it was a gray and cloudy day and the headline of the campus paper said 'Student Shot' and I thought there's no way you ever hear about something like that happening in Bloomington." And he was right. It was a unique time, and IU in the 1960s was a unique place.

In my own case, there had never been any question that I would go to college and that my parents would provide much of the financial support that would make it possible. But there had also never been any question that I would go someplace where the costs were manageable. The fact was, I had never taken seriously any option other than Indiana University. But coming from a small town, that prospect was a bit daunting. My classmate and best friend growing up in Remington, Ron Gillam, remembers his own trepidation: "I was scared to death that when we met up with guys from the big schools in Indianapolis and Chicago, we wouldn't be able to compete—they would all be smarter. I didn't know what I was doing there. But guess what? The first week I was at IU, I took some placement tests and got credit for six hours of English. I remember coming back to the dorm and finding out that only two other people had done as well. I decided maybe they weren't so damn smart after all. I think the school system in Remington was superb for the time, and especially for its size."

I began my freshman year with little idea of what I wanted to do beyond college. In the back of my mind, I saw law as an eventual possibility, but I was also intrigued by the thought of a career in broadcasting. I was ultimately attracted to the School of Business. I found the courses in advertising and marketing (my eventual major) particularly interesting, and I was mesmerized by Professor Charles Hewitt's introductory class in business law.

In the dining room of my fraternity house as a freshman pledge, I learned such things as the intricacies of properly passing the cream pitcher, and other social details that had not been on my radar screen before. I learned that if I didn't get out of bed and to class in the morning, no one else really cared, and that I and I alone would bear the consequences. Serving as the head of a committee for a student activity, I first learned the necessity of following up to see if others had carried out their assigned duties. It was not good enough to assume they would. All lessons with lifelong implications.

Almost immediately in the fall of my freshman year, I became involved in various extracurricular activities on the campus, so much so that in a way, I was as focused there as on my major. It began with the IU Fall Carnival, a major campus event sponsored by the student union that took place each fall in the university's old field house, formerly the home of IU basketball. Fraternities and sororities and men's and women's housing units paired up to design and build booths which contained complex and creative games of chance or shows. There was a competition for the best design, the most original, and so on, with the proceeds from ticket sales going to something called Campus Chest, IU's version of the United Way. I volunteered for a committee assignment and was placed on a subcommittee charged with overseeing the construction of the booths. The subcommittee chairman soon resigned, and I was asked to step in and take on the leadership of this small effort. My work there produced a wonderful letter of commendation to my parents from the dean of students, one of my first lessons in the importance and the impact of that kind of thoughtful gesture. It also led to an invitation to be a part of the Fall Carnival Steering Committee the following year, a role a bit unusual for a sophomore. The year following that, as a junior, I was asked to serve as general chairman of the entire Fall Carnival, which was a great success and gave me a major feeling of accomplishment.

Meantime, I'd gotten involved in campus politics. Student government at Indiana operated at the time with a structure built around the Organized Party, with its historic roots in the fraternity and sorority culture, and the Independent Party, run by those who

Members of the Indiana University Student Senate in 1962–1963. Among those shown are my longtime friends Dave Frick (on the left, third row), Indianapolis civic leader, former Deputy Mayor, and now Executive Vice President of the insurance company Anthem, Inc., and Jim Kittle (second from the right, fourth row), Chairman of Kittle's Furniture Stores and Chairman of the Indiana Republican Party. I am on the right, third row. Photo courtesy of Indiana University.

lived in the dormitory system. What the Organized Party lacked in numbers, it made up for in an ability to get out the vote. Campus elections were held periodically for class and student body officers and for the members of the Student Senate. During my sophomore year, I was elected to the Student Senate, representing the area of campus where my fraternity was then located. That, plus my growing name recognition from my role in other activities, led to my election as president of the IU senior class of 1964. It was a position of limited practical significance but a heady experience that put me on the stage with a small speaking role for my graduation ceremonies. And it turned out to be important on my résumé—the fundamental reason AT&T first identified me as a candidate they wanted to pursue for their Initial Management Development Program (IMDP).

Many of the students with whom I lived or with whom I worked on these campus political activities have been my lifelong friends and have gone on to significant leadership positions in Indiana and elsewhere, including my cardiologist friend Tom Hayhurst; Jim Morris, longtime Indianapolis civic leader and visionary, former president of the Lilly Endowment, and currently Executive Director of the United Nations World Food Program in Rome; Dave Frick, top aide to former Mayor and now U.S. Senator Richard Lugar during his service as mayor of Indianapolis and now Executive Vice President of the insurance company Anthem, Inc.; Jim Kittle, Chairman of the Kittle's Furniture Stores in Indiana and Ohio and currently Chairman of the Indiana Republican Party; Tom Huston, former aide to President Richard Nixon and now a successful attorney and real estate developer in central Indiana; and retired Brigadier General Fred Buckingham, the first graduate of the IU Air Force Reserve Officer Training Corps (ROTC) program to reach that rank.

During my senior year, I was cohost of a student-run radio program on Sunday evenings called *University Showtime*, on Bloomington's commercial radio stations, WTTS-AM and WTTV-FM. For three hours every Sunday, we played records, interviewed guests, and generally had a wonderful time. This was the closest I ever came to the career in broadcasting I'd once considered.

One fall afternoon in my senior year, I left a class at the business school and walked over to the student union to attend a meeting. When I entered the lower lobby of the union building, the scene was quite surreal, as if everyone had been frozen in place. There was also an eerie silence. I began to realize that instead of the usual background music, everyone was listening to a man's voice coming through the ceiling speakers. He was saying, "I've just been handed a bulletin from Parkland Hospital here in Dallas . . ." President Kennedy was dead, and the world would never be quite the same.

When I look back on those years, there are not many major

life-altering episodes that I see. Rather, it's a series of seemingly minor events, a connecting of the dots, if you will, from a variety of smaller experiences. I can't really point to one or two unique influences along the way that made me who I am today. In large part, college was made up of the kinds of experiences you don't realize are significant at the time. You simply don't comprehend the effect they are having on your life. But when you look back at them in the aggregate, you realize their impact.

As I graduated in June 1964, I recall a hesitant but growing sense of confidence in myself. It had been an enormous change for me to leave Remington for the IU campus in the fall of 1960. The size of my freshman class was several times the population of my hometown, and the diversity of backgrounds and experiences of my classmates was vast compared to anything I had known. When I arrived as a freshman, I was hopeful, but I simply did not know how well I could do in this larger and more complex environment. Over those four years, I had been tested, in many ways, and for the most part, I was pleased with what I had accomplished. I had been accepted by my new peers. I had generally enjoyed my course work, particularly my courses in the School of Business, and I felt I had received a good education. In most ways, I'd held my own. Maybe I *could* compete with those I would meet in the years ahead, those whose backgrounds were even broader and deeper than what I had now experienced. But along with the self-confidence I had gained, there was clearly a very big dose of humility and apprehension. I recognized that the world I was about to enter was an even bigger place than anything I had seriously contemplated while growing up in Remington or during my time as an undergraduate.

My years at Indiana University clearly marked the point in my life from which I can trace everything that has happened since. And in reality, what has served me best from those years were the lessons from outside the classroom—the excitement of accepting

I share a laugh with an Indiana University icon, the late Herman B Wells. Wells served as IU president between 1938 and 1962, and later as the university's chancellor until his death in 2000 at the age of 97. The photograph was taken in our Florida vacation home in the late 1980s.

new challenges, of managing multiple activities at the same time, of leading people with competing and often conflicting ideas, of finding myself with responsibilities in areas where I had little prior knowledge or experience to guide my actions and decisions. Through my extracurricular activities, I had my first taste of what it would be like to be a business executive. I had learned to deal with a lot of different, competing, and sometimes ambiguous issues all at the same time—and I loved it. I would soon learn that not everyone with whom I would work had enjoyed the benefits of similar experiences.

The World of Ambiguity

Several years ago, shortly after assuming responsibility for a new organization, I began to get acquainted with the skills and strengths of the various managers who carried the label "high potential." One manager in particular became a puzzle to me. He was viewed as having an outstanding track record and possessing the ability to continue to move ahead in the company. But I could not observe evidence of that capacity. Over time, as I discovered what his strengths and weaknesses really were, I concluded that in all likelihood I was right, but so were those who had observed him in the past. It was just that my arrival had changed the rules of the game and he was unable to operate as effectively in the new environment. During much of his career, he had been in jobs structured functionally, where there had been a great deal of very specific top-down direction. His role had been to take that direction and implement it. And he did that well. Under the new rules, he was responsible for an integrated piece of the company, from beginning to end. No one was providing that strategic direction any longer. In the current environment, he simply could not cope as effectively with the uncertainty and the ambiguity he faced. He was a great *manager*, but his *leadership* capacity was more limited than had been assumed. My fears were confirmed when I learned that in response to the initial coaching he received about the need to address these shortcomings, his first instinct was to seek out the "rules" for dealing with ambiguity.

Among those who aspire to be leaders, different people have different instincts. In part, that is the simple result of the skills they've been required to display in climbing their particular career ladder. I may risk offending my colleagues who come from certain educational or professional disciplines, such as engineering or accounting or copy editing, by suggesting that in my experience, individuals who spend their careers in highly structured jobs may have additional developmental challenges to overcome to become broadly focused leaders. The more a particular discipline requires, and rewards, strict adherence to process and procedure, requires coloring strictly inside the lines, so to speak, the more likely it is that people who have excelled in that environment will experience discomfort in dealing with uncertainty and ambiguity. For many, it's often a completely foreign way of looking at things. But like most generalizations, this one is dangerous if applied blindly across the board.

My good friend Norm Augustine, an engineering graduate of Princeton, has been recognized by his peers with many of the highest honors the field of engineering can bestow. When something *does* require a rocket scientist, Norm's the one to call. He's very proud of his educational background. When he's traveling overseas and has to fill out an immigration or customs form, in the blank marked "occupation" he always writes "engineer." And skilled as he is as an engineer, this retired Chairman and CEO of Lockheed Martin Corporation is also one of the most gifted leaders I've ever worked with. He's been widely recognized and honored for his many leadership achievements across a broad range of responsibilities. He's living proof that engineers *can* do it all.[1] So don't misinterpret my observation to mean that *all* specialists in highly structured fields can't deal with ambiguity. I'm simply suggesting that it may require a more discerning eye to uncover and develop what might otherwise be the hidden leadership potential in managers from certain backgrounds and experiences who have been rewarded for a more rigid kind of thinking and now must deal with the so-called soft issues, often so steeped in ambiguity. To fully determine

1. To illustrate my point, in 1983, when Norm was elected to membership in the National Academy of Engineering, the election citation read, in part: for the "imaginative blending of the skills of engineer, analyst, and manager in the accomplishment of important aerospace engineering projects."

their real capabilities or limitations as potential leaders may simply require more developmental attention.

Interestingly, Norm himself has an observation that I find quite consistent with my own. "It helps to have some depth in one field," he says. "I think it helps one better understand the problems six or seven layers below. If you work your way up from the bottom in one area of a business, chances are you will have learned just about everything you need to know about running it. If you can have depth in one field in addition to breadth, that's far and away the biggest advantage. [But] if you can only have one or the other, depth or breadth, concentrate on breadth if you want to be a senior manager."

The depth-versus-breadth question is one I get asked a great deal. And as is often the case, I agree with Norm's observation unconditionally. I think that depth in some professional field is a big help. Somebody who knows only a little bit about a lot of things is not likely to find it as easy to be an effective leader. There's a certain mind-set that comes with depth that enables one to form useful relationships with other such people, even if they are in very different fields.

In an industry like pharmaceuticals, which depends on scientific innovation for its driving force, these relationships lie at the heart of good leadership. Someone who is seen as a broad but shallow generalist often can't cope with a population of experts. In the end, such a person is sometimes thought of uncharitably as an "empty suit." At the same time, it's seldom a good idea to elevate someone who's an inch wide and five hundred miles deep. Future leaders absolutely must have breadth, even without great depth, which begs the inevitable question: How is that achieved?

As a former part-time professor and holder of the Poling Chair in Business and Government at IU's Kelly School of Business, and as the retired Chairman of the Board of Trustees of Duke University, let me make one think patently clear: I believe in the merits of a quality academic education. I am not suggesting that eschewing a serious and focused classroom education in favor of pursuing a laundry list of outside interests is a smart strategy for climbing to the top of anything. I am simply suggesting a somewhat broader definition of what constitutes a quality education. While the academic part of higher education is quite necessary, I think it's unfortunate when it's also seen as wholly sufficient. Too many students miss the other aspects of the educational opportunity. From my point of view, my involvement in extracurricular activities had at least as much to do with the development of the skills that helped me become a corporate leader as the lessons I learned in the classroom. And I don't think the importance of having those skills will diminish anytime soon. Why? Now more than ever, corporations are looking for people who can operate in the softer, more ambiguous areas of the business, the places where it is impossible to have all the answers. In short, they will be looking for people who can learn to be comfortable with discomfort, people who don't feel the need to ask questions like "Which do you want, long-term results or short-term results?" Rather, people who understand that if you're going to run the business successfully, you've got to have it all. You've got to be able to strike a balance. These are skills that can best be honed someplace outside a classroom.

Perhaps one of the key indicators for separating those who most likely have the potential to become successful leaders from those who probably do not is their level of comfort with ambiguity, their ability to be comfortable in an uncertain environment. How eager are they to continue to learn? Nearly every issue that arrives on the desk of the CEO has no right or wrong answer. If it did, it probably would have been addressed and disposed of at some lower level in the organization. Ambiguity and learning almost define the job.

Basketball and Music

My years on the Bloomington campus, coupled with all of the influences on my life that came before, provided me with something else that I have come to believe was an equally valuable part of my undergraduate experience: the desire and the instinct to build on my mother's influence and to keep learning. This need might seem obvious to most, maybe even trivial. But I have known leaders who thought they knew it all. I've also known those who are wise enough to start with the assumption that they know very little and want to find out more. Let me give you an example of two such leaders.

Donnie Walsh, President of the Indiana Pacers of the NBA, has been in and around the game of basketball all of his life, as a player, as a coach, and as an executive. An outstanding high school basketball player in New York City and a 1962 graduate of the University of North Carolina where he was a Tar Heel guard, and then the UNC School of Law, Walsh has been leading, building, and improving the Pacers organization since 1986 and is generally regarded as one of the premier executives in the game today.

Maestro Raymond Leppard, Conductor Laureate of the Indianapolis Symphony Orchestra and for fourteen years its Music Director, was born in London and educated at Trinity College, Cambridge. Well known to serious music lovers around the world, he's conducted most of the great orchestras in the United States, in Europe, and in many other countries. His work can be heard on more than 170 recordings.

My wife Marianne and I are proud to count both Donnie and Raymond among our friends. In many ways, they are probably as different from each other as any two successful leaders could be. Several years ago, on a Sunday afternoon in the fall, both were our guests at an Indianapolis Colts football game, where they became acquainted for the first time. That afternoon, as Donnie found himself explaining American football to Raymond, a very serendipitous thing occurred. These two leaders, who had achieved success in very different fields, discovered they were really in the same business. They seemed to conclude that they were each in the business of assembling, organizing, leading, and motivating groups of very talented individuals, causing them to work together as a unit, all for the pleasure of those who purchased tickets to enjoy the product of that effort. For the remainder of the afternoon, both men discussed various aspects of their experiences, sharing ideas and learning from each other. Some weeks later, Donnie and his wife Judy joined us for a concert of the Indianapolis Symphony followed by dinner with Maestro Leppard. And again, the same fascinating exchange occurred.

Leaders almost always think out of the box. They listen, observe, share ideas, and shamelessly borrow from the experiences of others. Both Raymond and Donnie are effective leaders, demonstrating traits to be sought and admired in those who will lead in the future.

M-Dipper

As I reflect on my part-time job experiences, I see that they all had one thing in common. They provided some incredible mentors early in my life, all of whom made a lasting contribution to the values and experiences that have guided my life and my career. That certainly included the final one, the mentor I was to have during the summer of 1964.

On June 8, 1964, I graduated from Indiana University. As a result of my choice to participate in the ROTC program at the university, I was also commissioned a second lieutenant in the field artillery branch of the U.S. Army. At the same time, I received orders directing me to report to the artillery school at Fort Sill,

Oklahoma, in October 1964, to begin a mandatory two-year tour of active duty. I had applied to and been admitted to law school, and my general game plan was to find something meaningful to do between June and October, spend the two required years on active duty, go back to school, and then get on with my life.

So far, things were working out as planned. Earlier in the spring, I had been hired by AT&T's Indiana Bell subsidiary to join a new and unique program with an unusual name. Those of us given the opportunity to sign on (about six or so in Indiana, as I recall) were called "M-Dips"—a term derived from the acronym IMDP. The idea was very simple. Candidates were identified, screened, and evaluated in many of the usual ways common to corporate re-cruiting on college campuses, with one important difference: The bottom line objective was to identify college seniors entering the job market who had demonstrated significant peer-supported lead-ership outside the classroom and had done so while performing well in the classroom. The program was seeking team captains, class presidents, dorm leaders, fraternity presidents, and the like. The theory was that if an individual had emerged as a leader among his peers on campus, chances were he would likely emerge as a leader in the corporation.

The M-Dips who were hired by AT&T were given challenging assignments from day 1 and often had several subordinates. They were expected to demonstrate within their first year that they were likely to advance into the leadership ranks of the company. If not, they were out the door. This was, in a nutshell, the IMDP way: Results mattered most.

There was one additional and important aspect to the IMDP. Each employee was assigned to a boss who was already in middle management, usually seven to ten years more advanced in their careers, and also identified as having very high potential.

In June 1964, at age twenty-two, I reported to my first assign-ment in Evansville, Indiana. I was responsible for seven employees, most of whom were several years older and at least that much more experienced in what they were doing. I was assigned to a bright, energetic, and very laid-back boss who (according to hallway scuttlebutt) at age twenty-seven was already on his way to very big things. And as usual, the grass-roots-level employees had the situation sized up correctly. The District Manager who was my first leader was Robert E. Allen, who two decades later would become Chairman and CEO of AT&T.

Bob was a superb mentor during those first few months. Remembers Allen, "Randy and I hit it off very quickly. I very happily took on the challenge of giving him some assignments and getting out of his way to see how he would do on his own. That was an important element to the program, to give young leaders a lot of responsibility at a very early stage with a little coaching. We washed out a few that way, but overall, I think it worked very well."

But it wasn't just the M-Dips who were expected to perform from the get-go. Accountability for performance was a company-wide practice. "The company was so service-oriented then that the great leaders would cut through red tape widthwise to get results quickly," says my longtime friend and colleague at Indiana Bell, Jim Irwin. "My first day on the job as a district manager in Indianapolis, I get a call from [former President] Tom Nurnberger's office. I hadn't even had my first cup of coffee. I thought, 'Unbelievable. The president is calling to welcome me aboard.' So I call back and reach his assistant, Julia Dawson, who says, 'You've got a service problem with one of your customers and Mr. Nurnberger would like to know what you are going to do about it. And I bet he would like to know by the end of the day.' That's the way the company operated. When you were placed in a new job, you were responsible that minute. And in those days, top-quality customer service counted for everything."

My experience in Evansville that summer was quite unexpected. I enjoyed it so much and was so impressed with Bob that I left in

October thinking I just might come back to Indiana Bell and AT&T instead of going on to law school. In the meantime, I was hardly aware of what had been happening half a world away.

Fire for Effect

Beginning in 1962, the United States had escalated its efforts in support of the South Vietnamese government, sending a stream of "advisors" and support aircraft, ships, weapons, and supplies to assist their military. By the summer of 1964, little or no progress had been made, and the South Vietnamese military found themselves giving up more and more ground to the Viet Cong. On the night of August 4, 1964, two U.S. Navy destroyers, the USS *Maddox* and the USS *Turner Joy*, were patrolling in the Gulf of Tonkin, off the coast of North Vietnam. The *Turner Joy* reported that it had picked up indications of high-speed vessels nearby, assumed to be attacking North Vietnamese gunboats. To this day, there are conflicting accounts about what actually happened. Some believe the boats were there; others do not. Nonetheless, both the *Maddox* and the *Turner Joy* responded with heavy gunfire, and the incident was immediately reported to Washington. Events began to escalate. President Lyndon Johnson quickly addressed the nation, and on August 7, 1964, Congress passed the Gulf of Tonkin Resolution,[2] authorizing the president of the United States to "take all necessary measures to repel armed attack against the forces of the United States and to prevent further aggression." This was to become the basis for the U.S. escalation of forces in Vietnam and the consequences that followed. Many who voted for that resolution would later regret it.

Even though I was commissioned as a second lieutenant from

---

2. The resolution was passed by a vote of 416 to 0 in the House and 88 to 2 in the Senate.

IU's ROTC program at the same time I received my degree, I had no interest in a career in the military. But with the Selective Service System in full operation, mandatory military service looked highly probable. Active duty as an officer seemed preferable to the other options I could imagine.

In early October 1964, some sixty days after the passage of the Gulf of Tonkin Resolution, I set out on the two-day drive to Fort Sill to report for my first assignment—fully expecting that I would soon be on my way to Southeast Asia. At that time, the first active-duty assignment for every newly commissioned second lieutenant from the college and university ROTC programs across the country was the school of the army branch to which they had been assigned. Fort Sill, the "Home of the Field Artillery," was first used as an army garrison in 1869 by troops sent into what was then Indian territory to stop raids on white settlements. Many of the original stone buildings constructed during that period are still in use. According to the official history, the U.S. Army Field Artillery School, as it is known today, was founded at Fort Sill in 1911 because it "was considered the best location for a field artillery school, since its 15,000-acre reservation allowed ample room for target practice and its great variety of [extremely rugged] terrain offered an excellent area for different types of tactical training." I had no trouble believing that. My first impression was that if Fort Sill itself wasn't the end of the earth, then the end must surely have been just over the next hill.

Along with a hundred or so other young officers, I was clearly entering a very different world. Some were eager to begin what they hoped would be lifetime military careers, but most were eager to get their two years over with so that they could get back to their civilian lives. All of us had attended ROTC classes several days a week for four years. We'd studied leadership, military history, military law, military courtesy, and a long list of other subjects. And we'd spent many hours learning to march with rifles in

Standing at the main gate to Fort Sill, Oklahoma, in 1966 while serving on active duty as a U.S. Army artillery officer.

close-order drill. We'd also spent six long weeks on active duty during the summer preceding our senior year in the ROTC equivalent of boot camp. By an act of Congress, our commissioning might well have made us "officers and gentlemen," in an official sense, but we surely were not yet prepared to take on the roles that would be expected of us.

For the next twelve weeks or so, we would be taught as much as we could absorb about what was required of an active-duty army officer, and of a field artillery officer in particular. There were courses in communications, tactics, map reading, and a number of other necessary skills. But the heart of the program was gunnery class, where, among other things, we learned the skills of an artillery forward observer, a role with a combat life expectancy of about fifteen minutes. In gunnery field exercises, we were taught to locate a distant target, usually an old car body on a hillside out on the firing range, through binoculars. We then attempted to identify the precise location of the target on a detailed map. At that point, one student officer was selected by the instructor to call the map coordinates he had determined to the fire direction center. There, the calculations were made for the appropriate settings required on the artillery pieces (the cannons) that were to be fired. The troops in the artillery battery, the basic artillery organizational unit, usually consisting of six artillery pieces, then prepared two of the guns to fire, setting the proper direction and elevation of the barrels and placing the proper powder charges in the shells. When all was ready, the order was given to fire, and if you were the one who'd been selected, you prayed that you would see white puffs of smoke through your binoculars, the indication of shells landing somewhere close to the target. The idea was to place two rounds slightly in front, then two more slightly behind, called bracketing the target. If that happened, you could then pinpoint the target exactly by splitting the difference and radioing those coordinates along with the command "Fire for effect." At that point, you hoped that shells from all six guns would come raining down on the target and that it would literally disappear into oblivion. Our early skills were such that seldom did it happen quite that way, but we felt great satisfaction when it did.

At some point, well along in the course, we all received orders for our next assignment. Some were assigned to artillery units at other military installations in the United States. Some were sent to units in Europe or Korea or elsewhere around the world. But many were sent to units in Vietnam, or clearly on their way to Vietnam. To my amazement, I was assigned to duty as an instructor right there at the artillery school, specifically to the Communications and Electronics Department. My mother was convinced, as mothers always are, that I had been hand-picked for this assignment on merit. I was more realistic about it. In the wake of the Gulf of Tonkin Resolution, the army was clearly in need of rapidly increasing its capacity to train personnel for assignments in Vietnam or in support of those in Vietnam. That meant more students would be coming through the school, which meant more instructors were needed. In my view, I'd simply had the good fortune to be in the right place at the right time.

After completing instructor training, I spent the next twenty-one months teaching students in various programs such as the one I had just completed, in Officer Candidate School, in the Artillery Officer Career Course, and eventually in private customized briefings for colonels and generals who were mostly on their way to command units in Vietnam.

There were several assistant instructors whose job it was to support me and the other officers who were primary instructors. All were senior noncommissioned officers who were veterans of World War II. All had been around for a long time. Most had in fact been promoted to officer rank during the war, only to be set back to their former enlisted rank when the size of the army was reduced after World War II. They were serving out their time as enlisted men to accumulate the years of service necessary to retire with their military pensions. As you would expect, they were not entirely happy campers. I soon discovered that I had the wherewithal to make their lives much more palatable, and they mine. We quickly came to an unspoken understanding. When they were assigned to assist me, I expected them to be on time, look sharp, work hard to help get the necessary equipment set up and working properly for class, coach me to do a good job with my assignment, and later put everything away properly. In return, rather than thinking up some kind of busywork to occupy the rest of their day, my approach was "if our real work is completed and you have nothing important or useful to do, don't do it here." They happily disappeared. It was amazing how productive we became as a team.

During my two years at Fort Sill, I also took advantage of the opportunity to take affordable flying lessons. Fort Sill had a flying

At the controls of a Piper PA-18 owned by the Fort Sill, Oklahoma, flying club in 1965.

club, subsidized in a number of ways as part of the army's efforts to make off-duty time as tolerable as possible. The club owned several Piper PA-18's, often referred to as Piper Cubs. These particular planes had seen service as artillery spotter planes and had been retired from that duty. After soloing, I spent many happy afternoons and weekends alone in the sky, flying around over the state of Oklahoma.

Sometime during 1965, I was invited to a party at the home of an acquaintance, a teacher in the school system serving Fort Sill. That evening, I met a delightful young fourth-grade teacher who worked in the same school. Her name was Marilyn Salyer. I discovered that she was driving back and forth at night to the Norman campus to finish her master's degree at the University of Oklahoma, a fact that impressed me because it was an unusual discovery in the Fort Sill social scene. I called her a few days later, and she agreed to join me for a movie. Afterward, we went to the officers' club for a drink. The rest, as they say is history. On September 2, 1966, we were married in a small family ceremony in Oklahoma City. I had accepted a job as the Indiana Bell Telephone Company manager in Lebanon, confirming my earlier decision to forgo law school for at least a while. After giving my final salute to the active-duty army, we were on our way to civilian life in Indiana and the extraordinary adventures in store for our twenty-eight years together.

I'm not sure I recognized it at the time, but my experience as an army instructor would later serve me well in my business career. For nearly two years, I had found myself standing before classes of student officers who often outranked me, who mostly had far more practical experience than I did, and who, without exception, would have loved nothing better than to embarrass me by catching me with the wrong answer to their questions. It was through that experience that I became quite comfortable testifying before Congress, addressing security analysts, presiding at annual meetings, and in general, communicating to audiences, friendly and hostile, large and small, formally or informally—a skill that is one of the hallmark responsibilities of any corporate executive.

SIX

The Hierarchy of Secrets

*The world of the 1990s and beyond will not
belong to "managers" or those who can make
the numbers dance. The world will belong to
passionate, driven leaders—people who not only
have enormous amounts of energy but who can
energize those whom they lead.*

—Jack Welch

Answer the Door

On a blustery but memorable Windy City morning in early
1978, the lights on the telephones in the repair center at Illinois
Bell's North Suburban Area—where I had recently been appointed
General Manager—began to light up like a Christmas tree. In rapid
order, the technicians on duty received a flurry of complaints from
major corporate customers in the area that something was dread-
fully wrong with their telephone service. It was soon determined
that two major underground cables passing through the Chicago
area and connecting the coasts had somehow been severely damaged. Once the origin of the problem had been generally located,
repair crews were dispatched to locate the precise source of the
problem, determine what had happened—and fix it. For employees who had worked in this part of the business for some time, the
probable root cause was an easy guess. Somewhere along the North
Shore, under a sign reading CAUTION: DO NOT DIG HERE—UNDERGROUND
CABLES, someone—a construction crew or a farmer, most likely—

---

had decided to dig a trench or a posthole and, in the process, had gone right through the cables.

It soon became apparent to those involved that this was more than a routine cable cut. I was notified by the repair center supervisor and briefed about what was known. I immediately contacted several of the major customers who were being affected—Motorola, for example—to inform them that we were on top of the situation, that their facilities were being temporarily rerouted to provide them with some partial relief, and that I would personally see to it that we were doing all we could to correct the problem and return them to normal service as quickly as possible. I then called my boss, Vice President John Clendenin. John was an executive of significant talent, and I admired him greatly. I suspect that during my time in his organization, I learned as much from him as from anyone for whom I ever worked. But I also found it was sometimes a challenge to keep up with him because his mind was so fertile and he knew so much about the business. It was never possible to get ahead of him. On this occasion, he had questions about the size and type of cables affected, whether they were pressurized, the name of the repair foreman on the scene, and so on. From experience, to the best of my ability, I had equipped myself with the answers to his questions. After concluding my report to John, I prepared to leave my office to drive to the trouble site to see what I could learn there, but just as I was leaving, John called back. He had a question about the size of pumps that were being used to remove the water from the manholes on either side of the cable cut, where work would also need to be done. His own instincts exemplified one of the characteristics most admired within the Bell System's management culture of that time: No detail that might be relevant was ever too small to be noted and communicated up the line.

I was joined by the Division Plant Manager, one of my key lieutenants who had responsibility for this part of the business, and together we drove to the location of the damage. We pulled up next to a telltale backhoe and a sheepish-looking construction crew that had been installing a drainage culvert when they cut into the cables. As I looked down into a recently excavated hole surrounding the damage, I could see an Illinois Bell repair crew already hard at work, led by a wizened and white-haired foreman who looked like an off-season Santa Claus tinkering in a makeshift workshop.

The damage to the cables had been precisely located and analyzed; the excavation around the damage enlarged to provide room to work; the sides of the excavation shored up to avoid a cave-in; the cable cleaned, propped up, and supported to contain the damage; and lights strung to illuminate the work area. In short, these people knew exactly what needed to be done—and they were doing it. Four experienced splicers were working their magic. Like vascular surgeons, they were patiently but swiftly splicing into the existing cable a section of new cable that would replace the severed wires that had been damaged.

"How's it going down there?" I asked.

The splicers paused momentarily, looked up at me, smiled and nodded, and then resumed their work. They recognized me because I'd already had early-morning coffee with them in their garage on at least one occasion as part of my get-acquainted efforts.

"How much longer do you think this will take?" I inquired, in part because I wanted to be able to pass that information along to the customers affected, and in part because I knew I'd be expected to pass frequent updates up the chain of command.

"We're estimating another couple of hours," the foreman responded.

"Do you need anything more? Do you have the equipment you need, and would you like me to get more people out here to help?" I asked, probably sounding as if those thoughts had not occurred to anyone else.

The foreman turned slowly and, with a gentle smile and a respectful but measured tone, said simply, "Son, we can only put so many men into this hole at one time. The fastest way for us to get this problem fixed is to just fix it."

And with that, he turned and resumed working.

Over the years, I've thought of that experience on a number of occasions. The man knew what he was talking about. There really is something to be said for the Nike slogan "Just do it." That concept applies in many ways to running a successful business, but it's also true when it comes to the factors that affect one's own career.

To be sure, those who emerge as successful leaders have to possess certain innate abilities and characteristics: the ability to motivate others, to communicate effectively, to withstand the rigors of long hours and travels. Beyond that, and in my own case, I attribute the development of my own leadership skills in large part to the sum total of my various and somewhat unique experiences: parental influence, education, early job assignments, extracurricular activities in college, mentors, and, significantly, early successes and failures. But assuming that two people seem to have comparable capabilities, and one moves ahead in the business while the other does not, what is the explanation if they both seem to be deserving of advancement?

Beyond sheer ability, there are many factors that come into play. But to steal a line from Clint Eastwood's aging gunslinger in one of my all-time favorite movies, *Unforgiven*, when success fails to come to those who are deserving, it's largely because "deserve's got nothing to do with it."

In my view, having the capabilities is absolutely necessary, but it's not sufficient. Success also requires opportunity. Making one's own fate by effectively addressing the opportunities that do come along is critical. With every opportunity seized comes the potential for growth and development, which opens the door to even more opportunity. And so it goes.

The Hierarchy of Secrets

In the spring of 1977, a career move came to me with roots in an opportunity that had occurred four years earlier. This was a move I would not have anticipated in my wildest dreams, not when I began my career with the Bell System, and not even on the day it came. The powers that be at AT&T headquarters had signed off on a decision that I would be transferred from Indiana Bell's headquarters in Indianapolis to Illinois Bell in Chicago. This was a very big deal. First of all, a transfer of someone at my level within the Bell System, from one operating subsidiary to another, meant you were on the high-potential list for career advancement and your performance was being watched at the top of the parent company. And whether true or not, getting transferred to Illinois Bell was thought to present an even more unique opportunity. If the Bell System's twenty-three operating companies were like the teams in a minor-league baseball league feeding talent into AT&T's New York–based major-league team, then Illinois Bell had seemed to serve as the perennial training ground for all-star players. That perception would continue for some years.

Then current Chairman and CEO of AT&T, John deButts had at one time served as President of Illinois Bell. Charles L. Brown, the most recent President of the company, had just been moved from Chicago to one of AT&T's seniormost positions in New York, and before long, he would replace deButts as Chairman and CEO of the parent company. My former boss at Indiana Bell, Jim Olson, had replaced Brown in Chicago, and he would one day replace Brown at the AT&T helm. And Bob Allen, another longtime mentor, had just been named Chief Operating Officer at Illinois Bell, the number-two position in the company. Some years in the future, he would replace Jim Olson as AT&T's leader.[1]

---

1. In the years ahead, Chuck Marshall, then a former Illinois Bell officer who had been sent in to run the company's Texas operations after something of a scandal was uncovered there and who had then moved on to become AT&T's Treasurer, would return to replace Olson as President

In my new Chicago assignment, my title was General Manager for the North Suburban Area. For the first time in my career, I was charged with responsibility for all aspects of telephone service in a geographic area of the company. It was my first experience running an integrated business. The managers, engineers, salespeople, operators, service representatives, and maintenance and repair crews working in this arm of the Bell System all reported to me.

I found myself in a job that, quite frankly, exceeded the best-case career plans I could have laid out for myself as a young college graduate entering the workforce. And I didn't get there as the result of some complex detailed career-planning strategy, such as the ones I'm often asked about by college students and young managers planning their own careers. So how was it that at age thirty-five I had already surpassed any longer-term career goals I might have outlined at the beginning of my career? Mostly by trying to do the best I could every single day and then letting my performance speak for itself. Career planning would take care of itself.

While I do not discount the influence of either the nature or nurture factors on my success, I have come to believe that there are two important components in determining whether one enjoys steady career advancement. The first is whether you have the capacity to repeatedly demonstrate both the ability to excel (the intangible factors, coupled with intelligence, creativity, judgment, and the like) and the drive, desire, energy, and enthusiasm to be

---

of Illinois Bell and would later become Vice Chairman of AT&T. Jerry Freche, my initial boss in Chicago, was soon promoted to Chief Operating Officer of Northwestern Bell. John Clendenin, an Illinois Bell vice president at the time of my arrival in Chicago, would become a senior officer at AT&T and then move on to become Chairman and CEO of one of the split-off regional Bell companies, Bell South. Bud Staley, a former Illinois Bell officer, would become the Chairman and CEO of NYNEX, another of the regional companies. Beyond Chuck, John, and Bud, a remarkably long list of others would move through Illinois Bell on their way to more senior assignments in the company. There was good reason for this. Illinois, with its massive urban Chicago area, its vast rural agricultural areas of small and medium-size communities, its Chicago political machine, and its rural-dominated state legislature, provided the ideal proving ground to test both the inside and outside capabilities of future leaders of the Bell System.

motivated by *all* of the jobs you find yourself working in, even if some assignments don't readily fit into your well-considered career plans. Beyond capabilities, the second factor is fate, or luck, or whatever you believe creates the opportunities to demonstrate your capabilities. I have come to believe that the defining events in any career, more often than not, have to do with the intersection of those two factors. One must have both the ability to consistently deliver results and the opportunities to demonstrate that ability, including most particularly at that rare, unexpected, and often unrecognized moment when career-altering opportunity presents itself. When the glare of the spotlight suddenly shines on your stage, you've got to be able to dance, to be sure. But you've also got to be ready to dance at every opportunity, because you won't always know when you're being called to the stage for what will potentially be the career-determining performance.

In fact, for me, the circumstances that have turned out to have the most influence on and significance in my career, the proximate causes of the turning points, more often than not came from totally unanticipated opportunities. Let me give you an example.

For the Bell System and for me, 1973 was a watershed year. Students of AT&T history will remember it as the year AT&T Chairman and CEO John deButts made his infamous "decision to decide" speech in Seattle, unintentionally solidifying in the minds of regulators, some have suggested, the need to break up the company. I had just been promoted to a job in the public-relations department at Indiana Bell. It was my first assignment outside the mainstream operations of the business, and even though it was a promotion, I was a bit apprehensive about what might be next, because this did not seem to be the kind of assignment where careers were built. My new position included the responsibility for planning and overseeing all of the company's advertising programs. At that time, Indiana Bell was the principal sponsor of the telecasts of the Indiana State High School Basketball Tournament.

In effect, I was the executive producer of that telecast and devoted much of my time and energy during the winter and spring to working with those who would be carrying out the details. However, one of the part-time responsibilities of my job was also to act as a kind of executive assistant to the president of the company. What that meant was that if the president of Indiana Bell was asked to take on some responsibility in the community, to be the chairman of some event, for example, then more often than not, the bulk of that task devolved to me.

So on an otherwise very ordinary day, in what I have come to view as one of the defining moments of my career, Paul Reinken, the Vice President in charge of the area of the business where I worked and an early mentor, called to tell me I was to go up to the executive suite to see the company's president. On my arrival in his office, Jim Olson, Indiana Bell's charismatic CEO, informed me that he had agreed to cochair an event to support the Business Committee for the Arts in Indiana. His cochair, and the person who had asked him to take on this role, was one of the most respected leaders in the state, J. Irwin Miller, the retired Chairman and CEO of the Cummins Engine Company of Columbus, Indiana. It's also worth noting that Mr. Miller was then a member of AT&T's Board of Directors. The purpose of the two-day symposium "we" were to develop was to encourage doing more than simply writing checks to support local arts and cultural organizations. The conference would bring together the presidents of Indiana's colleges and universities, the heads of the major arts and culture organizations in the state, the CEOs of Indiana's major corporations, and other state leaders. The specific purpose was to help the state's leaders recognize the importance of arts and culture to the state's quality of life and to motivate corporations in particular to look for ways to expose their employees to the arts. It was hoped that CEOs could be persuaded to be broadly sensitive to the arts and culture in all that they did, through relatively simple acts such as including the preservation of green space in the construction of buildings, loaning needed talent to not-for-profit organizations, or displaying traveling art exhibitions in company lobbies for employees' pleasure.

If the event went off well, it would have the potential to make a positive impact on the quality of life in Indiana. Beyond that, Mr. Miller would be pleased, it would be a very public and positive reflection on the company and on our commitment to the quality of life in the state, and it would reflect well personally on the president and CEO of Indiana Bell.

My leadership, along with that of someone from Mr. Miller's staff, would be required to bring the right people together to creatively plan the event, attract all the right leaders to attend, and then see to it that it was executed well. Taking on this task was not exactly what I would have chosen as a top priority that spring. Nonetheless, I devoted a great deal of time to the event, getting personally involved in all of the small details despite the fact that I had a full-time job worrying about the basketball telecast (which, in the hoops-crazed Hoosier state, was pretty serious business) and the rest of my regular job assignment.

The event went off without a hitch—even better than expected. A large number of business leaders signed up for the necessary follow-up. Mr. Miller seemed elated. Olson was a hero in the arts community. He was pleased with what I had accomplished, and very grateful that my efforts had kept him from having to devote much of his own time to the planning.

Although I didn't know it at the time, fate or luck or chance had presented me with an opportunity to provide at least a glimpse of what I was capable of doing to an executive who would soon move up in the business ahead of me. I took full advantage of that opportunity, not because I had any understanding of the future implications but because I was focused on doing the job at hand. If I had simply carried out the assignment, adequately but without any particular distinction, then this opportunity I'd been given would not have mattered to my career. Or if Jim Olson had not been moving ahead in the business himself, what I had done with the opportunity would not have affected my future.

Why was I driven to do the best possible job I could on an assignment that was only a marginal part of my mainstream responsibilities? Parental influence, early job assignments, early mentors? Certainly I was well aware this was the president of the company, but I was not sufficiently prescient to understand the possibilities. Over a lifetime, I had developed an ingrained work ethic that simply required doing the best I could, no matter what the assignment. It was not until years later that I came to realize that success in the corporate world is sometimes like the proverbial frog in children's literature—the happy endings often lie behind the guises and forms where you least expect to find them. For many would-be leaders, opportunities for career advancement are often missed because they get too hung up on finding what they believe to be the most obvious, most programmatic ways to the top, forgoing opportunities that don't readily fit into their formulas for career success. Or even worse, they refuse to go the extra mile for work that seems only marginally related to their job descriptions when it's not clear what's in it for them.

So when I'm asked how I became a successful CEO, my response is disappointingly simple. I believe I was blessed with some of the requisite abilities, certainly. But I also thought it was important to do my best to be ready when opportunity knocked. And then I always tried to answer the door.

Managers or Leaders?

Beyond the issue of seizing the opportunity, why are some managers able to become true leaders, while others are not?

Why did Charlie Brown find time to write that note to a young senior officer, while a similar gesture would not have occurred to others? Were there indicators early in Charlie's career of his enormous capacity to lead? What were they?

Why was Roberto Goizueta such an effective CEO at Coca-Cola, while his hand-picked successor, who had flourished in every prior job, was seemingly unable to master the requirements of leading the company?

Are some managers capable of being highly successful chief operating officers but less well suited to be chief executive officers? What are the signs?

Why was Lou Gerstner a consistently successful leader in such diverse companies as McKinsey & Company, American Express, RJR Nabisco, and, ultimately, IBM? Was that breadth of capability visible early in his career?

Are there early predictors of leadership capacity? And how dependable are they? The question of greatest interest to those whose careers lie mostly ahead is this: Can managers develop the competencies and characteristics necessary to become leaders?

I think perhaps the best answer to this last question is "Yes . . . but. . . ."

I've come to believe that almost every leader is born with at least some degree of the inherent capabilities that are required for effective leadership. But it's even more important to know that managers with modest innate skills have risen to become great leaders, while others with the potential to develop into strong leaders have never realized their full capability. So it seems logical that nearly all aspiring managers can enhance their leadership skills if they focus on developing the capabilities and characteristics that are most likely to help them succeed.

What are those?

Quite often, at the conclusion of a presentation I've made in a college classroom or of a speech I've given somewhere in the corporate world, a young student or employee will approach me with a legal pad full of questions. While they usually find a creative and polite way to frame their queries in the context of my remarks of the day, what they're often asking is, "How did *you* do it?" How was I able to climb the corporate ladder and achieve what they see as enormous success? What they really want to know is how *they* can do it. What types of leadership traits should they try to develop? Are they taking the right courses? Should they enroll in a master's program? What qualities are corporations really looking for on a résumé? In other words, what is the secret formula for becoming a CEO?

The honest and perhaps obvious answer is that there is no magic formula. But there are predictors that over the years I have come to believe are important and reasonably dependable indicators of leadership capacity that have been important to all of the organizations I have been associated with, either as a full-time employee or a member of the board of directors, including AT&T, Eli Lilly and Company, Kimberly Clark, ConocoPhillips, Agilent Technologies, Chemical Bank, Knight Ridder, Inc., and others.

In conversations with corporate leaders, I have always found it somewhat remarkable that while the job-specific talents and skills that corporations are seeking may vary from industry to industry, by and large leadership standards are the same everywhere. The leadership skills that a CEO in, say, the computer industry is looking for are not all that different from those that CEOs in biotechnology or magazine publishing want to cultivate in their own high-potential employees.

Unfortunately, while the leaders of many companies go behind closed doors to discuss the attributes they believe are necessary in those who may be rising to the top levels of their enterprise, they spend far too little time communicating those attributes to their employees, if those attributes are even codified at all. Indeed, years ago, a colleague at the telephone company always referred to each of his promotions as one more step up "the hierarchy of secrets."

And yet, what possible sense does such a practice make? What strategic purpose can possibly be served by preserving a sense of mystery around the characteristics that are key to filling the most important appointments in the company? Wouldn't it be helpful if everyone in the organization could see what the predictors for success are thought to be? Why not let everyone understand what it takes? Who knows which employees at what levels might be inspired and take aim.

The Secret List

During my time as Chairman and CEO of Eli Lilly and Company, several times each year I set aside significant time to work with Sidney Taurel, then the company's Chief Operating Officer, and Pedro Granadillo, the company's human resources officer, to develop and refine a shared understanding about the attributes we were looking for in candidates for senior leadership positions, including candidates who might one day become the CEO. Since my retirement, Sidney and Pedro have continued that practice, and their list has continued to evolve. So has mine. It would be a mistake to believe that the identification of leadership talent could be reduced to something as straightforward as a list such as the one that follows. Nonetheless, here is *my* list, based on that work and my own thinking in the years since, of some of the attributes that I believe are effective indicators of future leadership potential and are worth the effort for aspiring managers to try to develop. Welcome to the hierarchy of secrets!

Indicators of Leadership Potential
- A leader inspires confidence and trust and consistently displays the highest ethical standards
- A leader communicates effectively, internally and externally
- A leader consistently achieves superior results, and produces results through other people

- A leader pursues continuous learning and fosters a learning environment
- A leader produces other leaders
- A leader develops cross-functional knowledge and versatility—breadth
- A leader embraces change and looks for ways to use it as an advantage
- A leader is constantly on the lookout for innovative ideas—particularly in unlikely places
- A leader builds alliances to further corporate goals—internally and externally
- A leader balances the short term with the long term by focusing on both
- A leader embraces ambiguity
- A leader practices and encourages thoughtful risk taking
- A leader champions cultural diversity
- A leader's contributions leave "footprints"

Leaders on Leadership

In conducting interviews to gain historical perspective in preparation for our work on this book, Todd Tobias was struck by what he heard from friends and colleagues from various stages of my career. They come from completely different backgrounds, with careers that have been in very different fields. But all have one thing very much in common—they've found their way to the top of their chosen field. In spite of the different paths they've taken, they speak with an amazingly consistent voice when they reflect on aspects of leadership. Here is some of what they have to say:

> The more I think about leadership, the more I realize that leaders are not necessarily born—they are made. I think experiences are extremely important in shaping a leader. And of all the characteristics that are necessary to be an effective leader, to me the most important one is

the ability to learn. If you have that, if you never lose intellectual curiosity, if you continue to ask the right questions and grab every piece of information you have around you, [you will become a] better leader.

The environment changes all the time, [so] a leader has to have, first and foremost, the ability to foresee, as much as is feasible, where the environment might go and [must] have the foresight to say, "Okay, this is a general direction in which we want to go." Then a leader needs to complement that very quickly with the ability to translate that general vision into more concrete strategies. But the vision part—which is really an adaptation to the environment—is what I think differentiates a leader from a manager.

Leadership has to do with change, and therefore, the [critical] characteristic of a leader is the ability to adapt to change, the ability to learn. This implies also the discipline of sitting down and asking yourself, "What have you learned about any success?" or, more painfully, "What have you learned about mistakes?" I have really tried to institutionalize that at our company. Our senior management spends time looking at our performance and saying, "What lessons have we learned, both from our successes and our mistakes?" Recently we did that, and we nailed it down to five points. Then we broadcast that message to the whole company and talked about how we are going to spend more time on what we have learned[, instead of] simply saying, "We've met this objective and we've missed that one." It's just the basis for a more fruitful discussion of what we have learned, because that is how we prepare for the future. (Sidney Taurel, Chairman, President and CEO, Eli Lilly and Company)

I never aspired to be a CEO. I was happy in 1957 to get a good job. I was persuaded that if I did my best and worked hard and stayed out of trouble, I would somehow be rewarded commensurate with my achievements. I had really no ambitious goals that drove me. And I always believed if I did the right things, the next opportunity would present itself. I believed that the world was fair. And I have never once been disappointed with that belief system. Secondly, I've always believed—and I still do—that you have to be very careful in selecting the people who are going to work with you or for you. Once you do that, you kind of follow the idea of giving them a job—plenty to do—and getting out of their way. And then you provide coaching when things don't seem to be going in the direction you agreed upon. Even in that case, I would look for that person to take the initiative to come and talk to me. Now, there's risk in that. Occasionally, I picked the wrong people. Some would call my approach a hands-off approach. It's not totally hands off, but it is more hands off than somebody who is a hovering supervisor. I always believe that people will grow to their maximum if they have that opportunity—if they have that freedom. A focus on values is very important. I cannot overstate the importance of integrity. History books are written about people who have taken companies under because of a lack of integrity, or have lost their leadership position because of it. (Robert E. Allen, Retired Chairman, President, and CEO, AT&T)

I think the key to career success is the same ingredient that drives leadership success: encompassing enthusiasm for new ideas. Great leaders demonstrate that ability, and it becomes contagious. You want to be around people like that because they energize you, and I find, in my life in particular, that when I am around people who are very bright and very thoughtful and very questioning and very engaged, that turns me on.

I don't ever like to have a situation where you take a vote and it comes out 6 to 5—in any setting, whether it is a church meeting or a university meeting or a corporate meeting. If there are those kinds of nagging concerns that make people step aside, or be on the other side of the issue, then we haven't had enough conversation. We haven't had enough education. We haven't shared enough information. We haven't talked it through. Truly great leaders are masters of building consensus. (Steven C. Beering, M.D., President Emeritus, Purdue University)

I think a great leader is someone who not only focuses on the needs of the organization but is also able to focus himself or herself. Concentrating time on the things that matter most—and certainly wanting to know about the lesser things, but leaving them for others to handle. Not trying to manage everything—making sure that somebody, other than the man at the top, is accountable for decisions before they reach his desk. A true leader is someone who can not only look at the short term but also see [the] long term, someone who looks at the fundamentals in the enterprise and tries to strengthen them. Above all, being a psychologist, an understander of people and savvy in the way he deals with people and cultural entities. (Mitchell E. Daniels Jr., Director, Office of Management and Budget, the White House)

The Hierarchy of Secrets

There is nothing in the technology or processes of a business that is not created by individuals—all the way through the organization. Everything in an organization is about intellectual capital. So, the question is for aspiring leaders: Can you impact the psychology of the organization in ways that can help create intellectual capital? Can you motivate people? Can you inspire innovation? The foremost responsibility of senior management is to increase the value of the firm. Everything you do must be directed toward increasing the value of the enterprise. If you understand that value creation is only going to be achieved through the creation of intellectual capital—then you will understand that leadership is about the psychology of helping cause people to do exceptional things. That's what business is all about. And that is what will bring a leader success. (Ronald W. Dollens, President and CEO, Guidant Corporation)

The most important thing I learned in college at Indiana University is how important it is for a leader to create consensus for a decision, so that ultimately the team can feel like they decided the issue instead of its being dictated by one person. I also learned how to care deeply for and be proud of the work I was doing, no matter what it was. (James T. Morris, Executive Director, the United Nations World Food Program)

Leadership begins with the enjoyment of what you are doing. If you don't enjoy it, I think it is very difficult to display the kind of positive leadership people are looking for. You also have to enjoy working with people. You have to recognize that a very important part of leadership is helping them grow and develop. I have always felt that one of my major responsibilities is mentoring others. We try to do that at the national office with our interns, helping them gain as much experience as they can so they can select which path they want to travel as they begin to mature—so broadening their experience base, helping them find out what they enjoy doing, I think, are very critical parts of that mentoring.

At the same time, as a leader you have the responsibility for an organization or function, which requires decisiveness. But bringing people along with you is extremely important in the process. In fact, many times it's the process involved in providing leadership that's important as much as the end result. If you march down the street and look around from where you are and the band hasn't followed you, you haven't accomplished very much by decisively making a decision. I think it is very important that you work in concert with others to accomplish your goals. (Dr. Cedric W. Dempsey, President, the National College Athletic Association)

Don't try to become a CEO. Try to do whatever your current job is to the best of your ability, and then you may eventually become a CEO. But if you start out at the beginning saying, "I want to be a CEO," you spend so much time looking at the next rung on the ladder [that] you fall off the one you're standing on. Do whatever your current job is so well that people notice you, and the future sort of takes care of itself. (Norman R. Augustine, Retired Chairman and CEO, Lockheed Martin Corporation)

I think what makes a great leader is clarity of mind—the ability to pick from a bewildering set of potential issues or concerns for the organization to focus on. In other words, someone who can set agendas and help work through those agendas by keeping the team focused on the key issues rather than letting people get distracted and wander off into something that might seem fascinating but have relatively little to do with the long-term issues of strategy. So clarity of mind is very important—identifying issues with a sure sense of what is important and then keeping people focused on it. This might include being a diplomat. In the university setting, that might mean keeping trustees of a board from crossing some boundaries in terms of their interest in getting involved in aspects of the university where trustees really shouldn't be involved in terms of details of management. A great leader is able to do this by keeping people focused. (Nannerl O. Keohane, President, Duke University)

[First,] I think you need to show energy and excitement around a vision and a purpose of the business. I think once you do that, the next step is to ask, "Okay, if that's our vision and our mission, how do I get everyone aligned with our goals?" You have to get people to mirror the strategy by defining for them the values the organization is going to live by. When you don't have shared values, the business comes apart. The values piece requires galvanizing good employees toward a purpose that is larger than just being a quarterly profit machine. Second, I think the simplification—in other words, the communication—of a vision and a mission and strategies and objectives—and doing [so] while recognizing the importance of core values—[is] a huge part of leadership. You've got to communicate, communicate, communicate. One of my failings when I came to work for AT&T out of Sidley & Austin was that as a lawyer I had the mind-set that if I didn't have an original idea that hour, either that hour was not billable or I was not productive. So why would I want to communicate that which I've already figured out? But my experiences at AT&T have helped me learn otherwise. Recognize that none of this counts if you don't have the discipline to say [that] if it's not inside the vision, if it's not consistent with our values, it has to go. Otherwise, you don't channel the capital. You don't stay on course. Last, a good leader makes it fun to be together in a group. Makes it fun to win. Makes each person of the group believe that the leader likes and trusts them and feels good about the effort they are putting forth. (John D. Zeglis, Chairman and CEO, AT&T Wireless)

Many people have asked me which is more important, the strategic side of leadership or the more "soft side"—the people and cultural issues. The answer is: both. Neither is sufficient by itself. I see, in my career as a consultant, large numbers of executives with great strategic vision and tremendous intellectual capabilities who nevertheless failed because of their lack of understanding of what it takes to get things done in a human organization. How do you change? And what are the limits of change that people experience? It's the soft issues that often make the most difference. The issues of: How do I bring execution? How do I think of the process that has to be in place? On the other hand, there are people who are leaders who are very compassionate people but don't have the right strategic vision to make things happen, so it isn't one or the other. You need both. (Dr. David A. Nadler, Chairman, Mercer Delta Consulting)

SEVEN

Bond Traders

Good character is more to be praised than outstanding talent. Most talents are to some extent a gift. Good character, by contrast, is not given to us. We have to build it piece by piece— by thought, choice, courage and determination.
—John Luther

Adding Value(s)

One of the most vivid memories I have of my first few weeks on the job at Eli Lilly and Company is the look I received from a then-senior executive when I suggested that one of my priorities as Chairman and CEO would be to reenergize, reinterpret, and reinforce the company's core values. His reaction reminded me of the scene in *Hoosiers* in which the town elders sit down with the new high school basketball coach to explain that zone defense, not man-to-man, is "the way we play ball around here."

Because the Lilly values—*people, integrity, and excellence*—were already so much a part of the company's culture, he insisted, why would I want to devote time and energy to them? And reinterpret them to make them even more relevant? That would be almost a sacrilege. Those three words were visible on plaques that had been hanging throughout the company's facilities for years. Employees knew what the words were, and spending time talking about our values was, well, "not the way we do it around here." I'm afraid he was slightly out of touch.

He was certainly correct that the Lilly culture has always placed a premium on honesty and integrity. And in contrast to other corporations where the values over time become just slogans that are part of the woodwork, at Lilly there's an incredible sense throughout of what's ethically right and wrong. I'm sure Lilly retirees and long-time employees would confirm my observation that integrity has historically been ingrained so firmly in the culture that anyone at any level in the company who intentionally ignored or even bent the laws and regulations governing the business would likely have been chewed up and spit out by the organization before he or she even got started.

And though a strong values-based foundation was clearly in place when I arrived, I knew that maintaining it was not automatic. The world around us was changing dramatically. People were retiring. New people were joining the company. The industry and the company were expected to produce earnings growth and increased shareholder value. The pressures to find shortcuts would mount. Keeping our values as fresh and vibrant drivers of the way we conducted ourselves would require ongoing attention. Nothing I could think of would be more important to our future success.

Unfortunately, events that would unfold in the years ahead would prove my concerns about the importance of these issues to be well founded. Enron. WorldCom. Tyco. Global Crossing. Waste Management. Xerox. Qwest. Arthur Andersen. All, in one way or another, have provided evidence of what happens when values are not at the top of the priority list. It's been enough to cause a general public that usually ignores the intricacies of the business pages to challenge the integrity of America's corporate leadership.

The flurry of activity to determine the details of these corporate accounting scandals has led to a politically popular push for new laws and regulations, with the expectation that as a result, such high-profile business quagmires won't happen again. That's all fine. Maybe those actions make us feel better. And unless these additional constraints add appreciably to the costs of business that are ultimately borne by the end consumer, they may not even do great harm. But this is not what's required to really address the issues.

The law says the speed limit on I-465, the beltway encircling Indianapolis, is fifty-five miles per hour. Drive at that speed, though, and you're likely to be rear-ended. That's because the accepted culture places the "real" speed limit at sixty-five miles per hour or more. If we really wanted to slow down the flow of traffic, would changing the speed limit to fifty really help? If everyone feels it is acceptable to disobey the current speed limit, why would people obey a new one that's even lower? If we were serious about the fifty-five-mile-per-hour speed limit, we would all express our out-rage when we observed others exceeding the speed limit, and those who ignored the law would be held accountable under the laws that already exist. But we're not serious about it, and so we don't, and they aren't.

Without attention, it's possible for these same kinds of "wink-wink" attitudes toward the laws and regulations governing the corporate world to creep in and then become ingrained in the culture of a company. When the pressure is on to produce, if you are serious about expecting adherence to certain standards of be-havior, you have to make that clear—by your words, certainly, but more importantly, by your actions.

Not unexpectedly, many of the board members or senior ex-ecutives involved in the oversight of this recent rash of corporate egg on the face have feigned ignorance to the specifics of their companies' problems. Perhaps in some cases this is true, at least in a strictly legal sense. But from a leadership perspective . . . well, I submit that all of the board members and senior leaders involved are at minimum guilty of leadership negligence.

Why? What did these leaders do to ensure that their organiza-tions instilled a value system that would help keep such problems from occurring? What was done with companywide emphasis to ensure that those engaged in the well-being of the organization understood which actions would be tolerated in the pursuit of results and which actions would not? What did the boards and the executives of these companies do to ensure that the values of their organizations not only were well-defined but actually guided the thinking and behaviors of the employees?

Granted, even the most values-driven companies are susceptible to greedy, misguided, or ignorant employees, or even CEOs. Having well-defined and emphasized values won't necessarily prevent the possibility of a few bad apples. But it will certainly help to identify them—if those responsible are really paying attention.

Unfortunately, for many business leaders the thought of "working on values" is not very exciting. It's a subject some senior executives would just as soon ignore in order to spend more time on what they see as the more important issues. But when I hear corporate leaders refer to values and culture as soft issues, I wonder what they regard as being hard. In my experience, cultural beliefs are the heart and soul of all business matters. To suggest that there is somehow a separation between a business and its culture is like suggesting that we can draw a line between society and politics. One begets the other. The outcome at Enron or Arthur Andersen or Waste Management might have been drastically different if their leaders had shared this view. And while the knee-jerk reaction in Washington to addressing these problems has involved looking for solutions in new and tougher rules and regulations—and rhetoric—there is ample evidence that those responsible for the problems were simply behaving according to the accepted values and cultures of their institutions—accepted by their boards or their CEOs and senior executives, by the cultures and values pervasive in their organizations.

The August 26, 2002, edition of the *Wall Street Journal* reported that when "Enron Corp. was riding high, Chief Financial Officer Andrew Fastow had a Lucite cube on his desk supposedly laying out the company's values. One of these was communication, and the cube's inscription explained what that meant: When Enron says it's going to 'rip your face off,' it said, it will 'rip your face off.'" According to the *Journal*, "It was a characteristic gesture inside Enron where the prevailing corporate culture was to push everything to the limits: business practices, laws and personal behavior."

In my experience, the vast majority of corporate directors and executives are honest, hard-working people who seek to operate well inside the rules and laws that govern American corporations. And they expect everyone else in their companies to behave in the same way. Nowhere are the standards higher than at Eli Lilly and Company. But simply having the expectation is not enough. Cultures require continuous nurturing. Maybe there weren't many cases in corporate America where boards or chief executives were literally saying, "We want results, even if it means breaking the rules to get them." But in the absence of an active emphasis on core values clearly saying the opposite—a message of getting results the right way or not at all—was just not delivered.

The solutions to all of this will not be found in new laws and regulations. They will be found only in clearly articulated expectations of behavior, and accountability when those expectations are not met. There's an old saying: "Your actions speak so loudly I can't hear a word you are saying." The actions—or, more accurately, the inactions—of the boards of directors and CEOs involved in creating the cultural environments where these scandals occurred have spoken so loudly it's deafening.

During my first few weeks at Lilly, I became focused on our need for a new standard beyond an ethically grounded sense of right and wrong. As I observed the way employees related to one another, it seemed to me that even though a strong values-driven culture was clearly in place, there was a significant opportunity to enhance that culture by encouraging employees to embrace the broader meaning that I ascribed to the company's core values. Certainly employee behavior was not inconsistent with the core definitions of those three words. But I was looking for much more. If *integrity*, for example, was defined simply as "We don't lie, steal, cheat, violate the laws, or even push the limits of the intent of the regulations that govern our conduct—or tolerate those who do," then the ethical sense of right and wrong that was so evident in behavior throughout the company was clearly consistent with that definition. But if integrity included sincerity, as I believed it should, and therefore also meant "If I don't agree with the position you're taking, I'll be open and honest and tell you exactly what's on my mind," then living that value to the fullest was another matter.

I was beginning to sense the extent of the gap that existed between what the employees understood of the corporation's values and my own expectations. And that was before I even got to my feeling about the need to reinterpret the values in a more contemporary fashion.

This was an issue certainly not unique to Eli Lilly and Company. For me, it was, in the words of Yogi Berra, the Yankee catcher turned desk calendar poet, "déjà vu all over again." Like the Bell System in its heyday, Eli Lilly and Company had a deeply ingrained culture. There was an understanding about how things were done, and there were traditions the company had come to honor. And the underpinnings of this culture were the words found on plaques and posters throughout the company—*people, integrity, and excellence.*

Many in the company could, when pressed, recite those words. But only a handful of individuals at any level could articulate, in any detail beyond the obvious, the relationship between these words and behavioral expectations.

The first of these three words had largely come to serve as an icon for a strongly embraced employee sense of entitlement. The conventional meaning assigned to valuing people was the commitment and obligation that was expected from the company for taking care of Lilly employees. Maybe employees were once the only group of people this value was meant to include. But times had changed, and unless we began to take care of all the company's stakeholders, it would be difficult to continue to take care of the employees themselves.

Lilly's stated values had become a symbol richly rooted in the past but devoid of the freshness that must drive future behavior for the vast majority of employees. Clearly, it was time for us to redefine our values and our culture.

Crisis Center

How could the need for values-driven behavior and cultural change be balanced with the strong needs of Lilly employees to belong to an institution with unique and meaningful cultural traditions? Could we aggressively embrace change while dulling the sting of uncertainty in a constantly changing work environment, and at the same time honor the past?

I had come to believe strongly in a simple principle for managing change: *When an organization is engaged in wrenching and fundamental upheaval, it's important that all of the people touched by the organization have something comfortable and familiar to hang on to.* Whether it's a mission statement, a quotable blurb, or a familiar slogan, for all the something new that a sea of uncertainty brings, reenergizing a meaningful symbol from the past can act as nothing less than a floatation device.

When too much change is implemented on a wholesale basis, it risks *adding* to the sense of turmoil and further alienation of workers, but by relating new ideas to an organization's past successes, the new concepts can, in fact, serve as a comfort, even a rallying point for the entire organization.

Mitch Daniels, at the time President of U.S. Operations for Lilly and later Director of the Office of Management and Budget in the White House, had seen it done both ways. "In times of crisis, it's very easy for someone to say, 'Out with the old and in with the new,'" says Daniels. "Under Randy's leadership, we chose not to do that. We blended a reverence for the past with an understanding of the future, and it turned out to be a real advantage in helping to change the Lilly culture. I think a great example of this is the renewed emphasis we put on company values. We didn't pick three new values of our own. Rather, we modified the existing values for the world in which the company was operating at the time."

At Lilly, by *redefining* for the entire organization—rather than *changing*—the company's values of people, integrity, and excellence, by specifying what these words actually must mean in the current context, we were able to express how our past values would continue to guide the way we do business. And by providing clarity in the interpretation of what those words really mean, we were able to demonstrate that our values were not simply words hanging on a break-room wall—our values would continue to serve as the very foundation of our culture and our success.

"I think a great counterpoint to the way we went about reforming Lilly's culture would be the Jack Welch model of the early 1980s," says Ted Planje, a longtime Lilly writer. "Posterity has proven that Welch's style of sweeping changes and massive reform worked out pretty well, but if you knew people at General Electric in the 1980s, as I did, it was not a pleasant place to be working. It was the corporate equivalent of the SS. What Randy saw at Lilly was the potential to create reform based on the strengths of the institution. . . . He saw the opportunity to institute change by focusing on the company's core values."

Just how was this possible? Take, for example, the crisis involving the Lilly compound in clinical trials, FIAU, being discussed by the company's senior leaders on my first official day as CEO. As Rebecca Kendall described it at the time, "We had the nightmare that we all feared. . . . People died because we gave them our drug. That's as bad as it gets. . . . To have it happen so quickly and so dramatically is every pharmaceutical company's nightmare."

Yet in spite of the enormous pressure from all of the surrounding events, almost immediately the company's leaders began to act as one. As they began to set priorities, what they saw as first and foremost was consistent with my priorities—to do what was right, beginning with seeing to it that the patients involved received the very best care possible, without regard to how that might compromise our legal situation in the months ahead. And, importantly, the decision was made to go public immediately. No finger-pointing. No excuses. No ducking. No spin control. While I signed off on all of this and made my own views clear, the fact was that I had not really needed to make any of the decisions that were agreed to that morning. The decisions came from a shared set of values. There was clearly a strong foundation from which to begin the cultural transformation I had in mind.

Recipe (Reciprocity) for Success

During the course of my tenure as Lilly's CEO, I spent a good deal of time talking—in speeches, in meetings, in published reports—about the relationship of our core values to the company's financial success. Truly living those values would have a major impact on the successful implementation of Lilly's business strategies. I even made it the keynote of our 1997 annual shareholder meeting. Why was I so focused on values? Why did I not choose to devote that annual meeting's agenda to a more "serious" business concept like strategic planning or new science? As important as those concepts are, I have never believed that changes in strategy or in organizational structure, in and of themselves, are any guarantee of success. They may be necessary but are likely never sufficient. After all, if the analysis of the business and its opportunities is accurate, at least some competitors are likely to come up with similar strategies. Thus, organizations can't expect to win in their industry simply because they have the best strategy.

Look no further than the National Football League, where the San Francisco 49ers' "West Coast" offense, thanks to its adoption by several teams around the league, is now about as West Coast as a Brooklyn deli. Yet year in and year out, on any given Sunday, some teams who use it succeed, while a handful of teams using essentially the same offense fail miserably. In corporate America, as in professional sports, organizations win not because they have the best game plan alone, important as that is, but because they also do the best job of implementation.

More than heroic working hours, more than pay incentives, certainly more than strategy alone, shared beliefs—*values*—can be the key to unleashing the talents of all of the people in an organization. Values can be the very foundation of success.

When I arrived at Eli Lilly, I knew it would be necessary to instill a culture in which employees could continue to expect to be valued for all they had contributed and achieved in the past but would also understand that they could not rest on their laurels. Employees should expect to be measured by and rewarded for what they were contributing currently. A new understanding of Lilly's commitment to its people and, just as important, their commitment to the company had to be established.

During the time I was focused on revitalizing our core values, I received a wonderful note from one of our retired employees in which he brought to my attention a letter to the shareholders in the company's 1975 annual report. In that letter, written on the occasion of the company's one hundredth anniversary, Mr. Eli Lilly, the longtime Chairman of the company, grandson of the founder, and by then the Honorary Chairman at nearly ninety years of age, wrote about the importance of understanding that loyalty must be a *reciprocal bond*—that there must be reciprocal expectations of behavior between company and employee. I was delighted to read it, and to use it to demonstrate my interpretation of reciprocity—Lilly's commitment to its people and theirs to the company.

But there was something even more pernicious behind the sentiments employees were expressing to the media and around coffee carts during the course of my first few days on the job—a sense of *entitlement* about their roles in the company. It was hard to fault Lilly employees for their world view. After all, this feeling of entitlement about their jobs, about company culture, about the way things are "supposed to be," had been unwittingly fostered by the company over time.

Eli Lilly and Company can remarkably boast that it has never in its 127-year history initiated significant job layoffs of any kind in the United States. Not even during the Great Depression. Lilly values its employees that much. More recently, while certainly well intentioned, my predecessor had been quoted as saying, in effect, "There will never be any layoffs on *my* watch." No wonder employees were so upset to see him go.

While as much as anyone I didn't want to see any employees lose their jobs, I began to express, on my very first day, a point of view that was somewhat different from what Lilly employees had been accustomed to hearing in recent years. Through the media, internal publications, and speeches, I suggested that while I didn't see any need for involuntary job cuts in the immediate future, I believed no CEO actually had the power to promise whether there would or would not be layoffs. Employees are never axed because CEOs want to do it. It's always the marketplace—not company policy—that determines job security. It would be our success in our markets, working together, that would determine our future stability and growth or lack thereof.

Employees received that message in the spirit in which it was intended. The new CEO didn't want layoffs any more than they did, but it would be up to the organization as a whole to pull together to determine our collective fate. A strengthened set of shared values would drive that fate.

"The only Lilly people who have a right to feel entitled to anything are our shareholders" was the philosophy I would espouse throughout my tenure. While I wanted the entire organization to begin to feel a sense of urgency about our goals, what I was really trying to convey to our employees was that the bond of reciprocity was about to replace the mind-set of entitlement as the underlying theme in our culture. Of course, this wouldn't happen overnight. Reciprocity works only if leadership is capable of demonstrating its end of the bargain. Which is exactly what transpired.

Just as competitive pressures and the urgent need for preeminent organizational effectiveness require a company to do more for its employees these days, those very same pressures require that today's employees do more for the company. In other words, because Lilly believes that employees are the foundation of its success, the company expects a lot of them.

The bond of reciprocity begins with the premise that in these times of continuous change, any guarantee of job security is anachronistic. Accordingly, in recent years Lilly employees have become more responsible for their own work lives, for managing their performance, upgrading their skills, and planning their careers. That's their end of the deal. Of course, for this to work, companies are more obliged than ever to provide mentoring, career resources, and opportunities for training. That's management's end of the deal.

But it doesn't stop there. The reciprocal bond between employers and employees still demands that at times, people must make the extra effort and adjust to the company's needs. These relationships may even mean that people have to move or take new jobs. This kind of flexibility has been a fact of life during all eras in business and certainly remains so during this era of revolutionary change.

Critics who see the concept of reciprocity as a way for organizations to unburden themselves of the commitment to provide stable jobs miss the point. Reciprocity is about organizations weeding out the entitlement mind-set that has employees putting their own needs ahead of the needs of shareholders. Ironically, for the employees' needs to be met, they have to run in parallel. Success is a two-way street. In fact, I think you could make a good case that *the very promise of job security is the first step in destroying it*, because after all, what is entitlement, really? It's employees' feeling that they don't have any stake in looking out for their own future because somebody else is going to do it for them. How can that possibly be a productive way to work?

Companies that allow complacency in their culture are numbing themselves to the painful reality of change. The desire is understandable, but it's fatal. In spite of good intentions, that's the kind of thinking or lack of thinking that eventually leaves management with no path to survival except by the avenue of consolidation and cost-cutting. I believe that when you see radical downsizing, when you see massive job losses, it is, at least in part, a sign of the failure of leadership to adequately and creatively plan, to anticipate, to accept responsibility for shaping the future.

At Lilly, I believed, as does my successor now, that there is a reciprocal bond that ties employer and employee. Lilly's work ethic tries to recognize and harmonize the mutual needs of the company and its people. Reciprocity defines not only how companies set the terms of employment but also how they address the conditions of employment, how the work is to be done. That means any decision that company leaders make must take into account the impact that decision will have on their people.

Not all companies and CEOs have consistently embraced my views of the importance of reciprocity, including those identified by the media in the mid-1990s as the so-called corporate killers. At least one of the self-styled corporate leaders of that period, the one who flaunted his power-tool-inspired nickname, always seemed to me to be more like a character to be found in a professional wrestling ring than in a corporate boardroom. But I honestly believe that some newfound level of understanding of this concept is now leading many of these same U.S. companies to very much the same sort of conclusions I've described. A number of those companies are now trying to rebuild the bond with their own people in order to compete more successfully.

Reciprocity, by its very definition, must work both ways. By helping employees hone their skills and careers and providing them with services and programs that enable them to better manage their personal lives, businesses help their workers to feel more positive about their company and optimistic about their futures. That's good for the bottom line.

Life Savers

There is a broadly held view that Lilly is a good place to work because the company takes care of its employees. There is good reason for that view. From the very beginning, from the time of private ownership by the Lilly family on through to the present, the company has always placed a high priority on its human resources programs. When I arrived at Lilly in 1993, I was reminded of the corporate era when *The Man in the Gray Flannel Suit* reigned. Many of the company's highly respected policies and work-life programs were quite literally created back then. Were they still relevant? So that I could get a better understanding about that issue, one of the first reports I asked for was an analysis of exactly who Lilly employees were.

In examining the data, we soon discovered that Lilly people were living very different lives and had very different needs than the employees of twenty or thirty years before. What we learned dramatized the fact that many managers of my generation have an outdated view of American lifestyles—a view, I might add, that parallels many corporate policies that have survived over the years.

For instance, at the time we took the survey, only 18 percent of our 14,500 employees in the United States were part of a traditional nuclear family—a married couple with the father going to work in the morning and the mother working at home and raising the children. That meant that 82 percent of Lilly employees were living under some other model—with large numbers of single people without children, single parents, unmarried couples, dual wage earners with children and those without children, multigenerational families, same-sex couples, and so on. Therefore, 82 percent of our people had needs that were not anticipated and often could not be met by personnel policies and programs created in the era when all employees were assumed to live in the same neighborhood as Ozzie and Harriet. Today, it would appear that "father" doesn't necessarily "know best."

For many in the working world, accomplishing the daily chores needed to keep a household running can be a logistical challenge. Dealing with a snow day in the school system can be a crisis. Coping with the sudden illness of an elderly parent can be a catastrophe. For all employees, including the minority living in the traditional family structure, the effort to make not just a good living but a good life can be a continual source of stress and strain.

Since the early 1990s, Lilly has initiated a wide array of work-life programs to help its people cope with these new needs.

- On-site shops and facilities to help employees with daily needs: a full-service credit union offering nearly all the services of a traditional bank; a dry-cleaning outlet; a shoe repair shop; a convenience store stocked with greeting cards, soft drinks, pantyhose, and just about anything else you'd find at a typical convenience store
- Two child development centers at corporate headquarters providing day care for four hundred children of employees. Pro-

grams to help parents with back-up care when their regular care falls through are also available.

- A company cafeteria that prepares ready-to-serve take-home dinners four nights a week.
- A latchkey program offering workshops for both parents and children, ages nine through twelve, to assess children's readiness for self-care after school and to provide the skills needed
- Personal leaves of up to three years for dependent care
- Nursing stations for new moms
- Five (additional) paid vacation days for employees getting married
- Excellent on-site medical care and a broad range of exercise and wellness services; a twenty-four-hour employee assistance program makes counseling and referral services available to employees
- Assistance to families who are adopting a child
- Elder-care consultation and referral services addressing the needs of the approximately 35 percent of employees who report that they have elder relatives in their care

Obviously this is just a partial list. I'm not suggesting that Lilly is leading the parade in this area. But the company takes great pride in having been named one of *Working Mother* magazine's "top 100 companies for working mothers" several years in a row and counting. In fact, just as the corporate attitude about embracing innovation outside the company's walls was being changed, we also began to foster a similar attitude about cultural policies.

For instance, employees said they would appreciate having coffee bars available where they could go on a break or in the morning to enjoy a hot beverage a little more elaborate than the typical tepid brown liquid in a Styrofoam cup. So that's what they were given. Now they can begin their mornings with cappuccinos, lattes, espressos, herbal teas, whatever suits their tastes. I suspect that for a few employees, the coffee may very well be regarded as

Marianne and me with pioneer children's television host Bob Keeshan, also known as Captain Kangaroo, at the groundbreaking for the first Lilly Child Development Center. In the foreground are five children of Lilly employees who were the real stars of the event. Photo courtesy of Eli Lilly and Company.

the highlight of my leadership legacy. And that's the point—finding whatever it takes to boost morale.

A company with the scale and resources of Lilly can implement a number of programs that would be difficult for smaller organizations to duplicate. And yet there are many actions that organizations of any size can carry out that do not require large expenditures and can make a major difference for employees.

As the CEO of the company, I received a great deal of recognition for our work-life initiatives. In 1996, *Working Mother* magazine named me CEO Family Champion of the year, truly one of the most welcome awards of my career. That included an appearance on the *Today* show and a conversation on the topic with Katie Couric. By then I had become a spokesperson for the importance of work-life initiatives. I began to accept opportunities to speak to business audiences about work-life initiatives whenever my schedule would allow. I also served on a White House commission to make recommendations on public policy regarding work-life issues, and on behalf of that group I presented our report to the president in a Rose Garden ceremony.[1] But all I was really doing was playing the role of cheerleader, embracing and encouraging the suggestions of others like Pedro Granadillo, Lilly's Senior Vice President of Human Resources, and Candi Lange, the company's Work-Life Director.

---

1. Candi Lange, Lilly's Director of Human Resources (Workforce Partnering), remembers that "Randy served on a White House commission concerning work-life balance issues and had been asked to speak at a press conference in the Rose Garden. I accompanied him to provide staff support. Although he had been to the White House many times before, this was my first trip, and I was very excited. He introduced me to the White House Chief of Staff and to members of the President's Cabinet who were there. While we were sitting in a meeting, he took a notepad off the conference table that said 'The White House' across the top of each page and dropped it in my briefcase. When we met the President and First Lady in the Oval Office, he had a photographer take our picture, and then later sent it to me, framed and with a handwritten note. These gestures of personal attention and acknowledgment were very typical of him and meant a lot to me. But what I also learned from him is that such gestures from a leader can be incredibly motivating to employees."

After being selected 1996 CEO Family Champion of the Year by Working Mother *magazine, I was interviewed by host Katie Couric* (right) *on NBC's* Today. *Video capture.*

For example, when I arrived as CEO, the company had already put in place a summer science camp that allowed any Lilly employee to enroll his or her children for all or part of its eight-week run. It's a wonderful program and a terrific idea. I wish I had thought of it. When I first saw it in action, I was delighted with the whole concept and let it be known that I fully supported whatever appropriate measures could be taken to improve it. A swimming pool was built on Lilly property where the camp was held. Various experts from around the Indianapolis community were invited to be camp counselors for a day—like volunteers from the Indianapolis Symphony Orchestra who helped with a module on the science associated with air by explaining how string instruments or brass instruments make sounds. They were followed by a professor from the Indiana University School of Medicine who is also

In 1997, I served on a White House panel to develop suggested approaches to encourage businesses to support family-friendly programs for their employees. Here I am presenting the panel's recommendations to President Bill Clinton in a White House Rose Garden ceremony.

a fighter pilot in the Air National Guard. He came in full flight suit and helmet to explain how planes can fly. Because the summer science camp was so successful, the entire program was expanded to serve children and parents for holidays and school closings.

From the smaller initiatives like the coffee bar to the larger ones like the summer science camp, the company recognized that its people had new needs and that new tools needed to be offered to meet them. So why was Lilly doing all of this? Because the development of preeminent organizational effectiveness is one of the company's critical capabilities. Because "people" is one of its core values. And because reciprocity is the philosophy of the business. By addressing work-life concerns, company leaders are addressing the needs of the people on whom they depend. These issues are as important as ensuring that their facilities have lights that enable them to see, that company PCs are positioned so that op-

In 1998, after I announced my upcoming retirement as Chairman and CEO of Eli Lilly and Company, the children of Lilly employees attending the company's summer science camp posed for this thank-you photograph. Photo courtesy of Eli Lilly and Company.

erators are less likely to get carpal tunnel syndrome, and that employees get their paychecks on time.

You can ask employees to leave their personal lives at the factory fence. In the old days, that was the culture of most corporations. But you're just kidding yourself if you think they can comply. You can't hire part of a person. You get the sore back along with the skillful hands. You get the anxious heart along with the educated brain. So your policies and programs will be effective only if they bow to this reality and address the whole human being.

The bottom line is that Lilly's effort to support work-life priorities is good business. These are neither perks nor giveaways. These tools have helped the company attract, motivate, and retain people who are more likely to be more dedicated, more focused, more innovative, and more productive. In response to the skeptics, I believe Lilly's work-life efforts generate excellent returns on investment. Moreover, there is hard data from employees themselves that they welcome what the company is doing in this area, that these are not intrusions. And, importantly, everyone in the company benefits from being part of an effective organization that excels in the marketplace.

"I am living proof that Lilly's work-life initiatives have true business value," says former Lilly Investor Relations Director Patty Martin, now Executive Director of Lilly's Office of Alliance Management. "I could not have done the [investor relations] job without the Lilly day-care center," says Martin. "Full stop. Could not have done it. The job is a lightning rod for headhunters, but even if I wanted to, I could not walk away from a working arrangement like the one I have at Lilly. I mean, there was a tornado warning one day, and I was able to run down to the day care to check on my daughter and make sure everything was all right. You hire me, you hire my family. [Not only do] the company's work-life programs make a huge difference in my family's quality of life, [but] I think it helps me to be more productive on the job."

Flex Appeal

If work-life initiatives represent a competitive advantage, and they do, then today's leaders must address the barriers to change that will otherwise stand in the way of the realization of those benefits. They must do everything they can to accelerate the transition from talking about enlightened values, commitments, and policies to implementing consistent actions and behaviors that support organizational effectiveness. It's not enough to simply offer benefits and programs. The underlying cultural issues need to be assertively addressed.

For many years, the official work hours at Lilly's U.S. operations had been from 7:30 A.M. to 4:15 P.M. What was originally designed as a family-friendly policy intended to help employees spend more early evening time with their families increasingly caused problems, particularly in single-parent or dual-income households with children who were still at home when parents needed to leave for work. So to help solve those problems, flextime was instituted, with core hours from 9 A.M. to 3 P.M. Employees began using flextime, choosing the specific additional hours before and after the core period that best fit their own needs. But it was soon discovered that we needed to communicate our intentions much more clearly. Some supervisors simply didn't get it on their own. For example, there was a case of a single father who chose to work from 8:30 A.M. to 5:15 P.M. Early in this experience, when he arrived at his desk on time, he found that his group's regular staff meeting had already begun as usual at 7:30 A.M. His supervisor's interpretation of flextime was simply that this person was automatically excused from 7:30 A.M. meetings. We had to make clear that if anyone in a workgroup was on flextime, the entire group was affected. Meetings that formerly might have been held at 7:30 A.M. now needed to be held after 9:00 A.M., or the schedules of all employees had to be accommodated in some other way. Mitch Daniels, then President of Lilly's U.S. Operations, took it one step further. He had signs made and placed on all the conference-room doors in his organization that read NO PARKING BEFORE 9:00 A.M. OR AFTER 3:00 P.M.[2]

2. Daniels was also addressing another issue high on our change agenda: There were simply too many meetings. The culture was accustomed to decisions by committee, and we were working hard to change that. Reducing the hours when meetings could be held caused a number of managers to reevaluate whether the meeting they were planning was really necessary at all.

"There were detractors initially who felt like our work-life initiatives weren't 'business related,'" says Candi Lange. "For example, I gave a talk about flextime to a group of Lilly employees. A company vice president who was making a speech after mine got up and made a comment about not being able to speak very long because he was on flextime and had to get home. He turned the whole thing into a joke. But once the data started coming in, employees felt the programs were helping them be more productive, and we heard less and less from the detracting voices."

Lilly began to foster the understanding that the company, rather than employees, has flextime. A job-sharing program was introduced allowing two employees to fulfill the responsibilities of one full-time position. Telecommuting was introduced, which allowed employees working in certain types of positions the option of working from home. The point of implementing flextime was to help all people and workgroups do their jobs better. But working hours weren't the only cultural barrier that had to be overcome.

Let me give you another example. We all know there are people who regularly work twelve, thirteen, or more hours a day and rarely take much, if any, of their vacation time. When asked why they behave that way, and frequently expect others to do the same, the answer, in most cases, is that they've been rewarded for this work style. Or they've seen others rewarded for it. In many cases, these employees are striving to create, and reinforce, an image of heroic commitment. All too often, this work style may deflect their managers and their colleagues from focusing on their actual results. What's more, this style not only leads to imbalances in employees' personal and professional lives but can also create similar problems for colleagues whose schedules are controlled or affected by these employees' work style. Says Lange, "There used to be managers who would walk the halls at 7:35 to see who was late in getting to work. There were managers who would brag about how many of their people came in regularly on Saturdays. And employees were forced to try to beat the system. They would keep the lights on in their office and keep their coat hanging on the door and their computers on at night. If anybody walked by, well, they were trying to create the illusion that they had just stepped out for a minute."

When I observed that people were consistently working late into the night and on weekends, I frequently questioned them directly about their personal effectiveness and asked them point-blank about the reasons why they could not do a better job of managing their time and working more efficiently.

"I spent a good portion of my career at General Motors, and grew up in a business climate that didn't value output as much as we now do here at Lilly," says Lilly Chief Financial Officer Charlie Golden. "I will never forget Randy saying to a particular manager, 'I don't want to see you hanging around your desk at 8:00 at night. It doesn't impress me. It tells me that you are basically not organized enough to get your job done during regular hours.' That was a counterintuitive thought to me because of the previous culture I had come from. But I've come to embrace this thinking whole-heartedly. Focusing on output rather than input gets you to the root causes of issues much more quickly."

I am not suggesting that I don't value hard work and extra effort. What I am suggesting is that Lilly's culture needed to stop rewarding or encouraging managers to expect this type of ongoing heroic commitment from their employees—for no reason other than appearances. From time to time, there would be periods when employees would be asked to provide extra time and effort at the office—that's part of the reality of corporate life everywhere and can't easily be helped. What *could* be helped is that Lilly's culture not only would refuse to reward leaders who consistently demanded of themselves and their people that they never see the sunshine— it would even frown on such behavior. It was far more appropriate to value and measure output than input.

"We spent quite a bit of time in recent years talking to employees about output versus time on the job itself," says Pedro Granadillo, Lilly's Senior Vice President of Human Resources. "I think the articulation of the concept really helped employees get a firm idea of what we expected of them. It really helped to change the culture in dramatic and positive ways."

Organizations today cannot succeed except by and through the efforts of a fully committed workforce that is continuously growing, learning, and retooling for the future. Lilly's work-life efforts helped its employees, as did the company's newly defined core values.

The pursuit of shared values, like the pursuit of work-life support for people stretching for business excellence, is a journey, not a destination. It won't happen in fifteen days, fifteen weeks, or fifteen months. It takes time, a great deal of conscious effort, and then a lot of role-modeling that begins at the top of a company and extends throughout its organizations. Ultimately, it requires that all employees bear in mind the basic business logic for everything the company is doing on their behalf.

While the child development centers at the Eli Lilly and Company corporate headquarters[3] serve employees with young children, all the company's stakeholders benefit from these facilities that help Lilly people focus their undivided attention on their responsibilities.

For more than thirty-five years, I've watched corporations search for an alternative to people as the single most important source of business success. They haven't found it yet, and they won't.

In the conclusion of the book that was arguably one of the most influential business studies of all time, Peters and Waterman's *In Search of Excellence: Lessons from America's Best-Run Companies,*

---

3. I was honored and delighted when—on the occasion of my retirement—the company renamed the first facility the Randall L. Tobias Child Development Center.

the authors tried to synthesize everything they had learned about excellence from their anecdotal investigation into the practices of consistently outstanding companies. They said it all boils down to something quite simple: "treating people decently and asking them to shine."

The simple truth is, there is no alternative to human resources, and that requires attention to the entire lives of people. People are the ultimate competitive resource, and I, for one, have enjoyed embracing the responsibility for nurturing that resource to the best of my ability. Not just because it's good for business but because it's simply the right thing to do.

I'm pleased with all that was accomplished in revitalizing the company culture during my time at Lilly. But the fact remains that revitalization is a journey and not a project. The job is never done and requires continuous attention, particularly in a culture where the sense of entitlement has been so strongly ingrained. Long after I stepped down as Chairman, Sidney Taurel, my successor as Chairman and CEO, is still at it. Speaking to Lilly employees regarding the road ahead, he recently said, "Some companies focus, first and foremost, on results, on performance. Others primarily concentrate on their people. But people and performance are not mutually exclusive. Lilly is perceived as an extreme case where the emphasis on people is very high. We must elevate our focus on results and squarely face what went right, what did not, and why. We will maintain our values regarding people; we will never waver on that score. And we must balance those values with the same emphasis on integrity and excellence. We must have the integrity to take a stand and to do what we have agreed to do. We must aspire to the excellence that drives innovation and performance."

Communicating values, defining them, redefining them, and making sure they translate into meaningful actions are all part of an ongoing journey, not a one-time process. It's like striving for the perfect game of golf—there will always be room for improvement.

In the final analysis, values, I have come to believe, are the basis of all business success. And values at Eli Lilly and Company are no longer simply words hanging on a break-room wall. They are the underpinning of the company's culture and behavior, and thus the very foundation of Lilly's success.

EIGHT

Focusing the Boxes

*No institution can possibly survive if it needs
geniuses or supermen to manage it. It must be
organized in such a way as to be able to get
along under a leadership composed of average
human beings.*

—Peter Drucker

The Rules of Soccer

When my daughter Paige was eight years old, she joined a
soccer league. Until the afternoon she proudly brought one home,
I had not held a soccer ball since a high school physical education
class, so it goes without saying that I knew very little about the
rules of the game. But that mattered not to her. What was most
important was that when Saturday mornings rolled around, I was
willing to pack an army of screaming eight-year-olds into our station wagon, shin guards and all, and cart them off to the local park
for their weekly exhibition. Perhaps I can count myself a member
of the first generation of soccer moms.

Roaming the sidelines every Saturday morning, the rules of
soccer initially tenuous in my mind, I came to observe one inevi-
tability with eight-year-olds who are on a soccer field for the first
time in their lives:

Without guidance to the contrary, wherever the soccer ball is on the field, 100 percent of the players from both teams will be right on top of it. The rest of the field will be vacant.

Over the years, I have found that a corollary holds true in the corporate world: No matter how many important issues demand attention, everyone on the management team, without guidance to the contrary, will invariably gravitate toward the highest-profile issues. And the rest of the field will be vacant.

This "law" was the prevailing culture at Eli Lilly as well. One of the early internal meetings I attended, following my arrival in 1993, was a gathering of senior managers with responsibilities that in some way included the company's insulin business. For the most part, these were the same people I'd been with earlier in the week for a meeting about plans in the central nervous system part of the company. And we'd been together for presentations on a number of other issues. It was starting to remind me of a soccer game.

These were very capable senior people who had narrow but deep responsibilities for overseeing functions—development or manufacturing or marketing or sales or finance and the like. That meant they were more likely to think in terms of their function rather than the company's businesses, which, in the end, would determine its success. It also meant that each of them attended most meetings like this, when one of them could have been responsible while the rest were off addressing other businesses. We didn't all need to cluster around the soccer ball.

I don't recall the specific purpose of the insulin meeting. What I do recall, with great clarity, is a chance comment made by one of the participants, a comment which had a profound impact on my understanding of the company's organization and focus, and on later decisions I would make to change the company's organizational orientation. In describing another company in the business, an aggressive competitor that was very dependent on insulin because it represented such a large part of that company's corporate revenue and profits, the Lilly manager said, "They are very tough competitors because they are so focused on their business and they act as if the very future of their company depends on their success in that market."

Why, I wondered, did it not occur to him that we had to do the same thing if we were going to be successful ourselves?

Shortly after that meeting, I took a look at the organization chart to determine who in our company actually was responsible for the insulin business. I was amazed when I learned the answer. I was! Not until the Chairman's office did the focus narrow to a single individual with responsibility for all activities in the diabetes business. The scary news was that I knew I wasn't spending a lot of time on that area of the business.

Add to that the company's predisposition for using committees to make decisions by consensus. That meant decisions were often compromises rather than hard choices. It also meant that no one was really accountable. I couldn't live with that. From that day forward, I did all I could to create an environment in which decisions by committees were out and decisions by leaders were in. We needed to quickly identify just *who* was accountable for what and get focus within the company.

But before we did that, it was imperative that the company itself get focused. We needed to address the essential question: *What businesses are we really in?*

The place to start was with the development of a vision for the company, and a strategy to realize that vision. From my years as a part of AT&T senior management, I had experienced enough of the problems that come from the lack of a clear and compelling vision that the organization understands, accepts, and knows how to execute. We had similar challenges to address at Lilly, and I was eager to get on with the task at hand.

So where to begin? Well, I made a list. It was really that simple. As I began to understand the issues the company was facing, six priorities emerged. The list was really the first step in beginning to get some clarity about a strategic focus. It was my view that the priorities were to

1. Get the company operationally under control
2. Restore stakeholder confidence in the company, its leadership, and its future—beginning with employees and the financial community
3. Move quickly to increase shareholder value
4. Make some important and needed strategic choices
5. Rekindle and refocus the company's core values
6. Strengthen and deepen the company's leadership capabilities— at the top as well as in other key parts of the business—with the skills and experiences that would be required for success on the road ahead

With this list as an informal template, we began a process that would evolve into our company's new vision.

"Not long after Randy arrived, he began a push for strategic clarity," says speechwriter Ted Planje. "There had been a complex and extended strategic planning effort in recent years that frustrated a lot of people. When Randy came on board, he very quickly wanted to go for a more simplified corporate strategy, which we have in place today. We began to ask some fundamental questions about the organization and its parts and whether they fit into our new strategic plans. We worked very hard to get clarity around our strategic focus, and I think it accelerated a process that was urgently needed."

Item 4 on the list addressed perhaps the most important question of all: What businesses are we really in? This was the start of asking employees to look at the various parts of the organization and address some fundamental questions about the company's future.

Retaining the Wait

Of course, there were no easy answers to such questions. I did know from experience, however, that we needed to make some choices. Even if a strategy is wrong, if an organization enjoys the full support of its people, is focused on what it does best, and moves collectively toward a shared goal, a shared vision of the future, it will have more success than going down the best path, but not as a team. It is only with the shared support of the entire organization that a company can quickly come to a full understanding of what strategies are working and what strategies are not. Through my AT&T experience, I had come to believe that success in a complex environment comes to those who are completely focused on the businesses they know how to operate successfully, businesses that fit compatibly side by side under the same owner, businesses for which the company is an appropriate owner. For some organizations, like the General Electrics of the world, focusing on what they do best might include managing several very diverse concerns. But those skills and cultural capabilities are rare. For many, if not most, companies, spreading the focus too broadly is often detrimental to the success in any of the company's businesses.

Lilly had some experience in owning at least one business that was not a good cultural fit. At the time I joined Lilly's board in 1986, the company owned the Elizabeth Arden cosmetics company, including the Red Door salons in major cities and the Main Chance spa in Arizona. The acquisition had been made some years earlier under the theory that products might be developed in the pharmaceutical laboratories that could scientifically have an impact on skin tone, for example.

That theory was brilliant in, well, theory, but not in the real world. In the pharmaceutical industry, the big driver of expense is research and development because science truly drives the success or failure of any product brought to market. Without intending to offend anyone in the cosmetics industry, let me simply say that the rules are different. In the cosmetics business, it is advertising and promotion that drive expense and success or failure. Research is a very small fraction of a company's costs. Perception is reality. The successful creation of customer perception is what creates shareholder value. Package inserts are developed by the marketing department, not by the U.S. Food and Drug Administration (FDA). Maybe it was best explained some years ago by Charles Revson, the founder of Revlon, who said, "In the factory we manufacture cosmetics, but at the counter we sell hope."

Just imagine the frustration of the managers of a cosmetics division owned and controlled by a pharmaceutical company where it is part of the culture to have every word in the promotional materials for prescription drugs approved by the FDA. If the FDA hasn't approved it, you can't say it.

These two cultures are highly incompatible. In the late 1980s, Lilly wisely sold the company and got out of the cosmetics business.

When I became Lilly's Chairman and CEO, I concluded that we were still not as focused as the company needed to be, in several important ways. The situation was much like that at AT&T in the mid-1980s and early 1990s: Lilly's senior leaders were spreading their time across a wide collection of assets, and not in proportion to the importance of each of the company's activities to our strategic future. Lilly was in the human pharmaceutical business; the plant science business, albeit through a joint venture that had been established in the late 1980s by combining the company's assets with those of Dow Chemical Company; the animal health business; and a number of medical device businesses.

The Elanco animal health and Elanco plant sciences businesses were the products, over time, of the company's own laboratories. The animal health business was in some ways a natural extension of the human pharmaceutical business. It was very well managed and indeed was one of the few parts of the company really organized with a focus toward the profitability of a business rather than with a focus on the functions. I concluded that if we had not already been in the animal health business, it would not be a business to enter. But because we were and it was doing just fine, we would leave it alone.

The plant sciences joint venture had been established to create better critical mass and scale and, at the same time, take the first step in positioning it so that the entire business could be sold to a strategic or financial buyer, or Lilly's interest could be sold to Dow later on; eventually, it was.

The real issue was what to do long term with the medical device businesses, a debate that had been going on for some time. It was time to decide, one way or the other.

The decision to invest in device businesses had been made sometime before with a good deal of thought. The theory was that from time to time, there would be dry periods in the pharmaceutical business, and the more opportunities that could be created to generate revenue during such periods, the better off the company and its shareholders would be.

Since 1977, Lilly had spent more than a billion dollars to build its medical devices and diagnostics division. All told, Lilly had acquired nine companies scattered across the U.S. which specialized in products ranging from heart defibrillators to balloon angioplasty catheters to diagnostic tests used in hospitals and laboratories.

In 1992, the year before I became CEO, the medical devices and diagnostics division generated $1.2 billion in sales, or roughly one fifth of the company's total revenue. The revenue figures looked great. But that wasn't the entire story. Owning these businesses was not creating shareholder value, one of my top priorities. When we looked at the price-to-earnings ratio the pharmaceutical industry was producing, then multiplied that number by the earnings from just our pharmaceutical division, that was about the price of Lilly stock. When investors purchased stock, they perceived that they were buying shares in a pharmaceutical company. They were not paying much of a premium beyond that to own the other businesses in Lilly's portfolio. There was hidden shareholder value that had to be unlocked.

But that wasn't all. "When I had a return on investment calculation run," remembers Jim Cornelius, at the time Lilly's Chief Financial Officer, "it was quite startling for me, as the CFO, to present it to the executive committee and show that while it had a 15 percent return, it was barely earning its keep in the overall scheme of things. Couple that with the amount of time it took to manage nine companies all across the United States and the amount of time the senior corporate management was spending on running them, the expense [to] the core pharmaceutical business was immeasurable. It was getting increasingly competitive in the pharmaceutical business, and I think from a shareholder's standpoint, we were better off to put our eggs in one basket—for each of the businesses."

From this work, we made a number of decisions about the company's future course, including the following:

1. The focus of the company would be primarily on human pharmaceuticals.
2. Lilly would exit the medical device businesses, using the best approach we could develop to unlock the potential shareholder value that wasn't being realized. We would try to find an approach that would also harvest some of the value of the assets in cash for the Lilly parent to invest in the pharmaceutical business.

3. The best opportunity to harvest cash from our investment in the Dow–Elanco plant science joint venture would be pursued— probably a sale to Dow.
4. Unless new facts caused a need to reevaluate, Lilly would remain in the animal health business.
5. A different approach would be taken to the research and development driving the pharmaceutical business, focusing efforts on selected therapeutic areas with essentially three characteristics:
   a. Disease categories with significant unmet medical needs
   b. Disease categories where Lilly's research capabilities already were or could be a match for what was required to effectively address these unmet medical needs
   c. Disease categories where the likely profit margins available were attractive, avoiding, if we could, probable low-margin businesses.

After looking at a number of options, including a sale of the device businesses to two other players in that market, the decision was made to launch a new company, Guidant, as a stand-alone device company. With the help of the investment bankers at Morgan Stanley, we decided to do a "splitoff," something that had not been used before in a transaction of this size. Essentially, Lilly shareholders were given two options. They could trade their old Lilly shares for new Guidant shares, which would transfer their shareholder value from a combination of pharmaceuticals and devices in the old Lilly to devices only in the new Guidant. Or they could just sit still, in which case, after the transaction, they would own only new Lilly shares in a pharmaceutical company. But each of their shares should have greater value because of the share repurchase characteristics of the transaction, caused by the Lilly shares that were traded in being removed from the market. We also placed a prudent amount of debt on the Guidant balance sheet while it was still 100 percent owned by Lilly, then issued a special dividend of the resulting cash to the Lilly parent. All in all, it was a very successful transaction. It is my strongly held belief that both companies, Lilly and Guidant, have done far better than either could have had the device businesses continued under Lilly ownership. Indeed, at its high in September 2000, the market capitalization of Guidant alone was well above the value of the old Lilly, including the businesses that became Guidant at the time I became CEO.

As for the change in focus in pharmaceutical research, Gus Watanabe and I had a very positive collaborative effort from the beginning. Gus did heroic work in fundamentally reinventing the way research is done at the company. "We both agreed that we needed greater focus," says Watanabe. "Specifically, we needed to refocus the business on a small number of selected therapeutic areas such as cardiology, oncology, and neuroscience, as opposed to disciplinary areas such as chemistry, biology, and molecular biology. . . . The exact areas we would focus on was something that I worked out with Randy's full support. What Randy brought to the table was an insistence on customer focus. The prior philosophy was that R&D did not interface with business. Randy did away with that. He instilled in the R&D people the notion that customer focus begins with research. That was a big change in philosophy and helped us to develop a vision."

It was my view that instead of playing the "if we build it, they will come" game, we needed to understand where there were major unmet medical needs that we had the capabilities to do something about, and then we needed to focus our attention in those areas. Gus put together a team that reconsidered all of the areas where Lilly was then focusing its research and development. The analysis led to the conclusion that efforts would be focused on five therapeutic areas of research.

Beyond Gus's work, the rest of our early strategy effort culminated in two other major decisions. We would need to develop or enhance capabilities that would be critical to our success going

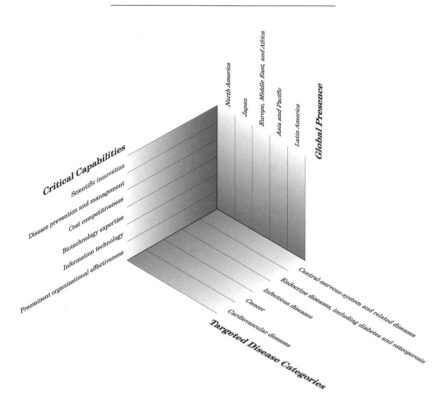

*"The Cube," which we used to illustrate the three elements of Lilly's new strategy
—Targeted Disease Categories, Global Presence, and Critical Capabilities. It
appeared in the company's 1993 annual report to shareholders, entitled* Three
Dimensions of Strategic Focus, *and was the principal subject of my seven-page
letter to shareholders. It was also used widely in our communications with
employees and other stakeholders. Photo courtesy of Eli Lilly and Company.*

forward, and we would need to focus more aggressively on building our businesses in markets outside the United States to reduce
our dependence on our home market. To communicate this vision
to our stakeholders, we developed a device called "the cube," which
provided on a single slide or a single piece of paper the basis for
describing our strategy in terms our employees and others could
clearly grasp.

Focus Group

To put it quite simply, "structure must follow strategy."

My inability to find anyone in charge of Lilly's various businesses, beginning with the diabetes business, is not uncommon in functional organizations where the units of the business are managing isolated activities such as manufacturing or sales or research. However, functional organizations do have clear advantages, too. If a manager is focused only on manufacturing and that's essentially all he or she thinks about, learns about, and works on over an extended period, then that manager will likely become an expert at manufacturing, far more skilled than managers who spend only part of their time on that function. The issue is not about doing away with functional managers. Rather, the issue is where and when and how and how quickly does integration take place? Who is accountable for the integrated business activities?[1]

Let's say the salespeople in a company want to sell a product in eighteen different configurations of color and size, to meet what they see as the varying needs or preferences of the broadest range of customers. And let's assume they are right, that more customers would buy the product if there were that range of choices. But let's also remember they are probably not measured or rewarded on

---

1. With the benefit of twenty-twenty hindsight, it is now my view that in spite of my best intentions and those of some very capable people around me, we fell short, during the process of making all of these strategic and organizational changes, in our efforts to properly deal with the management of change in certain aspects of our manufacturing operations. On the one hand, our focus on the extreme importance of experienced scientific and technological skills in manufacturing may have inadvertently taken a backseat to other issues whose importance needed to be elevated. On the other hand, we might have been too willing to continue doing some things as we always had when change was desperately needed. These things are never totally clear in the aftermath. Nonetheless, I believe that issues facing the company some years later might well have had their early roots at least in part in decisions I made nearly a decade earlier, and I want to note that here.

the basis of the company's profit. They are probably rewarded mostly on the sales revenue they produce. And let's assume the manufacturing people want to make the product in only one or two colors and sizes because they know that they can dramatically lower the manufacturing cost per unit manufactured if they can have longer manufacturing runs. And let's assume *they* are right, that manufacturing costs will be lower with fewer product variations. But let's also remember they, too, are probably not measured or rewarded on the basis of the company's profit. They are probably rewarded mostly on manufacturing costs. The issues go on and on, but at some point, decisions have to be made that integrate all of these points of view. Chances are, if hard choices are made, the best interests of the company may not be in the best interests of every individual part of the company. So where and when and how and how quickly will the tradeoff decisions be made? And beyond that, how can reward systems be better aligned with the interests of the entire company?

These same issues exist not just with functional versus integrated decisions but also with local versus global, centralized versus decentralized, and on and on.

Lilly in the early 1990s was largely a functionally organized company. That structure had served the company well for a long time. With only a few exceptions—the animal health business and the medical device businesses in particular—almost no one at Lilly had the integrated responsibility for any one business, for the company's total approach to any specific market opportunity. For many years, the industry had not changed very quickly, so time had not been a critical factor for a company to use in gaining competitive advantage. The culture had produced many effective function managers, but few business managers. The structure and the culture had also inhibited the quality of information reaching the executive floor. It was no longer adequate. There were plenty of experts in the functions we performed, but there were too few to be found who were senior-level experts in the businesses we were in. All of this had a strong feeling of familiarity.

The Changing Boxes

During much of its history, the Bell System was also structured around the functions it performed, in the extreme. For most of my career, one could enter just about any district office in the Bell companies across America and find, lined up in a row, the offices of the district plant manager (installation and repair), the district traffic manager (telephone operators), and the district commercial manager (the company's business offices—its face to the public). For the most part, my rise in the business had come through the commercial department. But now the structure was changing. Late in the 1970s, as competition began to enter the scene and one-size-fits-all solutions no longer fit, the organization began to move away from having very senior functional jobs in an operating telephone company. In its place, the organization was being structured, where possible, around sets of customers. The heart of that change created organizations focused on the needs of residence customers and business customers. It seems very straightforward now, not even very revolutionary. But for many employees then, it was absolutely gut-wrenching. The organization was just not culturally prepared to deal with change, and I was about to be thrown right into the middle of leading it.

In 1978, I was appointed Vice President—Residence at Illinois Bell in Chicago. But that did not last long. In the fall of 1980, I received the biggest and most unexpected promotion of my entire career. At the time, I was working for the Vice President and Chief Operating Officer of the company, Phil Campbell, who in turn worked for the President and CEO, Chuck Marshall, truly one of the nicest people I've ever known. As Chuck remembers, "I got a call one day from Charlie Brown, who was the Chairman of AT&T by then. He said, 'Chuck, I understand you have a guy out there at an early vice president level who looks pretty good. Olson thinks very highly of him.' I said, 'You're talking about Randy Tobias.' Charlie said, 'That's right. What do you think of him? Is he ready to be promoted?'" Chuck later told me he'd said some very nice things, which were apparently convincing to Charlie, whom I did not know well at the time. A few days later, I was told that at the beginning of 1981 I would be moving to AT&T's corporate headquarters to become Vice President—Residence Sales and Service. It was the equivalent of being promoted in Chicago not to my boss's job but to my boss's *boss's* job. I couldn't believe it. I would have corporate responsibility for the company's service to residential telephone customers, nationwide. That meant I would also become one of the fifty or so members of the Presidents' Council, the management group made up of the senior officers at the headquarters and the presidents of the operating telephone companies. According to Alvin von Auw, the erudite Assistant to the Chairman and company sage, I would be the youngest to hold such a position in the history of the corporation.

To put the company's leadership, culture, and organization in some perspective, in 1980 AT&T had approximately one million employees. Charlie Brown, the company's recently appointed Chairman and CEO, sat at the top of that organization. Brown was highly respected by AT&T people at all levels—and a bit feared by many. A graduate of the University of Virginia and a naval officer in the Pacific during World War II, he had worked his way up the AT&T Long Lines organization and, after demonstrating his ability in several other high-profile assignments, eventually to the top of the company. He never yelled. He didn't need to. A man of few words with a quiet voice and penetrating blue eyes, he did not suffer fools easily and had absolutely no patience for those who, in his view, had not done their homework or who made comments or assertions they could not support. Some years earlier during his tenure as CEO of Illinois Bell, after hearing a report he did not think much of, he reportedly told the subordinate responsible for the report that it would probably be a good idea if he started walking east (from the company's downtown Chicago offices toward Lake Michigan) and kept walking until his hat floated.

There was, however, another side to Charlie Brown that not many had the opportunity to see. After his retirement from AT&T, he invited Marilyn and me to spend a weekend at Colonial Williamsburg in his beloved Virginia. Shortly after, he extended an invitation, which I accepted, to join the board of trustees of the parent Colonial Williamsburg Foundation, where he was then serving as Chairman. This was an invitation I have always viewed as a singular honor, not only because of my high regard for the institution and its very distinguished board but also because of its source. Although I worked closely with him at AT&T, I always found him somewhat intimidating, perhaps in part because I viewed him with such great respect. Through the Williamsburg association, and later through my membership in the Business Council, I got to know him on a much more personal basis than when we were working together. I found him to be an extremely thoughtful, kind, and gentle man, when the occasion called for it. When Marilyn died in 1994, Charlie and his extraordinary lady, Ann Lee Brown, were among the first to come to Indiana to share my grief. In the years following my marriage to Marianne, they've both gone out of their way to make her feel welcome and connected to the relationships that preceded her arrival in my life. She and I have both been very grateful for our relationship with the Browns.

At the time I became part of the AT&T headquarters organization, immediately under Brown were Bill Ellinghaus, the company's

At the time of Charlie Brown's retirement as Chairman and CEO of AT&T in 1986, I arranged to have one of AT&T's cable ships renamed the CS Charles L. Brown. *Shown here at the surprise christening ceremony in San Francisco are Charlie, his wife, Ann Lee Brown, and the ship's captain. Photo courtesy of Mary O'Brien.*

President, and Bill Cashel and Jim Olson, both Vice Chairmen.[2] Together, these four officers formed what was then known as the Office of the Chairman, or the OC. Beneath the OC were four Executive Vice Presidents, each with responsibility for some part of the corporate headquarters operations.[3] In addition to these eight, also at AT&T Headquarters was the President of Bell Laboratories, the company's research and development organization; the Presi-

2. Ellinghaus had distinguished himself as President of the New York Telephone Company, leading the company and New York City out of the well-publicized telephone service crisis some years earlier. Cashel's last assignment before arriving at AT&T headquarters had been as President of the Bell of Pennsylvania company. Olson, of course, had been the President of Indiana Bell, had followed Brown at Illinois Bell, and then had been summoned by Brown to New York.

3. Tom Bolger, Dick Hough, Charlie Hugel, and Ken Whalen.

dent of Western Electric, the company's manufacturing entity; the President of AT&T Long Lines, the company's interstate and international network arm; and a dozen or so Vice Presidents, charged with oversight of various other parts of the business. In addition, there were the "cardinals" of the corporation, the "princes," the twenty-two Presidents of the operating telephone companies who ran their organizations with what I now regard as a surprising but enlightened degree of autonomy, particularly considering how oriented we were toward conformity. Short of the position occupied by Charlie Brown, these were the most coveted jobs in the corporation. And for the few who eventually found themselves as the CEOs of their "home" operating telephone companies, it was difficult to leave if the call came to move to a job in the corporate headquarters, even though such a move would likely mean, at least eventually, a promotion to one of the eight top jobs. Chuck Marshall remembers his own summons in late 1981. He received a call one day from Jim Olson, who told him, "I'm in town and I want to see you. And to make a long story short, Chuck, we want to bring you back to AT&T." Even though Marshall could see the train coming down the track, he told Olson, "Forget it. You and Charlie came through here, but you're not *from* here. I'm from here, and I want to stay here. I really don't want to go to New York again." Olson responded, "Well, you think about it."

As Chuck recalls, the very next day, he got a call from Charlie Brown, "who was God to all of us." Charlie said, "Chuck, I'm not going to argue with you. I'm just going to tell you we need you out here." Says Chuck, "What could I do? I went."

For an organization that had experienced little change, we were entering a period mostly characterized by change. Some changes were imposed by orders we received from the FCC, some by ourselves. But nearly all moved us in the direction of multifunctional organizations, bringing integration and decision making to much lower levels in the organization. And we discovered it was far more

Shown here sometime in the early 1980s are (left to right) me; Chuck Marshall, who later became AT&T Vice Chairman; and Jim Olson, later AT&T Chairman and CEO. Photo courtesy of AT&T.

complicated than just moving the boxes around on the organization charts. We had too few managers who were prepared to take on these kinds of roles. And we did not understand that for an organization to be effective, it really required a good deal of effort in addressing what Dr. David Nadler calls "the soft stuff." Initially, we didn't do enough of that. Many managers had known only a functional structure, and they were trying to manage multifunctional organizations without addressing the cultural changes that needed to take place. Just about the time we'd get something working, along would come another wave of organizational changes, at a speed the company was simply not equipped to absorb.

But we were even less well equipped to recognize the absolute imperative of a new vision to fit our changed circumstances. Those of us who argued for such a change were never able to mount a sufficiently persuasive case. The prevailing view remained that AT&T had signed on to the terms of the breakup of the Bell System, agreeing to nothing less than separating ourselves from our customers, to maintain our ability to extract that elusive synergy from "technological integration," from a singular approach to designing, developing, manufacturing, and selling telecommunications hardware. We had also paid a big price to be permitted to enter the computer business. Those with the power to do so were not about to give up on that vision. Rather, we continued to look for the answer in some different approach to the organizational structure we were using to pursue that vision.

I recently had a conversation with a former AT&T senior officer who was there at the time of the breakup. "Once the consent decree was announced," he observed, "and we started getting serious about how to build a business out of the left-over parts of the Bell System, I was truly astonished to discover how many [AT&T senior officers] really didn't have a clue about how we actually made money. So instead of devoting energy and creativity to the task of fashioning a coherent (new) strategy . . . all of the effort went into reorganizing and redeploying existing business units that had no chance in hell of ever becoming profitable over the long term. Moreover, we were paying high-priced consulting firms . . . to help us cobble together high-overhead, no-margin businesses."

In looking back over that period in my career, I believe the most basic lesson that was confirmed for me was the degree to which people who should know better somehow believed that changing an organization's structure would be the panacea— the magic potion—that would fix all the other problems. Organizational structures are seldom bad or good; they are just different from each other. Selecting the appropriate organizational structure is, quite simply, a question of choosing the appropriate tradeoffs.

More often, the tradeoffs involve issues such as the role of centralized product-oriented organizations, focusing on achieving efficiency and effectiveness through superior information, product uniformity, economies of scale, and the like, versus locally focused (country, region, city, etc.) organizations, which can generally move more quickly and can achieve superior local focus. It's probably human nature, but there is a lot of truth to the old saying, "Where you stand on an issue often depends a great deal on where you sit." In the old Bell System, most operating telephone company presidents favored a Bell System structure that was heavy on local focus, giving lots of latitude to each of the company presidents. When those same people were moved to senior positions in the AT&T headquarters, they were usually able to quickly see the benefits that could be achieved through more centralized decision making.

It's always important to sort out what is really needed and to match the organizational structure to the mission that's been assigned and the particular market circumstances that exist. For organizations that require deep expertise but do not have to move quickly, functional organizations are just fine. It's just difficult to find situations in today's competitive global markets with those characteristics.

It is true that occasionally the choice of a particular structure will create a situation that is so dysfunctional that success can never be achieved until the structural barriers are removed. I've been given at least one assignment in my career that I now believe was structured in a way that had almost no chance of being successfully carried out. The authority simply didn't match the accountability.

Whatever the circumstance, it's important to remember that changing the organizational structure alone will not create success; it will only create a structure where success may be more readily achieved. Changing from one type of structure to another in the belief that it will fix the problem—whatever the problem may be—is a big mistake. It just doesn't happen that way. Organizational structures are really only about tradeoffs. That's all.

Heavyweight Champions

Organizational culture is often closely attached to the existing structure and, by definition, very deep rooted, resilient, and enduring. Therefore, when changing a company's structure, the management team may find that changing the corporate culture is the single most difficult assignment it faces. Transformation cannot be achieved merely by issuing new policies and making a few speeches. It requires a patient, sustained effort to educate people about a new way of doing things, to eradicate the old habits that no longer work, and to validate the benefits of change as they occur. And it requires honest introspection and change at the personal level. This is one process that absolutely must come from the top down, for the simple reason that if a management team behaves according to the old culture, everyone else will receive implicit permission to do so as well.

There are some fundamental leadership concepts that I took away from my stint as an "officer and gentleman" in the U.S. Army that have served me well in the corporate world. When one is building or inheriting a leadership team, it is crucial to recognize the importance of assembling, structuring, teaching, and, above all, truly empowering one's troops to prepare to fight by the ground rules of the *next* war, not the last one.

In business, as in the military, history might be written by the winners, but that's largely because the winners knew when to disregard history. When organizations fail, their missteps can often be traced back to the moment their leaders succumbed to the allure of trying to fit round-peg formulas of past successes into square-hole strategic plans for future battles. While their strategies might have changed on paper, the plans of these would-be visionaries often go awry when the roles, the skills, and the very faces of the people driving their boldly hatched schemes have not. As a result, businesses can find themselves with teams of individuals who possess the ideal sets of skills and are aligned in a way to bring their organizations success . . . twenty years ago.

Don't get me wrong: Honing a strategy and understanding the initiatives that have contributed to past successes are key elements to any organization's growth and well-being. But in my experience, the thin line separating the winners from the losers is often determined by how well an organization chooses and structures jobs for its people in a way that is consistent with its plans for tomorrow, not yesterday.

Leadership, in my view, is about far more than producing results through one's own initiative—it's about being able to produce results through others. It's about building consensus and leading through a collective, team-oriented approach. It's about articulating clearly defined roles. It's about learning to be comfortable with delegation. And above all, it's about creating a structure and environment in which individuals are truly empowered to make, implement, and own decisions—even (and sometimes, especially) if they are not the highest-ranking individual in the room. In short, leadership is about setting up your people to succeed.

I cannot think of a better example of a team at work than the story of the 1997 launch of Lilly's now-blockbuster drug Zyprexa. Schizophrenia is rightly called "the cancer of psychiatry." It is a disease that so ravages the mind, it can be a living damnation. The antipsychotics before Zyprexa had limited efficacy against the symptoms of the disease and produced side effects nearly as unpleasant as the symptoms—uncontrollable trembling, severe facial contortion, and so on.

Terry Hotten and Dr. David Tupper in England, at Lilly's Erl Wood research facility, synthesized the molecule they named olanzapine, now marketed as Zyprexa. As subsequent testing and development would confirm beyond the researchers' best hopes, the molecule would be a breakthrough in both efficacy and safety and would offer the promise of several unlooked-for benefits as well. But time would pass before the company began to aggressively pursue the development of the compound.

When that time came, we decided to try a very aggressive new approach to development and regulatory submission—with an entirely new (to Lilly) organizational structure—and a new culture to go with it. The approach, first suggested to me by Dr. Gus Watanabe, Lilly's head of R&D, involved creating a dedicated team of some of our best people, a heavyweight team. The idea was to break free of the gravitational field of bureaucracy by pulling one hundred key people out of their various functional silos, putting them all in one place, and giving them collective ownership of the whole development and registration process worldwide.

The heavyweight team for Zyprexa was formed in January 1995 under the leadership of Dr. Gary Tollefson. Dr. Tollefson gave his team a goal of achieving regulatory submission in all our biggest markets by October 1995. It didn't look difficult—it looked impossible. He was proposing to do in nine months what the company had taken years to do in the past. The team came up with many, many innovations in pursuit of that goal. But working faster was not the only objective. They also worked smarter.

For instance, from the beginning, Dr. Tollefson saw a way to prepare the ground for commercial success early in the registration phase. And so the heavyweight team designed a 2,000-patient trial at sites in seventeen countries to answer many questions at once. This trial, the largest ever of a psychotropic agent in the development phase, set out to establish not only Zyprexa's safety and efficacy but also its positive attributes, such as impact on mood, stability in long-term maintenance, contribution to quality of life, and cost advantages over other treatments. All of this was powerful information that could be used beyond registration, beyond launch, in detailing the product to the physicians who would prescribe it and to those who would pay for it.

If one stream of innovation went into generating all that data, another went into managing it and packaging it all for submission. The paper version of the materials the FDA required ran to something like 1,100 paper volumes of 350 pages each. It would take 400 large boxes to hold the entire submission and a large truck to transport the boxes from Indianapolis to the FDA offices in Rockville, Maryland—typical for the submission of the information necessary when seeking approval of a new molecule.

But along with those mandatory boxes, Lilly's regulatory team submitted an electronic version on twenty-three CD-ROMs, along with software to make it faster and easier for the FDA reviewers to use.

Ultimately, the Zyprexa team members not only met their impossible October deadline, they beat it. They submitted the new drug application in September 1995. Not just in the United States but in sixteen additional countries—Canada and the fifteen nations of the European Union. Within just days, they accomplished a task that had once taken years.

Novel applications of information technology continued to be critical to the next chapter of the Zyprexa story—winning regulatory approval, getting the best possible official language on the label indicating the approved use of the drug. Along with the heavyweight team, the principal actors in this part of the drama were the people in Lilly's then newly created global regulatory group under Dr. John Lechleiter.

This group had been heavily involved in the preregistration effort as well. Its members brought a new kind of intensity to their task. At least one newcomer to all of this among the senior executives had been puzzled to observe that we had historically treated the regulatory submission of an application for a new drug as if it were tantamount to winning the Indianapolis 500: an occasion to celebrate the successful conclusion of something and break out the champagne. But that didn't happen with the Zyprexa submission. Rather, everyone understood the new paradigm. They recognized the moment of the submission of the application for what it was: a time to pause and thank everyone for what they'd contributed and accomplished so far, but with the understanding that we hadn't yet won the race—we'd just built the car and shipped it to the track.

In fact, when actively managed, the period between submission and approval is very dynamic, very tense, and very critical to the ultimate outcome. The scientists in the regulatory bodies don't simply ponder the data and render a judgment. They ask questions—often complicated questions that could reasonably take months to answer.

We were ready for that. A small group led by Jeff Ramsey and Ann-Marie Crawford created the Rapid Regulatory Response Database to capture, track, and coordinate responses to inquiries from authorities anywhere in the world. The database was really a way of capturing and focusing teamwork among people located in many countries. It was like a virtual rolling meeting, a way of pooling ideas and sharing solutions.

The database was also a strategic modeling tool. Many possible questions had been anticipated, researched, and answered by the time of submission. The tool proved its worth when the agency in charge of the then-new centralized submission process for the countries in the European Union asked a series of about thirty questions that stopped the review clock. Nothing more would happen with our application until these questions were answered.

John Saunders of the heavyweight team had the primary responsibility for responding. In the past, developing the answers might have taken John and his team anywhere from six to twelve months. But using the new technology, they were able to pull together an appropriate response and submit an answer, twenty-plus volumes of information, in just twenty-eight days.

Other teams were also gearing up for the race to market, the leg from approval to launch. There were plenty of heroes and plenty of innovators in this stage as well. On the other side of the Atlantic, Kay Loghrey and Katherine Brooks, the company's registration officers in Basingstoke, England, saw a way to cut months, even years, off the process of achieving registration in emerging markets. Many emerging nations link their own approval for marketing a new pharmaceutical product to the official document of approval issued by the United Kingdom, known as a Free Sales Certificate. The heavyweight team members had identified sixty emerging markets where they wanted to launch the product once this certificate was in hand. What Loghrey and Brooks asked was "Why not apply in all of them, all at once?" Moreover, "Why wait until after approval in the United Kingdom to get ready to apply in these sixty countries?" They worked with the embassies and consulates of all sixty nations to determine what each country would require in its application packet. They prepared custom-made draft packets for each, asked the consulates for review, and then went back and made the changes each consulate suggested.

The results were spectacular. Zyprexa was approved in the United Kingdom on September 27. The Lilly U.K. organization had applied for and received the Free Sales Certificate within forty-eight hours. Loghrey and Brooks were ready and immediately submitted all sixty registration applications in final form. Ninety percent were accepted and approved without further revision—something that was unheard of. And within three weeks, fifty-seven emerging markets granted legalization of the Free Sales Certificate—a critical step toward permission to market. It took Prozac three years to achieve that.

There are any number of great stories in the final chapter, the actual launch of Zyprexa. But my favorite is the story of the manufacturing source for the U.S. launch—the company's production facility at Carolina, in Puerto Rico. To be ready, Carolina began making ten-milligram tablets of Zyprexa in March 1996, six months ahead of the anticipated approval date. As the date neared, Carolina Production Manager Teresita Colon and her organization had to climb over a series of obstacles to stay on schedule. And then came Hurricane Hortense, twenty days before the target approval date. Modern storm-tracking technology is double-edged. It gives people warning, time to prepare. It also gives them time to be afraid. As Colon and her organization watched the monster storm churn its way toward the island, they all wondered, "How bad will it be? How long will we be down? What can we do?"

The three plants in Puerto Rico are equipped with a computer-driven energy management system that allows the engineers to shut down facilities or shunt electricity from place to place as needed if commercial power fails. The group's hope was to use this capability to keep the one plant making Zyprexa up and running. But to further cover the risk, the group brought in an additional backup diesel generator as well. The other critical measure was to carefully store the inventory of what had already been produced, as high and dry as possible, against the danger of flooding. That done, Colon sent nearly everyone home. All hands needed to secure their homes and their families in the few hours they had until Hortense came calling. But a small team of engineers, including Jimmy Varela, volunteered to stay at the plant through whatever was to come.

The storm made landfall on Tuesday, September 10, and pounded the island with eighty-mile-an-hour winds and torrential rains, flooding roads and towns, unleashing mudslides, dropping trees, and cutting power lines everywhere. Varela and his team stayed at the plant all through the storm, activating and then monitoring the emergency power system, keeping everything tight and dry.

When the rest of the workers came in on Wednesday morning, leaving their own battered homes and wading through flooded roads to get to work, the plant was still operational, ready to complete the production of the Zyprexa needed for the introduction of the product in the United States.

In the final days before the launch, employees from all the plants in Puerto Rico volunteered to help with the inspection and packaging of Zyprexa. This, too, was an amazing feat. To meet internal quality-assurance guidelines, a total inspection of the samples was performed, meaning that every single case had to be checked by hand. Approximately thirty people managed to sort through 60,000 finished sample cartons within twenty-four hours. Through such heroic efforts, the initial shipment of 97,000 sample bottles, six million tablets, was packed and ready in just three days.

What does this all mean? Why does it matter? Coming to market eighteen months early allowed Lilly to catch and to pass several competitors. Because of the extra eighteen months, hundreds of millions of dollars of revenue will be earned during what will be, in effect, eighteen additional months of effective patent life. And the lessons from the organizational approach created for Zyprexa have produced benefits for virtually every other product from that point onward.

Beyond the financial measures, there is another kind of payoff that cannot be quantified, cannot be converted into dollars. In the eighteen months between the product launch and the date that *would* have been the product launch, hundreds of thousands of patients, all around the world, were treated with Zyprexa and were given help and healing and hope. It is this power to improve, indeed to save, human lives that gives innovation its real meaning.

NINE

Risky Business

*The path we have chosen for the present is full
of hazards, as all paths are.*
—President John F. Kennedy, announcing the
U.S. blockade of Cuba after installation of
missiles by the Soviet Union

Gray Flannel Suits

When I began my AT&T career in the early 1960s, managers working for the Bell System were euphemistically referred to as "Bell-shaped heads." This colorful, if somewhat cynical, label seemed apt not only because of their unflinching commitment and loyalty to the company but also because the heads were the quintessential conforming army of "men in gray flannel suits," memorialized during that period in the Sloan Wilson novel. They didn't take a lot of risks. But AT&T was not unique. Signing on with a U.S. corporate behemoth in those days carried with it the likelihood that you would soon take on many of the characteristics of your colleagues. If you worked for IBM, for example, it was well known that you could wear to work any color shirt you wished . . . as long as it was white. Doing something other than that was a big risk.

Likewise, working for Ma Bell meant abiding by her strict cultural code. You might say that when you embraced change in the Bell System, you did it slowly, at the direction of those above you, and in lockstep with your fellow employees.

Some of the priorities of the company's leaders of the time seemed unusual to younger managers. By today's standards, they seem absolutely bizarre. Shortly before the time of my arrival at Indiana Bell, there was a chief operating officer who would regularly stroll out into the park diagonally across from the headquarters building in downtown Indianapolis for the purpose of ensuring that all of the venetian blinds in the building were adjusted identically to the prescribed height and angle. The windows of offending nonconformists were duly noted, and being on that list was not a distinction one coveted.

There were, however, those who were culturally ahead of their time and determined to beat the system. Until sometime in the late 1950s or early 1960s, men who worked for the company and had attained a certain level in the hierarchy were required to wear hats to work—straw in the summer, felt in the winter. One iconoclastic band of early-day Dilberts, working in a building a few blocks away from the headquarters, were said to collectively own an "office hat." Whenever one or another of them had business in the headquarters, he simply donned the office hat and went on his way. These were big-time risk takers.

In those days, demonstrating the right behavior and subscribing to the codes of the company's long-standing values was as much a part of the corporate fabric as dial tones and coaxial cable. The intricacies of this culture were sometimes difficult to articulate with any precision. While we knew the correct and expected behaviors of the company's culture when we saw them in action, we often had no clue why the organization valued them or the relationship these behaviors had to our business objectives. We did know that conforming was the way we were expected to behave, following the practices that had been written for nearly every aspect of the business and codified in rows and rows of black binders which lined office walls. We simply learned to accept the fact that how-we-do-it-around-here was, well, how we did it around there, even if we couldn't always begin to express why. It was quite clear that risk taking was not encouraged.

Making Candy

Sometime shortly after my first visit to a Lilly manufacturing facility, I began to think a lot about candy. Specifically, M&M's. I asked our manufacturing people to make contact with the Mars candy company and arrange for a tour of an M&M's factory. I wanted them to learn all they could about how M&M's were produced, mostly in the hope of getting them to think in new and different ways about how pharmaceuticals are manufactured, to think about the likely profit margin in a typical product made at Lilly, a single pill of some kind, for example—then consider the likely profit margin in a single M&M. It doesn't take great insight to conclude that over the years, the Mars candy people have had a far greater incentive to make an M&M as efficiently, effectively, and inexpensively as possible. And while in many ways we are talking about apples and oranges, nonetheless, an M&M does have some things in common with a pill. Each piece of candy has to be produced uniformly and in very high volumes, and above all, each one has to meet the strict standards required of a product being consumed by a human being.

By asking our people to visit an M&M's factory, I wasn't trying to suggest that I knew anything about manufacturing pharmaceuticals. I certainly wasn't suggesting that we should begin to make pills in the same way M&M's are made. I was just suggesting we should look outside our normal and expected sources of information, and that perhaps by looking at manufacturing from a new perspective, by thinking outside the box, we could borrow an idea or two for our own business. Beyond that, regardless of what our people actually learned, the trip could be beneficial, encouraging our employees to think in new and different ways about their jobs. Clearly, we needed to become less risk-averse.

Why? Over the years, probably without making a conscious decision to do so, we had developed a culture that rewarded *not failing* rather than *the achievement of success*.[1] Back when the pharmaceutical industry moved relatively slowly and predictably, we had not been significantly penalized by this culture. But now, unless we changed, it would simply not be possible to keep up with our competitors.

The decision to split off Guidant required a new willingness to take well-considered risks.

The decision to focus and reinvent our approach to research and development required a new willingness to take well-considered risks.

The decision to set up the heavyweight team to manage Zyprexa required a new willingness to take well-considered risks.

The decision to move away from functional organizations in favor of more integrated decision making focused on our businesses required a new willingness to take well-considered risks.

By encouraging more risk taking, we would make mistakes, to be sure. But the ultimate measure would be the *net* impact on the creation of shareholder value from everything that we did—not just the number of times we made a well-considered decision that didn't turn out the way we planned. One of the lessons I learned very early in my life is that a basketball team can avoid missing any shots if it never takes any. It just won't win any games.

---

1. For some aspects of the pharmaceutical business, such as matters impacting the safety and well-being of patients, the standard of *not failing* is totally appropriate. That standard, however, does not and should not automatically carry over to other aspects of the business where it does not apply.

Choosing between Risks

In the years preceding the 1992 election, Arkansas Governor Bill Clinton and his wife, Hillary Rodham Clinton, had forged a path to the White House based in part on promises of major changes in who would pay for health care in the United States and how health-care delivery decisions would be made. In the fall of 1993, having repeatedly painted the pharmaceutical industry as villains bent on forcing elderly Americans to choose between eating and paying for their prescription drugs, President Clinton unveiled a health-care reform plan that would call for the use of something new called global budgets,[2] forced rebates, threats of blacklisting, and other forces designed to bring down drug prices.

Government imposition of price controls on any industry is viewed by many as the first step toward dismantling the free-market system. Virtually no administration wants to be viewed as advocating such a move, and Clinton officials were no different. I recall a friendly but spirited debate I had early on with Health and Human Services Secretary Donna Shalala on this subject. She insisted that their plan did not include price controls. But that, of course, is dependent on what the definition of *price controls* is, so to speak.

The Clinton health-care reform plan promised to give every American insurance coverage for prescription drugs, either through Medicare, available to those over age sixty-five, or through large government-sponsored buying groups called regional health alli-

2. Global budgets refer to expenditure limits or prospectively defined caps on spending for some portion of the health-care industry. Global budgeting in the United States as envisioned by most proponents would establish binding targets for permissible growth in the U.S. health-care system.

ances. Both plans would encourage, and presumably eventually mandate, the widespread use of generic drugs, which are priced well below brand-name medicines.[3] Whether generic drugs or not, under the rules of the proposed reform, doctors could prescribe only those drugs on an approved list, called a formulary, established by the government. Because Medicare would literally dominate the market or, one might even argue, *be* the market, pharmaceutical companies failing to get their products on the formulary would be committing nothing short of financial hara-kiri. First, the plan, if approved by Congress, would give Medicare a strong hand in negotiations over price because the pressure to get one's drugs on the formulary list would be enormous. Second, the plan would give the Secretary of Health and Human Services the right to blacklist any drug deemed too expensive. While regional health alliances wouldn't be required to follow that lead, in reality we knew that they would. In short, such measures would serve to create de facto price controls.

While Secretary Shalala was correct that no formal price controls were spelled out explicitly in the plan, as a practical matter they seemed to leap off the page to me and my colleagues. Arguing that the Clinton plan did not in effect equate to price controls would be like arguing today that Wal-Mart does not in effect con-

3. This is, of course, because companies in the generics business manufacture and sell their products using, at no expense to themselves, the intellectual property information that has been developed and paid for by the brand-name pharmaceutical companies who earned the original patents—those patents now having expired. This work often costs hundreds of millions of dollars. The public policy arrangements involved here would be similar to someone's being given the right to publish and sell a version of a college textbook in competition with the original author and publisher, but without paying anything to those who originally researched, wrote, and published the text. As a result, the generic pharmaceutical companies have virtually zero expense for research and development, which is *the* major expense in the research-based pharmaceutical industry, and thus can make a profit at much lower retail prices. A lack of public understanding about these issues contributes to widespread feelings that brand-name pharmaceutical companies engage in overpricing their products, a perception that some in the public sector have been quite willing to exploit.

trol wholesale prices for many of the products it sells. Wal-Mart has so much buying power and accounts for such a significant share of the total sales in many manufacturers' product category that if these companies want their products sold in Wal-Mart stores, they either meet the price demands or they don't get Wal-Mart shelf space. And for many categories, not selling through Wal-Mart essentially means not being a player.

Under the Clinton plan, if you didn't meet the price demands of the only customer who would count, the U.S. government, how could you be a major player in your product category? And if you did meet their price demands, wouldn't that play a major role in determining the prices your other customers would pay? Sounded like price controls to me.

As if that weren't enough to contend with, drug companies would also be forced to pay rebates to Medicare patients, which would amount to a new industry tax. And additional rebates would be required if drug companies were to raise prices to Medicare faster than inflation. Because prices to Medicare could become benchmarks for prices charged other health plans, again, those rebates could become a form of price controls.

At the time the plan was announced, its successful passage looked to be about as much of a sure thing as you could get. To put the plan's prospects into some context, remember that the Democrats controlled the Senate, the Democrats controlled the House of Representatives, and not only was a popular Democrat, early in his first term, sitting in the White House, but he was also putting his very able spouse in command of the effort to get this health-care plan enacted into law. Who could possibly bet against the plan's probable enactment in at least some form resembling what was being proposed?

The future was, at best, uncertain. It wasn't clear to anyone exactly how this situation was going to play out. However, it was clear that the odds of successful passage of the Clinton plan were very high, and the odds of the pharmaceutical industry finding itself in a very different world were even higher.

What to do to prepare?

One thing that seemed highly likely was that firms known as pharmaceutical benefit managers, or PBMs, would play a major role in the new environment. PBMs had some of the critical capabilities that would be necessary to make the Clinton proposal operational. They had been created to help control costs of drug-benefit programs for the providers they represented, as well as to provide drug benefit insurance-claims processing services. As part of their approach, PBMs developed formularies, lists of selected drugs for which they would provide full reimbursement. Among other approaches, they also traditionally negotiated volume purchase agreements with manufacturers, negotiated prescription prices with pharmacies, and dictated mandatory generic substitution programs. From the beginning, there had been something of an adversarial relationship with the pharmaceutical industry, because of concerns that the decisions of PBMs could wipe out the market share of a pharmaceutical company when its drugs were not selected for a formulary. But in the new world, perhaps there would be a way to use PBMs' capabilities to advantage.

Sometime in 1993, Merck had announced that it was acquiring the PBM Medco Containment Services. This would, among other things, give Merck a role in getting its own products on the Medco formularies and would put the company in a much stronger position to participate in the market as it might develop. This was the first purchase of a PBM by a major pharmaceutical company. In the months that followed, SmithKlineBeecham acquired Diversified Pharmaceutical Services (DPS). The last remaining major PBM was PCS, at the time owned by McKesson.

If the political situation developed as it appeared it would, owning a PBM would potentially put Lilly in a much stronger position to compete. If we were to move in that direction, PCS realistically was the only choice that could make a difference. Under virtually any scenario, there were defensive considerations to take into account. "The concern that I had and others had," says Tom Grein, at the time, Lilly's Director of Investor Relations, "was that if PCS were to fall in the hands of someone other than Lilly, we would be at risk because of a dependence at that time on Prozac, and it could well have been that [another major pharmaceutical company] might have picked it up. The speculation was that it would likely be someone else with a major antidepressant, which would preclude Prozac from being on a formulary and in fact would bring about a substantial weakening of the company."

Whether to acquire PCS was one of the most difficult decisions I've ever had to make. The future of our market was unclear. The future of the political environment was unclear. The future moves Lilly's competitors might make were unclear. There were huge risks no matter what we did or didn't do. After a great deal of study and consideration, we decided that the best course for Lilly would be to acquire PCS if we could. What pushed the decision over the edge was that in the end, we saw the risks of not acquiring PCS as posing a greater threat to the company's future if the Clinton plan were approved than the risks associated with buying PCS and then having our assumptions turn out to be wrong.

Even though we'd been working on the decision for some time, the timing of the final presentation to Lilly's board for its approval could not have come at a worse time for me—Monday, May 23, 1994, three days after Marilyn's funeral.

"PCS was a risk, sure," says former Lilly executive Mitch Daniels, who at the time was the head of Lilly's U.S. Operations and had grave concerns about the situation. "But if we had gone into nationalized health care or something like it, Clinton Health Care, which very nearly happened, the model would have been a tremendous defense for the company and probably offensive, too."

But a number of things went wrong. The Clinton administration was not successful in gaining passage of their health-care reform initiative. We found we had not properly understood the impact of the relationship between the type of products in a portfolio and the ability of a PBM to be fully effective in helping to move those products. Beyond that, the Federal Trade Commission weighed in, unexpectedly, in effect changing the rules of the game. This put us in a more complex situation than we had expected, and had we had the latitude to do so honorably, I believe we would have called the deal off at that point. Commissioner Christine Varney of the FTC, speaking at the annual conference of the National Association of Retail Druggists in March 1995, summarized her position: "In the past year, drug manufacturers have acquired some of the largest PBMs—Medco, PAID, PCS, and DPS. . . . We worry that those manufacturers could use their PBMs to foreclose competitors' products from the market." The FTC's concerns led to the necessity of Lilly's entering a consent decree with the commission, after we were committed to the deal, agreeing to a number of their demands to even get the deal closed. Beyond that, we had always planned to bring in partners if we could, after the deal was concluded. But by then, it was too late.

As it turned out, had we taken a risk and not acquired PCS, we would have been better off. As it was, we took a risk in acquiring PCS, and we lost. Our assumptions turned out to be wrong in a number of ways, and the decision to acquire PCS became one I would very much have liked to take back. In spite of heroic efforts on the part of the managers who were responsible for making the acquisition work, in the end it was a loser. Several years later, we sold PCS for significantly less than we paid for it, thus creating a hit on shareholder value of some magnitude. The only thing to do was to say so and take the action required.

"Let me tell you about a leadership lesson that I still recall to this day," says Mike Eagle, retired Vice President, Manufacturing at Lilly. "Some people said that we paid too much for PCS and that it was a mistake and that we shouldn't have bought it and that kind of thing. Randy said that the strategy had been reasonable at the time, based on what we knew and the assumptions we made about the future. But that didn't matter now because the strategy was not right today. So we were going to fix it. He used it as an opportunity to talk about how the Lilly culture had, in the past, hampered our ability to be successful because we were so risk-averse. We would often not make decisions because we were afraid of making the wrong one, when not making a decision at all was sometimes worse. Basically he was saying, 'We took a risk because we thought it was the right thing to do based on what we knew. It didn't work. I'm accountable. Let's fix it. Let's learn everything we can. Let's move on.'"

The working cultures I have observed to be the most chaotic and directionless over the years were the ones in which people were not rewarded for their successes so much as for not failing. Lilly employees, for example, had been taught to think that if they made three decisions during the course of the year, all of which had been studied fourteen ways, and they were absolutely certain they knew they were making the right decision, even though the real benefit would have come from making some decision six months earlier, then probably from a career point of view they were going to be better off. The problem with that logic was that only a small number of decisions were made, even though they were all successful. I'd rather have somebody make twenty good decisions and two bad ones, if the bad ones are manageable, and managed, so that the damage is contained and we move on. In the meantime, we made eighteen good decisions. It's a difference of risk aversion versus taking thoughtful risks.

When decisions are made and things go wrong, what needs to be evaluated is not only the end result but also what did we know and when did we know it? When was the best time to make this decision? Was the risk of making the decision and being wrong outweighed by the likelihood we were going to be right, and the benefits if we were?

Often you can learn 70 percent of what there is to know before making some decision in 20 percent of the time it would take to learn 100 percent of what there is to know. Part of leadership is having the wisdom and the courage to understand the relative value of having the next 10 percent of the information and beyond, against the cost in time and dollars to learn that information. At some point, you are far better off making a quicker decision, even if it turns out wrong, than doing all the things that are necessary to be in a position to make a perfect decision later.

That, to me, is part of leadership. It's making judgments. It's taking informed risks. It's being intuitive. Intuition, after all, is really the collective wisdom of all our own mistakes and those we've seen other people make, as well as all the right things we've done or seen other people do. That why it's sometimes the best tool we have going for us.

Buying a Vowel

In 1997, we brought three hundred or so of the top Lilly executives from around the world to Toronto for our annual Global Management Meeting. Part of the program one evening was a unique awards presentation. It was unusual in that we were not recognizing the company's best achievers. Rather, we celebrated some of our most distinguished losers. With Sidney Taurel at my side, we presented awards to ten different employees who had shared a common trait during the preceding year: They had each taken a risk that hadn't worked out. These were decisions that had been made in a timely fashion and based on the best information available at the time. But for one reason or another, these choices hadn't panned out the way the "winners" had hoped. In each case, however, there was something to be learned from these decisions. I

The "Best Failures" awards ceremony at the Lilly Global Management Meeting in Toronto in 1997, hosted by (left to right) company President and Chief Operating Officer Sidney Taurel, "Vanna White," and me.

wanted the company's top leaders to recognize that sometimes it's okay to make a mistake if the decision was based on the best available information.

It was also important to make clear that over the longer term, we were not going to reward people whose careers are characterized by having made a lot of really terrific mistakes, and I don't believe anyone present misunderstood that message. Rather, our awards presentation that night was a way of acknowledging that not only were we not going to penalize someone for taking an occasional well-considered risk—we were, quite literally, going to reward them for it.

For me, the highlight of the evening was the willingness of Mike Eagle, then the company's vice president of manufacturing, and head of what is clearly the most "macho" division in any large corporation, to demonstrate what it really means to lead by example. He brought down the house when he appeared in drag as Vanna White from *Wheel of Fortune*, the television quiz show. In my book, his willingness to help communicate that it was time to loosen up made him the biggest winner in the room.

It was one of those wonderful unanticipated moments when you could almost see lightbulbs going on in the minds of those around the room, managers saying to themselves, "They're really serious, and I get it!"

TEN

When It's Time to Go

The final test of a leader is that he leaves behind him in other men, the conviction and the will to carry on.

—Walter Lippmann

Band-Aid

When I was in the second grade, I learned to play the cornet. This was not by choice. I would have preferred the saxophone. But students in the Remington Public School in my day rarely got a vote when it came to selecting the instrument into which we would channel whatever musical aptitude we happened to possess. In fact, aptitude or not, most of us came to appreciate the inherent pleasure of mastering a musical instrument. Like math or English composition, eventually playing in the high school band was not really an elective. It was an expected part of the local culture, making it virtually required. The musical curriculum of my elementary school was more than a way for students to touch the arts; it was part of the well-designed succession plan of Robert B. Shearer, the man who directed the music program in the Remington Public School.

In 1960, my graduating senior class consisted of forty-one people. We didn't have a marching band that performed at football games

---

213

ROBIN JOEL McGLYNN   ROSALIE RAE ULYAT   PATRICIA ANN HOLTCAMP   KATHERINE LOUISE RANEY   JANET KATHRYN BENNER   JAMES ANDREW NUSSBAUM

PEGGIE ANN BELL   JOHN R. ANSTETT   JUDITH FAYE McCURTAIN   RONALD L. ST. PIERRE   DONNA JOANNE BYRD   RONALD L. GILLIAM, JR.   LINDA LOUISE PITSTICK

EMIL JOSEPH ALBERDING   DONNA JEAN CULP   DANIEL WILLIAM BIDDLE   JUDY ANN OPENSHAW   RALPH MITCHELL MOORE   JENELL ANN WOODRUFF   MICHAL ALVIN MERKEL

KATHLEEN JO BAHLER   DONALD CARL WORLEY   ALLIENE THOMAS   CURTIS G. SIEBENTHAL   CAROL ANNE SCHANTZ   MARVIN EARL BAXTER   MARY BETH JONES

JOHN RUSSELL REES   SHARON SUE FLEMING   JAMES W. COCHRAN   CAROL ELIZABETH TYLER   WAYNE DOUGLAS GARRIOTT   CATHY COLLINS INSLEY   LOWELL EDWARD ALBERTS

CLASS
1960

MARY MAY
SPON.

DONALD D. UTTER
PRIN.

RANDALL LEE TOBIAS   SHARON ROSE SHAW   HAROLD EDWARD ARBUCKLE   CARILYN FRANCES CAIN   DONALD M. COCHRAN   LINDA JO THURSTON   RONALD E. SIGO

The forty-one members of the Remington High School senior class of 1960.

214

because we didn't have enough student bodies to field a football team. But that was just fine with our music teacher, who each year assembled a successful and well-regarded high school concert band. The band also marched—on occasions such as the annual tribute to veterans on Memorial Day in the community cemetery. But mostly, we played concerts. As part of our music curriculum, we diligently learned the works of Elgar and Copeland and Sousa, as well as various fight songs and school anthems. And once a year, our band would take a trip to some Indiana city to participate in a competition against other school bands—in many cases, the ones who also actually played and marched at football games.

Nearly every year, a remarkable thing occurred. The band without a football team earned first place. For a school our size, Mr. Shearer used the paucity of potential musicians to his advantage. At the beginning of each school year, he would examine the roster of each class, looking all the way back to the second grade, to determine how openings would be filled each year with the departure of the band's outgoing seniors—not only that year, but in years to come. And his expectations and aspirations were high.

"I started playing the flute in the second grade," remembers my former classmate and lifelong musician Carol Anne Schantz McDougal. "Mr. Shearer came around to our elementary school classroom and looked at our body types and our mouths and made a judgment about what instrument would be the most natural fit for each of us. He then made himself available to offer private lessons after school and during the summer, free of charge. So he was not only thorough in his planning and training, but by the time we got to high school and there was a vacancy in the band, we were quite prepared to take over."

The only thing I would add to my friend Carol Anne's account is that I don't recall that the free lessons were in any way optional.

My older brother Roger was a French-horn player in the Remington High School band and remembers our teacher's

Me as a third-grade student, practicing my "chosen" instrument, the cornet, accompanied by my mother on the piano.

influence to this day. "Mr. Shearer taught us that achieving excellence meant that you would devote yourself to practicing music year round and the results spoke for themselves. Of course, there were some challenges along the way for a school of our size. I was on the basketball team, and during the halftime of our games some of the players who were not regulars would move to the stage in our gym and take part in the halftime band performance. When it was over, they would make a quick switch back to basketball and get ready for the second half. You were talking about some true sixty-minute guys here. It would have been easier to just not have a halftime performance at all, but Mr. Shearer would not hear of it."

Although it was lost on me at the time, Mr. Shearer was teaching us more than simply notes and scales, and more than just the power of high expectations. He was teaching us an important lesson in succession management. Planning for a successful transi-

The Remington High School concert band in 1960. Conductor Robert B. Shearer is pictured standing at the right rear. First-chair flute Carol Anne Schantz McDougal is pictured just to the right of the conductor's podium. First-chair cornet Mike Merkel is pictured sixth from the left in the last seated row. I am next to him, seventh from the left.

tion does not begin when it's time for a leader to step down—when someone *ends* a tenure. In my experience, successful succession planning must begin years earlier. And it was only recently that I remembered where I first observed that concept successfully practiced.

This was certainly one of the first leadership lessons I took away from my hometown, and I have applied it a number of times in a number of jobs since. But it was far from the last lesson I would learn growing up in this one-stoplight (well okay, one-blinker-light) farming community. Remember that book *Everything I Need to Know I Learned in Kindergarten*? It was an interesting little tome that cleverly broke down life's essential lessons into easily understandable ideas that even a five-year-old would recognize. I was not that precocious. But it's probably accurate to say that a good deal of what I've needed to know about life, I learned by the time I graduated from Remington High School in 1960.

Onstage

The implementation of personnel choices and succession plans takes place in many ways. Consider the way Dan Quayle was introduced to the world as George H. W. Bush's running mate in the 1988 presidential election. In politics, as in business, first impressions can often make or break a career. As the world got its first real glimpse of the boyish senator from Indiana, he came across like . . . well, there's been more than enough written about that already. Suffice it to say that he perhaps looked a bit like a Broadway understudy who had unexpectedly been given the opportunity to perform onstage . . . only he had not been given the script for the part he was now being asked to play. It appeared that way because it happened that way.

As the world was forming an opinion of the little-known junior senator, it didn't know that there had been virtually no preparation for managing that moment. In his book *Standing Firm*, Quayle recalled, "We'd been told nothing about the platform arrangements at Spanish Plaza and I had no idea what sort of speech I was expected to give." Careful staging had been traded for the political excitement and energy that could come from springing a surprise "out of the box" selection. And even though Quayle had known privately that he was one of several people under consideration and had a strong suspicion that he might well be selected, there was no time for the realization of the actual selection to settle in, once he'd been informed that he was the one. From the time he received the call from Bush until his moment in the spotlight, Quayle had been given all of ninety minutes to begin to think of

At Pebble Beach in 1993 with former Vice President Dan Quayle.

himself as the actual candidate for Vice President of the United States, to consider how best to project an image of someone who was ready to be only a heartbeat away from the presidency. And most of that time had been consumed with trying to find a way, on his own, to simply get to the location of the announcement. It is true that when the glare of the spotlight suddenly shines on your stage, you've got to be *able* to dance, and you've also got to be *ready* to dance at every opportunity, because you won't always know when you're being called to the stage for what will potentially be the career-determining performance.

The fact is, it was a risk taken, and an opportunity lost, with costly future consequences for both Quayle and Bush.

I've known Dan Quayle for a long time. I know him to be a bright, well-informed, and passionate individual who has been an outstanding public servant. But that afternoon, to many he did not look like someone who was ready to be the Vice President of the United States, let alone prepared to step in as president. Had Quayle been given the opportunity to prepare more fully for that enormously important moment, history might view the former Vice President quite differently. After all, first impressions are difficult to overcome.

Allowing future leaders the opportunity to "feel presidential," to see themselves in a role before being expected to convey that image to the world, is a smart thing to do when trying to effectively implement a leadership succession plan.

In mid-1994, several months before the planned departure of Lilly's General Counsel, J.B. King, who would soon become the first General Counsel of Guidant, Inc. at the time of its launch, I invited one of the company's senior attorneys to come to my office. I had been pondering the selection of J.B.'s replacement for some time and had considered several well-qualified candidates, from both inside and outside the company's law department. After a great deal of thought, I had reached a decision and had recently shared the name of my choice privately with the company's outside directors. I would promote Rebecca Kendall to the role of Senior Vice President and General Counsel. My reason was very simple. I had concluded she was the best-qualified person for the job. Beyond that, I was well aware that in accepting this position, Becky would become the highest-ranking woman in the entire history of Eli Lilly and Company, and I was determined to do all I could to help her be successful.

When Becky arrived in my office, I promptly cut to the chase. I told her what I planned to do and that I had great confidence in her ability to do the job. I asked her how she would feel about taking on these new responsibilities. Becky recalls her initial reaction: "It was unexpected. I had concluded some time before that I wasn't a candidate for the job . . . and I had just moved on. . . ."

I told her that I had a very specific reason for laying out my plan months earlier than might normally have been expected. I reminded her what happened when Quayle was introduced as the vice presidential candidate and how unfair I thought that had been. I told her it was my guess that when she awakened the following morning, because it had been so totally unexpected, one of her first thoughts would be, "Did he really tell me that he wants me to be the Senior Vice President and General Counsel of the company?" This was an idea that would clearly take some time to absorb. But I speculated that as the days went by, she would increasingly get used to the idea and would in due course awaken each morning feeling like the General Counsel, totally comfortable with the role. In the months ahead, she would also have the opportunity to quietly and thoughtfully make plans, to decide what changes she would make, how she would deal with various people inside and outside her organization, what priorities she would establish. In short, she would have the opportunity to be fully prepared to hit the ground running. And in the end, which would really be the beginning, when I announced her appointment to the world, she would both act and feel like the General Counsel, and everyone would sense that.

She told me she needed some time to think about it. She wanted to understand my expectations, understand what it would take to do the job, and determine whether she felt she could deliver. Beyond that, she said, she wanted to discuss the opportunity with her daughters, sort through the pluses and minuses with them. I thought all of that was very reasonable, and I was doubly glad I hadn't waited until the morning of the announcement to raise the issue.

In the end, it worked out much as I had hoped. Today, Becky says, "I think Randy had the experience to see that in some cases, it really works better to give people the opportunity to begin to wrap their minds around what it is they are going to be doing, to start to visualize what it's going to be like before they actually have to start doing it. Maybe he just read me as someone who was going to need more time to get onto this. It certainly . . . was very valuable for me to have had that."

Timelines

In the corporate world, succession planning seems often not to get the attention it deserves. Sometimes there is an assumption on the part of CEOs that it is the board's job to do. Sometimes CEOs are not eager to get it started because they are reluctant to begin the process of giving up their own power. For whatever the reasons, it had not seemed to me that succession planning was very high on the priority list at AT&T, and retired Chairman and CEO Bob Allen agrees. "In looking back on my time at AT&T," he says, "I think probably the thing I would spend more time on, more than anything else in my whole career, is having a better definition of the succession process."

Clearly there was a need for a new approach at Lilly. The very fact that I was in that role was the direct result of a failed CEO selection, development, and transition process, and I was determined that must not happen again. Almost immediately on becoming Chairman and CEO, I set out to develop and put in place a comprehensive succession-planning process for the senior leadership—and most particularly, for managing CEO succession. In looking at AT&T and the boards on which I've served, it has long been my view that succession planning and implementation comprise one of the most important responsibilities of a CEO. If done properly, the process ensures leadership continuity and therefore the corporation's continuity. But to do it well sometimes requires putting the ongoing well-being of the corporation above personal considerations. For some, that seems instinctive, but for others, it seems a surprisingly difficult act. I believe the British do have it right: "The king is dead," they say, referring to the departed leader, followed immediately by "Long live the king," referring to the new one.

I began to meet regularly with Pedro Granadillo, Lilly Senior Vice President—Human Resources, to learn all I could about the existing talent identification programs and processes. I was generally impressed with what I found. But the process seemed to stop before it focused on the senior leadership needs at the top of the business. Over time, I began to include Sidney Taurel in our discussions, and together the three of us developed a set of criteria to use in evaluating the future potential of Lilly managers for the seniormost leadership positions in the company.[1]

At the beginning, we identified the top twenty-five or so leaders in the company, generally regardless of their level or age, who appeared to have the potential to go the farthest, to take on the most responsibility in the future. Using the evaluation criteria we had developed, we plotted our collective assessment of each individual's current performance on a four-cell matrix designed for that purpose. The vertical axis represented quantitative performance—the delivery of measurable results—and the horizontal axis represented demonstrated ability to obtain those results in a manner consistent with the changes in values and culture we were working to implement. So if a manager was highly effective in delivering results and highly effective in getting those results in the "right" way, he or she would have a mark plotted somewhere in the upper right quadrant of the chart—high vertically on the chart because of the quantitative results, and to the right horizontally on the chart because of demonstrated "soft" skills. If another

---

1. See the list in chapter 6 entitled "Indicators of Leadership Potential."

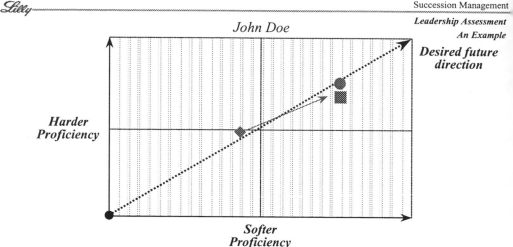

A sample of the chart I used with the Lilly board to show the relative proficiency of senior managers in providing leadership for the "harder" or more quantitative areas of job performance and the "softer" or more qualitative areas.

manager was delivering results but was "using up" people in ways that were contrary to our values and culture, then that manager's dot would be plotted in the upper left quadrant—high because of the results but more to the left because of limitations in the "softer" areas of the job. Over time, we began to replot those dots at least annually to see who was making progress and who was not.

At some point, I devised a spreadsheet of sorts, which was relatively simple in concept and allowed us to get a better picture of the forward-looking timeline for the career of each of these leaders. For planning purposes, and unless we had specific informa-

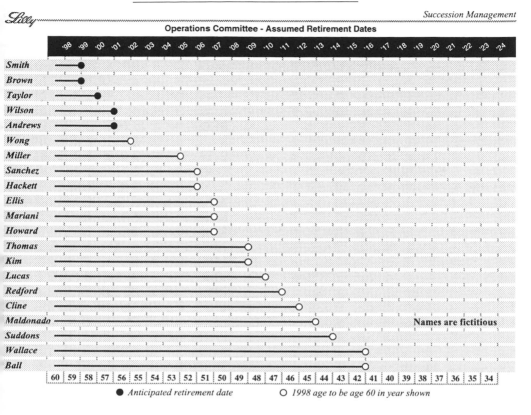

A sample of the chart I used with the Lilly board to provide a better picture of developmental actions that had to be made over time to prepare leadership talent for key assignments as needed.

tion to the contrary, we assumed each would likely retire at age sixty, even that being slightly older than the actual average officer retirement age at Lilly at that time.

Starting with the first vertical column on the left as the current year, and moving from left to right with each vertical column on the spreadsheet representing one more year in the future, we assigned a horizontal row to each candidate, beginning with the current year and extending to the right to the column representing the year of that individual's sixtieth birthday. This provided a useful picture of the length of the remaining career for each individual, and for the group relatively. We added to this chart a horizontal bar for each officer currently occupying one of the company's critical leadership positions—up through and including the CEO.

In putting it all together, it was now possible to see, in most cases, how little time there really was to get people moved to the positions they needed to hold to gain the developmental experiences that would prepare them for targeted positions of increasing responsibility later on.

This information then became the basis for discussions among the senior leaders, decisions regarding personnel assignments, action plans, coaching, and, eventually, periodic reviews with the board. In some cases, I included Sidney Taurel and Pedro Granadillo in those board discussions, but at least once a year, I met privately with the board to discuss, among other things, my thinking about my own successor. Before long it was clear to me and to the board that Sidney had the capacity to be an excellent chairman and CEO. It was also clear that it would be my job to be sure he had the opportunities he needed to be fully prepared when the time came, and to be sure that the eventual transition would be done in a way that would provide every opportunity for Sidney and the company to be successful after I was gone. All of this became a top priority for me.

Torch Song

On the morning of December 15, 1997, I walked upstairs from my office to the Eli Lilly and Company boardroom. As I made my way to my usual chair at the head of the table, I couldn't help but recall the first time I had moved across a similar room as the company's new leader. Back then, my first day on the job, it felt as if I were wading through the shallow end of a swimming pool, the tension in the room was so thick. On this day, however, it felt as if I were literally floating on water. I was feeling quite content about what the company had accomplished during my time there and about the decision I had made and was about to share with the company's board of directors as a result of those accomplishments.

I had learned long ago that when you are wrestling with a complex decision or when you are trying to develop a clear and coherent point of view on a major issue, a new strategy, for example, it's always a good idea to write it down. If you can't say it clearly and convincingly on paper, you probably don't have your mind firmly around the issue, and you need to keep writing and editing until you do. For several months, I had been working privately on such a memo as a way to lay out my logic and my conclusions about the subject I was preparing to put before the board.

Since taking over as Chairman and CEO in 1993, it had been my habit to spend some part of nearly every board meeting alone with the outside directors. At least once a year, I spent virtually the entire time that way, with the agenda devoted almost wholly to the discussion of succession planning and the planning process I had developed. Today would be such a day. Using the memo I had prepared as a guide for the conversation, I launched the meeting.

"In a very short time," I began, "I will have been Chairman and CEO of Eli Lilly and Company for five years. And certainly a lot has changed during that time. Perhaps one of the most obvious indicators of that change is the fact that only four of the fourteen directors who were on the board at the time I came to this role are around this table today. With my upcoming five-year anniversary in mind, what I want to do today is to review with you the one senior-level succession matter that I haven't fully discussed during our previous meetings, and that is my own personal plans for the future. . . ."

Prior to that moment, what no one had known, except for my children, Paige and Todd, and my wife, Marianne, was that for several months, I had been finalizing my own retirement plans. Today, I would lay them out.

I reminded the board that the circumstances which existed at the time of my arrival were, to say the least, somewhat unusual. There's been a good deal written on the subject, but I think the situation may have been captured most succinctly in a 1997 book entitled *Champions of Change*, in which author David Nadler describes how several CEOs addressed the need for decisive action and significant change in their companies. Nadler writes:

> Imagine you're Randall Tobias in June 1993. The board of pharmaceutical giant Eli Lilly and Company has reluctantly ousted the CEO, and you've accepted its offer to take his place. It's hard to imagine a worse time to be taking over. Political and market forces are buffeting the entire health care business; Lilly is in particularly bad shape, having lost an astounding 40% of its market capital value in the previous eighteen months. The takeover sharks are beginning to circle.
>
> As you show up for work the first Monday morning at Lilly's sprawling campus on the south side of Indianapolis, the financial community is screaming for results—and they're far from reassured by the appointment of a lifelong phone company executive. The good news is that your predecessor, after literally refusing to give up the job, has vacated the executive office on the twelfth floor of Lilly's administration building. He was immensely popular with the employees, who now are panicked by rumors of massive layoffs. And over the weekend, for the first time since anyone in the company can remember, several patients taking part in clinical trials for a promising new drug began showing signs of liver failure. (In the weeks ahead five of them will die.) That's what's waiting for you on your first day of work—so where do you start?

A good question! I reviewed with the board my assessment of the progress we had made, as an organization, in achieving the goals I had established on becoming CEO.

At about that time, a wave of anticipation about where my remarks were heading began to wash over the faces of those in attendance. Dr. Steven Beering, at the time the President of Purdue University, unconsciously paid me one of the biggest compliments I have ever received: He got up and left the room. At the time, I didn't think much of his quick exit, assuming that his cell phone had vibrated and he was quietly slipping out to field an urgent call. That assumption was reinforced when he returned in two or three minutes. It was only later that he explained that he could see where I was going with my remarks and he simply got a little choked up. "I had tears running down my face, I don't mind admitting," Beering remembers. "I think others did, too."

I told the board I felt the company had made significant progress toward the goals we all had in mind when I came. We were now seen as a leader in our industry on a number of dimensions. Certainly our financial performance reflected that leadership. But, I emphasized, I was equally pleased with the progress we'd made in the quality of our senior leadership, in our core capabilities, in our ability to plan and therefore shape our own future, in our progress in identifying and developing future leaders, in revitalizing our values, and in recognizing the need to balance work and family and to value diversity throughout our organization.

I told them I believed that one of the keys to our success was that we were much more focused and aligned than we had been five years before. That is to say, we had a clear and shared vision of our future, we had a strategy that was increasingly well understood throughout the company and was being aggressively implemented, and everyone in the organization was increasingly marching forward together, in the same direction.

I felt the business was generally being well managed, was largely under good operational control, and was heading in a very positive direction. Our people were feeling very good about themselves and about the future of the company. At the same time, I believed the leadership team and, increasingly, Lilly employees more broadly understood, perhaps for the first time ever, that there is no entitlement, that without full and continuous attention, success could evaporate overnight, and that it was the nature of our business that the next crisis was potentially never more than a

ELI LILLY AND COMPANY

Shareholder Value Creation
The Tenure of Chairman of the Board Randall L. Tobias
June 25, 1993 to December 31, 1998

MORGAN STANLEY

A Morgan Stanley chart looking back at the increase in shareholder value during my tenure as Chairman of Eli Lilly and Company.

phone call away. I told them I believed this newly found respect for reality was quite healthy for the future of the business. Clearly we had made some mistakes—the acquisition of PCS the biggest— but our mistakes had come as a result of a new willingness to take considered risks, risks that had turned out to be right far more than not.

I was very proud of what the organization had done to create significant shareholder value. The market value of the company, including what had since become Guidant, was about $14 billion on the day I became CEO. On the day of that board meeting, the market value of Guidant alone was over $8 billion and the value of

Lilly itself was well over $70 billion. And we had accomplished that growth in the context of very stiff competition from our peers. Even so, our own cumulative total return to shareholders had ranked first in the pharmaceutical industry over the past five years.

I reminded the board that we did have ongoing challenges. The long-term prospects from major compounds in the pipeline were quite extraordinary. At the same time, realizing that potential would present some significant challenges. Beyond the inherent high-risk nature of the business, the most prominent cloud on the horizon, the expiration of the Prozac patent in the United States, would provide a huge hurdle to overcome in the next few years. I told them I was very encouraged with both the planning and operational work under way to deal with it, under the strong and creative leadership of Mitch Daniels, and I was confident in our ability to come out the other side with renewed momentum. I believed we had the opportunity to take advantage of that event by learning to prepare for future expirations of major patents as part of the normal course of our business. After all, with the several potential blockbusters we had brought forward, Prozac would not be the last opportunity the company would have to face this issue in the years ahead.

I told the board I believed we had assembled a first-rate leadership team, starting with the current board and senior officers and extending on down through the current generation of leaders and well into the next. I provided specific observations regarding several members of the team.

I then began to address the questions I would be asked repeatedly in the months to come: Why would any CEO want to step down while things were going so well, the future looked so promising, and the company was in such great shape? CEOs just don't do that. And in particular, why would any CEO want to relinquish a position of such power and prestige at such a relatively young age—a few months short of fifty-six?

I began to explain. "After I took this job in 1993, and after I had some time to think about the longer-term considerations, I made a commitment to myself that at the pleasure of the board, I would remain until the six initial goals that I outlined here a few minutes ago had been appropriately addressed, but certainly no less than five years. Consistent with my thinking before I left AT&T to come to Lilly, I have given almost no consideration to staying past age sixty. So from the beginning, I've been focused on concluding my time here sometime during the four-year window bounded by my fifth anniversary in a few months and my sixtieth birthday in early 2002. Beyond that, I've always been mindful of the words of Peter Lynch, who, upon announcing his own unexpected early retirement after an extraordinarily successful career at Fidelity's Magellan Fund, was reported to have proclaimed, 'Nobody on his deathbed ever said, "I wish I'd spent more time at the office!"'

"In addition, and very importantly to me, in thinking about the more specific timing of my own departure, I've been mindful of my long-held observation that all too often, leaders in virtually all fields step down mostly when it's convenient for them, without regard to whether or not their own timing corresponds with what's in the best interests of sustaining the vitality of the organization they are leading. I've been determined not to follow that path. I have wanted to choose a time to leave that not only suited my own objectives but also fit well into the rhythm of the company's continued progress—not too soon, but certainly not too late."

When it comes to succession planning, too often, boards of directors and the retiring CEO don't take the time to agree on a shared set of assumptions before the plan is developed. If the departing CEO is staying until the end of the last month of his or her sixty-fifth year and that's the maximum expected retirement age, the board should know why that date happens to also be in the best interest of the company. If the former CEO is staying on indefinitely as nonexecutive chairman, or even planning to stay on the board of directors at all, the board should know and agree that it is best. If he plans to remain in the office he's occupied as CEO, or even in some other space in the executive suite, why is that in the best interest of the corporation? If the answers to these question indicate that the decisions are primarily for the benefit of the former CEO and not the company, then the plan needs to be revisited. Too often, boards acquiesce out of respect for the former CEO and his contributions. These are issues that really deserve serious consideration.

I know these words will offend some. Nonetheless, it's my view that when it comes to succession planning, all too often leadership transitions are handled with the principal objective of determining the best way to address the ego-related concerns of the person who is leaving. Too often, the timing and the manner of a leadership change have more to do with the personal objectives of the leader who is stepping down than with a combination of other factors that center around what is best for the future of the enterprise. The more appropriate questions which should be asked include "How can positive momentum best be sustained in the company?" and "What approach will contribute most to helping the new CEO be successful?" Too often, an outgoing leader's principal motivation is driven by a desire to hang on to power until the last possible minute, and that moose never gets put on the table. Without the right objectives, the implementation of a succession plan too often becomes an eleventh-hour fire drill.

Just as with the Remington High School band, corporate succession planning begins not on the day a leader decides to step down; it begins the moment a leader takes charge. And this is exactly what I emphasized to Lilly's board of directors on the day I announced that I was retiring.

"As you know, from the time I've spent with you in previous board meetings addressing these issues, I believe that succession planning, in all of its ramifications, is one of the most important [responsibilities]—perhaps the *most* important responsibility—of the leader of any institution, including this one. I want the success of my stewardship of Eli Lilly and Company to be measured not only by the results we achieve while I am here but also by the results we achieve after I am gone."

I also reminded the board that during the five years I'd been the CEO, a number of significant and unforeseen events had occurred in my personal life, and they would not be surprised to know those were also factors in my planning. During my first year at Lilly, Marilyn, my wife of twenty-eight years, had taken her own life to relieve her suffering from severe clinical depression. In the summer of 1995, I had married Marianne Williams McKinney, who'd been through her own life-altering tragedy. Finally, I had reached the point of needing to take multiple insulin injections daily for my type II diabetes, a disease I'd been dealing with for nearly fifteen years. While my condition was, and is today, generally under good control, my calendar and global travel schedule had made it somewhat difficult to manage the situation as effectively as I felt appropriate. "And much as I hate to admit it," I said, "I'm feeling less immortal than I once did. I'm recognizing the need to give this issue more of my attention, because I genuinely believe that having a schedule that makes it easier to take better care of my diabetes will add time to my life.

"Most importantly, from the succession planning we've done together, I know you share my view that Sidney Taurel is not only capable of leading this company, he is prepared to lead it and is the best person for the job, inside or outside the company. We've discussed and agreed to all the reasons why, and I won't repeat all of that this morning. Let me just say that he is, in my view, truly exceptional. Sidney and I have had a great partnership. We've developed genuine respect for each other, and I could not have been more pleased as I've watched him demonstrate his ability to take on more and more responsibility. When it comes time for him to fully take charge, I have no reservations about the transition. It will have been made in a way that will not cause any major waves with our employees or with Wall Street. And you can count on the fact that Sidney will continue to grow every day he is in the job."

It was time to get to the bottom line, something that every director now understood. Clearly they were surprised by the timing of my decision. But once we got past that, everyone in the room was well aware that the succession-planning process had been under way for several years. And even though it had been targeted toward a date more likely to be several years in the future, we were ready. What needed to begin now was the implementation of that plan.

"Having given all of these issues a great deal of thought for a number of months," I continued, "I want you to know today that I believe an appropriate time for a leadership transition here at Lilly is on the horizon, and I'd like to begin the implementation process. Therefore, I'd like to propose for your consideration the following actions:

- "Just prior to July 1, 1998—about six months from now—I'd like to announce my intention to retire from the company, effective one year from now, on December 31, 1998. At the same time, I'd also like to announce, and begin to implement, my plans for the transition of leadership.
- "To begin this transition process, at the time of the announcement of my retirement plans, I'd like for the board to elect Sidney Taurel to the additional position of CEO, to be effective July 1, 1998. I will continue as Executive Chairman for six months—from that time through the end of the year.
- "At the board meeting in December of 1998—twelve months from now—I'd like for the board to elect Sidney to the addi-

tional position of Chairman of the Board, to be effective with my retirement.

- "At the same time that I step down as Chairman, I will also be retiring from this board of directors and moving my office out of the headquarters building.

- "Beyond our discussion here today, and prior to our next board meeting in February, I plan to travel to your offices to speak with each of you individually to get on top of any additional input or concerns that you may want to be sure is considered as we develop the transition more fully. Those appointments are in fact already on your calendars, under the pretense of simply being one of my periodic individual meetings with each of you. At the February board meeting, with the benefit of your input between now and then, I'd like to obtain your endorsement of the outline of a more specific succession plan."

Assuming the board's concurrence with what I'd laid out, I planned to talk with Sidney after the February board meeting and tell him what we had in mind. I thought it would be useful to give him the opportunity to begin to think about his new role and to thoughtfully develop a transition plan that would address priorities, people, structure, and how best to fully take advantage of the energy that could come from a leadership change. I would obviously work closely with him on this planning, but in the end, it would need to be his plan, and the board's, not mine. I suggested that we make that plan the subject of discussion, to be led by Sidney, at an executive session at the April board meeting.

I emphasized the importance of taking great care not to increase the risk of rumors or leaks by not expanding the circle of those who were aware until we were ready to make an announcement, or the announcement would likely get made for us through unintended rumors or speculation and would become a distraction for the company.

I did not want them to conclude that this decision had been a no-brainer for me, because it had not. I'd thought about it, discussed it at great length with Marianne and Paige and Todd, and planned for it very carefully for some time. And much as there were reasons why I would have enjoyed staying on for a time, there were even more reasons why I believed it was time to prepare for this transition.

Gratifying as this experience had been, I still had a number of additional things I wanted to do with my life, including having additional time for myself and for my family and having more time for trying to give something back to a society that had been very good to me. I was proud of what we had accomplished so far during the five years I'd been there and optimistic about what I believed could be accomplished in the years ahead, through the remainder of my leadership and well beyond.

I felt extraordinarily privileged to have had the opportunity to lead and be part of this great company.

The Fire Department

Following the February board meeting, I invited Sidney in for the conversation I had been looking forward to with great anticipation. As I had hoped, there had been no leaks. He was totally surprised.

I reviewed the overall plan with Sidney in some detail. I told him I would be there to assist him in every way I could in developing his transition plan, but that it needed to be his plan. There is an important organization development concept that I learned years ago from perhaps the leading practitioner in that area, David Nadler. I've come to believe in it strongly. When you're putting a new organization in place, the planning *must* be done by the people who are going to be on your new team, not those on the old team. That's the only way they'll have total ownership. It's my view that

Sidney Taurel and me at the June 1998 press conference announcing my retirement at the end of the year and Taurel's selection as Lilly's new Chairman and CEO. Photo courtesy of Eli Lilly and Company.

it is just as true with a change in leadership. CEOs who stay around for a long transition after their successors are selected and announced (or hired) are, in my view, mostly doing so because they just don't want to let go. I made clear to Sidney that beginning on the day we made the initial announcement of my retirement, I would be stepping down as CEO. From that date until the date I also stepped down as Chairman of the Board, retired from the board of directors, and moved my office out of the headquarters building six months later, he should simply think of me as the "fire department." I would be there in case of emergency, to help if he needed me. But he would be in charge from that day forward, and through both my words and my actions, I would make that clear to everyone.

"In the months prior to the announcement of Randy's retirement," says Taurel, "I had the good fortune of being able to know I would be in the CEO role and to start thinking in that way. Also, I had the time for planning the reorganization that would be needed since I was not replacing myself as COO. That was invaluable. In the months after the announcement, he mostly—really only—played the role of Chairman of the Board, so people would very quickly get used to the idea of me as boss rather than him—which is what began to happen in those six months between June and December. When there was a problem, they began to come to me.

"With the two boards that I am on, there have been recent successions. At McGraw-Hill, there was succession from one CEO to another, where the old CEO stayed as Chairman of the Board for a while. We are going through the same thing now at IBM. [Our] succession plan [at Lilly] was an exemplary model, and frankly what I learned from that, I have been using to advise [my boards]."

Jack Welch has described an incident that took place at G.E. shortly after it was announced that Jeff Immelt would become his successor. The company's regular operating managers' meeting was scheduled a few weeks later—the first opportunity for the company's senior leaders to see Immelt in his new role as Chairman-Elect. At the last minute, Welch was called away for a meeting with then President-Elect George W. Bush, by default putting Immelt in charge of the G.E. meeting. As Welch describes it, it was "an unexpected and lucky break because it gave Jeff the chance to do his own thing without me sitting in the front row."

Welch may well be the finest CEO to ever hold the title. He would certainly get my vote. And clearly, he is the master when it comes to finding and developing executive talent. Nonetheless, it seems possible that what turned out to be "a lucky break" in his transition plan is at the heart of what I'm suggesting should *be* the plan. Sooner or later, all things must change. When it's time to go, it's time to go.

Redirection

Sunday, November 3, 2002, was a day I had been anticipating for a long time. I was going home. Novelist Thomas Wolfe said you can't do that, but I had spent the past two years trying to prove him wrong. Later that day, we would dedicate the brand-new Roy and Fern Tobias Center and Public Library in Remington, and I was ecstatic—about both what had been accomplished and the way it had happened.

It is difficult to express the feelings of gratitude and affection I have for my parents and for the place I grew up, for the values that were instilled in me at a very early age, for the experiences that helped shape my life and my professional career, for the support and encouragement I received, and for the people of that community in the 1940s and 1950s who, in many ways, were like an extended family. From the time of my mother's death in 1994 and my father's in 1996, I had hoped to identify something I could do in their honor, something that might also benefit the Remington community. But what?

After stepping down from my role at Lilly at the end of 1998, one of the initiatives I had taken on was the establishment of a more formal structure for our family philanthropy. Toward that end, in early 1999, I had persuaded Suzanne Hazelett, a respected Indianapolis development consultant with foundation experience, to come to work for me on a part-time basis as Executive Director of the Tobias Family Foundations. One of her principal assignments would be to create and implement a model results-oriented family foundation. If we were going to have a family foundation, I wanted to do it right, and from everyone I could find to provide expert advice, I soon learned that Susie was the one who would be most likely to make that happen.

Sometime in late 1999, I asked her to see if she could discreetly find the answers to two questions: Could anything be identified that I might be able and willing to provide that was needed by the Remington community to help improve the quality of life there? And, assuming that such a project could be identified, did leadership exist in the community that would likely be able and willing to help accomplish whatever needed to be done, and then carry on once my role in the project was completed?

To answer those questions, Susie enlisted the help of the area community foundation director, who soon quietly involved two or three leaders in the Remington neighborhood. After a good deal of discreet discussion with no commitments yet on my part, it became clear that one possible project would likely have great appeal for Remington, and it was an exciting prospect for me as well. When I was growing up there in the 1940s and 1950s, the school was the center of community life. Since the late 1960s, Remington children had been part of a consolidated school system located outside the community, involving a much broader area. As a result of this change in the local culture, a real need had emerged for a gathering place for the people of Remington itself, a local community center of some type. There was also a pressing need to bring the public library up to standards. The building was not in good condition, and the internal information technology was outdated. Perhaps there was a way to address the two needs at the same time.

This was a project with great appeal to me and to my family. In years past, both my father and my mother had served on the local library board, and in fact, my mother was deeply involved in the construction of the existing building, which had replaced the prior Carnegie library destroyed in a fire sometime in the 1950s. Beyond that, we were developing a real interest in literacy in our family foundation, helping address Indiana's pressing need to find more effective ways to teach Hoosier children to read.

My first meeting with the Remington representatives had a feeling of great comfort and familiarity. The local delegation included Ivan Reel, an area farmer who had been a longtime friend of my father and an usher in our church for as long as I could remember. It also included Jim Flickner, another longtime acquaintance and at one time my baseball coach. In short order, a third community leader named Gene Lehman came into my life. Although I had not met him before, Gene had lived in Remington for a number of years and was the current President of the library board of trustees. He had come on the scene sometime after I'd gone away to college and on to my career, but he had known my mother and father well. In our initial discussions, he expressed his own enthusiasm for the project and a personal willingness to lead the effort locally. Gene's inherent leadership skills were readily apparent; clearly, he wouldn't need to read this book. We quickly determined that we had a shared vision of what was needed and how it could be accomplished. Gene understood the need to get the decisions made and the work under way but at the same time the imperative of developing a consensus in the community that this project was needed and welcome and would enjoy the backing of the community once completed. Town meetings were held to discuss the project, including two public hearings called in the community firehouse. Standing-room-only crowds indicated the enthusiastic support.

We began to develop possible plans for essentially replacing the current library with a new structure and adding a connected facility that could expand the programming capacity of the library and serve as a stand-alone community center, a location for community meetings, piano and dance recitals, wedding receptions, the activities that are the lifeblood of every small community. After consulting with Paige and Todd, we agreed to make a commitment from the family foundation that would pay for construction of the community center. And with Susie's help and that of a number of other people, the library applied for and received a govern-

The renovated Remington, Indiana Public Library and the new Roy and Fern Tobias Center, named to honor my parents.

ment grant to help rehabilitate the building. In addition, Marianne surprised me with a wonderful gift of her own, a grand piano for the community center and a computer system for the reference desk of the renovated library.

Ground was broken in early 2001 and books were back on new shelves by May 2002. In the end, the entire project was completed early and under budget, just the way I remembered things being done in my hometown.

I had traveled a long and winding path from my earliest days in Remington, a path that had brought me right back where I started. On this November day, I would be reminded that I didn't really need to come home, because in so many ways, I'd never really left.

Epilogue

BY TODD TOBIAS

*If the relationship of father to son could really be
reduced to biology, the whole earth would blaze
with the glory of fathers and sons.*
                                        —James Baldwin

When I began working on this book, there were four words I
would never have imagined I would be writing now: *I'm a company President.* It's true. I am. My company is called Table Moose
Media. We get the moose on the table. It's sort of our reason for
being. We speak openly and honestly. It's how we define *integrity*.

Because, by dint of my job title, I'm the leader of this business,
I try to do the things I've learned effective leaders do. I focus on
the business I am really in. I talk to my employees about things
like "defining our core values" and "communicating our story before others do it for us." I try to treat all the people our company
touches with respect. I listen to the opinions of others. I have a
vision. And a succession plan. I embrace change. But most of all, I
try to lead by example. For this, in the final analysis, is what leaders do. At least, it's what my dad did. And as far as I can tell, it
served him pretty well.

Anyone who knows me well knows that the closest I have ever
been to a business school was the time I got lost in one looking for

a seminar on postmodern poetry. That's why, occasionally, when I see the word *President* attached to my name, I have to laugh a little. I'm not really a business guy. Writing has always been my passion, and it largely still is. Indeed, I am an author of this book. That's not to say that these ideas are mine—they're not. What I mean is, I now have authorship of them. They have seeped into my soul. I care deeply about them. This wasn't always the case.

Mark Twain once wrote: "When I was a boy of fourteen, my father was so ignorant I could hardly stand to have the old man around. But when I got to be twenty-one, I was astonished by how much the old man had learned in seven years." I can relate to that. As many of the experiences you just read about were unfolding in my father's life, I regarded them with the flinty-eyed indifference of the very young. But an interesting thing happened to me as I began to help record these thoughts on paper: Not only did I become a father for the first time but I also, literally and figuratively, became my father. While I was helping my dad capture his life experiences, I tried to adopt his voice. I tried to think as he would. I said things like "If writing this book is the answer, what's the question?" For me, it turns out it was a question I would never have imagined in my wildest dreams: "What will turn out to be an effective crash course in learning how to manage a business?"

It's not so much what my dad accomplished in the business world that impresses me most, it's the way he did it. I interviewed over eighty of my father's friends and colleagues for this project. If there was a common thread running throughout these interviews, it was that almost without exception, the interview subjects went out of their way to comment on my father's truly unique style. What is this little piece of leadership magic?

As my dad often says, "When I was growing up, I was taught to treat others with respect."

Turns out, that advice served him pretty well. It's advice I try to follow every day.

Tobias's Lessons in Leadership

On Leading

Leadership is about far more than producing results through one's own initiative—it's about producing results through others.

It's not always necessary for a leader to have all the right answers, but it's critical to be able to ask the right questions and to set the right tone.

Leadership is as much about listening, about building relationships, about providing encouragement when it's needed, as it is about communicating one's own ideas.

I had an early role model who taught me a great deal about how leaders get results. He simply led by example. He had high expectations of everyone, and set the example through his own work habits.

Leaders almost always think out of the box. They listen, observe, share ideas, and shamelessly borrow from the experiences of others.

Successful leaders possess certain innate abilities and characteristics, which always include the ability to communicate effectively and to motivate others.

Leadership is far more complicated than simply being an effective manager. Among other things, it's about leaving behind indelible footprints.

On Values and Culture

At an early age, I learned from my parents that when you have the responsibility to do something, you do it. Period.

From my father I learned an essential recipe for personal and professional success: Take the job seriously, but never yourself. And at the end of the day, always make time to separate the two.

From my mother I learned to keep learning, all of my life.

Success in corporate America, especially in a changing environment, begins and ends with a company's commitment to treating all of the people it touches with respect.

Just because a company clearly has a strong values-based foundation in place does not mean that maintaining it is automatic. Cultures require continuous nurturing. Nothing I can think of is more important to future success.

When the pressure is on to produce, if you are serious about expecting adherence to certain standards of ethical behavior, you have to make that clear—by your words, certainly, but, more importantly, by your actions.

When I hear corporate leaders refer to values and culture as "soft issues," I wonder what they regard as being "hard." In my experience, cultural beliefs are the heart and soul of all business matters.

More than heroic working hours, more than pay incentives, certainly more than strategy alone, shared beliefs, *values,* can be the key to unleashing the talents of all of the people in an organization. Values can be the very foundation of success.

It is simply a fact that certain actions, behaviors, and objects in corporate cultures become imbued with symbolic significance in ways that other company cultures would find utterly bizarre. It is important to understand what those icons are.

Companies that allow complacency in their cultures are numbing themselves to the painful reality of change.

The very promise of job security is the first step in destroying it.

It's always the marketplace that determines job security, not company policy.

When you see radical downsizing, when you see sudden and massive job losses, it is at least in part a sign of the failure of leadership to adequately and creatively plan, to anticipate, to accept responsibility for the future.

Loyalty in the corporate world must be a *reciprocal bond*—reciprocal expectations of behavior between company and employee.*

Reciprocity is about organizations weeding out the entitlement mindset that has employees putting their own needs ahead of the needs of the other stakeholders. Ironically, for employee needs to be met, the needs of all stakeholders have to be met in parallel. It can't work any other way.

Reciprocity defines not only how companies set the terms of employment but also how they address the conditions of employment, how the work is to be done.

It's important to understand who your employees really are. In 1993, we discovered that only 18 percent of Lilly's 14,500 employees in the U.S. were part of a traditional nuclear family. Eighty-two percent were living in some other model. For decades, the

---

*From a letter to the shareholders in the company's 1975 annual report, written on the occasion of the company's 100th anniversary by Mr. Eli Lilly, longtime Chairman of the company, grandson of the founder, and by then the nearly ninety-year-old Honorary Chairman.

company's human relations policies had implicitly assumed just the opposite.

It's not enough to offer benefits and programs. The underlying cultural issues also need to be assertively addressed.

By addressing work-life concerns, company leaders are addressing the needs of the people on whom they depend.

You can ask employees to leave their personal lives at the factory fence. But you're just kidding yourself if you think they can comply. You can't hire part of a person. Your policies and programs will be effective only if they bow to this reality and address the whole human being.

When managers are consistently working late into the night and on weekends, and asking their people to do that too, it's important to determine who is at fault. Is it because the demands of their jobs genuinely require it, or is it because they need to do a better job of managing their time more efficiently, or is it because the company has developed a dysfunctional culture of rewarding the image that employees have learned they must create in order to get ahead?

Communicating values, defining them, redefining them, making sure they translate into meaningful actions, are all part of an ongoing journey, not a one-time process.

The working cultures I have observed to be the most chaotic and directionless were those in which people were not rewarded for their successes so much as for not failing.

People are the ultimate competitive resource, and you should embrace the responsibility for nurturing that resource to the best of your ability. Not just because it's good business, but because it's simply the right thing to do.

On Vision

Without a shared vision that is compelling and truly embraced with passion, it's nearly impossible for any organization to be successful.

Most visions have many fathers. But in the end, people must be able to see and believe that their leader is the ultimate father, and truly owns the vision.

The words "vision" and "strategy" are sometimes confusing because they are often used interchangeably. Creating a vision involves deciding where the organization must go, and then, with some passion, communicating (and communicating and communicating) a simple message describing that destination. A strategy, on the other hand, is the plan that will be used to pursue the vision.

To make a vision stick, at least two very critical components must exist. The vision must be crystal clear. But even when it is, you cannot simply order people to "believe." For a vision to take hold, it must also be compelling.

If an organization enjoys the full support of its people, is focused on what it does best, and moves collectively toward a shared vision of the future, even if its strategy isn't quite right, that organization will have more success than one that has identified the right path but is not moving forward as a team.

On Change

In business as in life, one thing is absolutely inevitable—continuous change.

The sooner leaders recognize that change itself can represent the very core of competitive advantage, the sooner they will taste success.

Change is a lot like fire. Manage it, turn it to your advantage, and you will bask in the warmth of its glow; ignore it or manage it poorly, and one thing is certain—eventually you will get burned.

When the rules of the game have changed, decisions will often still be based on a world that no longer exists. Asking some senior leaders to deny a lifetime of corporate learning is like asking them to change the color of their eyes.

When one is building or inheriting a leadership team, it is crucial to recognize the importance of assembling, structuring, teaching, and, above all, truly empowering the troops to fight by the ground rules of the *next* war, not the last one.

Transformation cannot be achieved merely by issuing new policies and making a few speeches. It requires a patient, sustained effort to educate people in a new way of doing things, to eradicate old habits that no longer work, and to validate the benefits of change as they occur.

At the top of any change agenda must be recognition of the need to communicate deliberately and openly with all of the people the company touches.

When an organization is engaged in wrenching and fundamental upheaval, it's important that all of the people touched by the organization have something comfortable and familiar to hang on to.

When one is in the midst of enormous change and all of the ground rules are being thrown out the door, it's absolutely essential to ask—and to answer—*"What business are we really in?"*

On Risk Taking

By encouraging more risk taking, mistakes will be made, to be sure. But the ultimate measure should be the *net* impact of the successes and the failures on the creation of shareholder value, not just the number of times a well-considered decision doesn't turn out as planned.

When decisions are made and things go wrong, much more than just the end result needs to be evaluated. What was known and when was it known? Was the decision made at the most opportune time? Was the risk of making the decision and being wrong outweighed by the likelihood and benefits of being right?

At some point in the process of making most decisions, you are far better off to make a timely decision based on sufficient but partial data than to do all the things necessary to make a perfect but untimely decision based on waiting for all of the data.

On Communication

We have long known that the pen is mightier than the sword. We must now understand that the fax machine is mightier than the rifle.

Through experience, in crafting significant messages I have learned to be very sensitive in trying to understand and anticipate what will be *heard* and not just assume it will be what is being *said.*

Effective communication is more than simply delivering a collection of well-considered statements. It's also where and how and, above all, *when* these words are delivered that truly cause messages to take hold and behaviors to change.

Leaving an information void is always a terrible mistake. Whenever employees or the media or analysts or others have to fill such a void, they are most likely to fill it with the worst-case scenario they can imagine.

It's important to communicate early. The audiences for organizational communication are much like a blank sheet of paper. The longer that people have to wait to get information, the more they begin to add words and pictures of their own to that sheet—and the longer it takes to remove what's already on paper before you can communicate your version of the story.

Bad news does not improve with age.*

Organizations that are run on shaky ethics and questionable practices are destined to find themselves in hot water. There is no way they can "communicate" themselves out of trouble.

For some, "communication" is defined as a set of writing and speaking functions—a collection of specialized events. It is that, but it is much more. It is the sum of all the activities that demonstrate, through words and actions, what a leader—indeed, what a *business*—really is about.

The real challenge for many leaders is not only communicating per se, it's integrating the way they behave with what they speak and write.

Today, not having an effective communication capability in corporate America has a very real impact on the financial success of a company.

Communicating to audiences, friendly and hostile, large and small, formally or informally, is a skill that is one of the hallmark responsibilities of any corporate executive.

An American Life: One Man's Road to Watergate by former Nixon presidential assistant Jeb Stuart Magruder.

On Career Development

I attribute the development of my own leadership skills in large part to the sum total of my various and somewhat unique experiences: parental influence, education, early job assignments, extracurricular activities in college, mentors, and, significantly, early successes and failures.

Having the capabilities for senior leadership roles is absolutely necessary, but it's not sufficient. Success also requires opportunity. With every opportunity seized comes the potential for growth and development, which opens the door to even more opportunity.

I have come to believe that determining whether one enjoys steady career advancement has to do with the intersection of two factors. The first is whether or not one has the capacity to repeatedly demonstrate the ability to excel. The second is fate, or luck, or whatever you believe creates the opportunities to demonstrate your capabilities.

When the glare of the spotlight suddenly shines on your stage, you have to be able to dance, to be sure. But you also have to be ready at any time to give what may be a career-determining performance.

Success in the corporate world is sometimes like the proverbial frog in children's literature—the happy endings often lie behind the guises and forms where you least expect to find them.

The circumstances that have turned out to have the most influence on and significance for my career, the proximate causes of the turning points, more often than not came from totally unanticipated opportunities.

One of the key indicators for separating those who most likely have the potential to become successful leaders from those who probably do not is their level of comfort with ambiguity.

The more a career discipline requires—and rewards—coloring strictly inside the lines, the more likely it is that people who have excelled in that environment will have difficulty dealing with the uncertainty and ambiguity of more broadly based leadership.

Depth in some professional field is essential as preparation for taking on broader leadership. Somebody who knows only a little bit about a lot of things is not likely to be as effective a leader. There's a certain mindset that comes with depth that enables one to form effective relationships with other such people, even if they are in very different fields.

The ideal preparation for becoming a senior leader is having experience with both depth and breadth. Both are vitally important. But if you must choose one or the other, choose breadth. It's at the heart of leadership success.

When I'm asked how I became a successful CEO, my response is disappointingly simple. I always thought it was important to do my best to be ready when opportunity knocked. And then I always tried to answer the door!

Over a lifetime, I developed an ingrained work ethic that simply required doing the best I could, no matter what the assignment. That was my career planning strategy.

Nearly all aspiring managers can enhance their leadership skills if they focus on developing the capabilities and characteristics that are most likely to help them succeed.

My secret list of indicators of leadership potential:

A leader inspires confidence and trust and consistently displays the highest ethical standards

A leader communicates effectively, internally and externally

A leader consistently achieves superior results, and produces results through other people

A leader pursues continuous learning and fosters a learning environment

A leader produces other leaders

A leader develops cross-functional knowledge and versatility—breadth

A leader embraces change and looks for ways to use it as an advantage

A leader is constantly on the lookout for innovative ideas—particularly in unlikely places

A leader builds alliances to further corporate goals—internally and externally

A leader balances the short term with the long term by focusing on both

A leader embraces ambiguity

A leader practices and encourages thoughtful risk taking

A leader champions cultural diversity

A leader's contributions leave "footprints"

On Organizational Structure

To put it quite simply, "structure must follow strategy."

The thin line separating the winners from the losers is often determined by how well an organization chooses and structures its people in a way that is consistent with its plans for tomorrow, not yesterday.

For organizations that require deep expertise but do not have to move quickly, functional organizations are just fine. It's just hard to find situations in today's competitive global markets with those characteristics!

It's important to remember that changing the organization structure alone will not create success; it will only create a structure where success may be more readily achieved. Changing from one type of structure to another in the belief that it will fix a problem is a big mistake. It just doesn't happen that way. Organization structures are really only about tradeoffs.

Organization structures are seldom bad or good; they are just different from each other, with different benefits and different shortcomings.

When you're putting a new organization in place, the planning *must* be done by the people who are going to be on your "new" team, not those on the "old" team. That's the only way they'll have total ownership.

On Succession Planning

It has long been my view that succession planning and implementation are among the most important responsibilities of a CEO.

All too often, in virtually all fields, leaders step down when it's convenient for them, without regard to whether that corresponds with what's in the best interests of the organization they are leading.

The success of any CEO's stewardship should be measured not only by the results achieved while in power but also by the results achieved after the CEO is gone.

Without the right objectives, the implementation of a succession plan too often becomes an eleventh-hour fire drill.

Succession planning by a sitting CEO, if done properly, is the process by which leadership continuity, and therefore the corporation's continuity, is assured. But to do it well sometimes requires putting the ongoing well-being of the corporation above personal considerations.

CEOs who stay around for a long transition after their successors are selected and announced are mostly doing so because they just don't want to let go.

Planning for a successful transition does not begin when it's time for a leader to step down. It begins the moment a leader takes charge.

Whenever possible, allow future leaders the opportunity to see and feel themselves in an unexpected or unaccustomed role before they are expected to convey that image to the world.

I've always been mindful of the words of Peter Lynch, who, upon announcing his own early retirement after an extraordinarily successful career, proclaimed, "Nobody on his deathbed ever said, 'I wish I'd spent more time at the office!'"

Other Important Lessons

Coaching my daughter's soccer team years ago, I learned that, without guidance to the contrary, wherever the soccer ball is on the field, 100 percent of the eight-year-old players from both teams will be right on top of it. The rest of the field will be vacant. Over the years I have found that the same holds true in the corporate world. Every team needs a coach.

I have found that the simplest questions or the simplest actions are often the most important and can yield the most significant results.

In the corporate world, success and praise from the financial community has a shelf life about as long as that of a gallon of milk.

Excessive interdependence among the parts of a corporation often leads to the company being only as strong as its weakest link.

Take what you find and make it better.*

Treat everyone with respect, no matter their station in life.

My father never let his own success define how he related to other people, and he never let his career define who he was as a human being.

My camp duties added up to nothing less than a crash course in life. It was my first experience with broad and ambiguous responsibilities. If something needed to be done, job descriptions didn't count for much.

What has served me best from my college years are the lessons from outside the classroom—the excitement of accepting new challenges, of managing multiple activities at the same time, of leading people with conflicting and often competing ideas, of finding myself

---

*Colonel Eli Lilly, upon turning over responsibility for the company to his son J. K. Lilly, said, "Take what you find here and make it better."

with responsibilities in areas where I had little prior knowledge or experience to guide my actions and decisions.

It's obvious that the academic portion is the core of one's higher education. What's less obvious is that while this core is necessary, it's insufficient.

Adding more people to the task at hand is not always the answer to getting a job done more quickly or more efficiently or more effectively. You can put only so many men into a manhole at one time.

It is far more appropriate to value and measure output than input.

A predisposition for using committees to make decisions by consensus means that decisions are often compromises rather than hard choices. It also means that no one is really accountable. Building a consensus to support a decision is an important leadership responsibility. Making decisions by consensus is not.

Success in a complex environment most often comes to companies that are completely focused on businesses they know how to operate successfully, that fit compatibly with their other businesses, and for which the company is an appropriate owner. Rare are the skills and cultural capabilities for managing several very diverse concerns at the same time.

When you are wrestling with a complex decision, or when you are trying to develop a clear and coherent point of view on a major issue—a new strategy, for example—it's always a good idea to write it down. If you can't say it clearly and convincingly on paper, you probably don't have your hands firmly around the issue, and you need to keep writing and editing until you do.

Life has many twists and turns, not all with happy endings.

ACKNOWLEDGMENTS

I not only use all the brains I have, but all I can borrow.
                                        —Woodrow Wilson

In preparation for writing this book, more than eighty interviews were conducted with friends and colleagues who have been part of the times I've written about. Quotes taken from the transcripts of those conversations are clearly marked, as are references quoted from other sources. But for the most part, the book is based on my personal recollections, observations, notes, correspondence, and other papers accumulated over the course of the first sixty years of my life. In a number of instances, those who were there have generously read early drafts of sections of the book and offered helpful comments. While I have researched all of the material in the book to the extent possible, a work of this type is, by necessity, largely based on personal recollections of conversations, meeting, anecdotes, and the like. Therefore, in the end, any mistakes herein are entirely my own.

I began the introduction to this book with the story of my great-great-grandfather, David Tobias, and his son, Theopolis. In keeping with that Tobias family tradition of father–son ventures, I want to immediately draw your attention to the second byline on this book. My own son, Todd, who makes his career in the publishing world, has shepherded this project from a throw-away response I once made to him about my reluctance to seriously consider suggestions that I write a book about my experiences.

Colonel Eli, the founder of Eli Lilly and Company, once said to his son and heir apparent, J.K. Lilly, "Take what you find here and make it better." Those are words to live by, and that's essentially what I asked Todd to do, in conducting dozens of interviews, in helping me pull together the various notes and speeches and clippings—and sometimes fuzzy memories—that are the story of events over the course of my lifetime, including nearly forty years in corporate America. He's also responsible for some of the most creative and compelling writing in the book. I wouldn't and couldn't have undertaken this project alone. Having agreed to write this book, I simply can't describe the pure joy I've experienced from having the opportunity to work with my son, or the pride I feel in understanding more completely the depth of his talent and capabilities. If you learn something here, as I have, or even if you're just entertained, as I have been along the way, it is quite likely you have him to thank as much as me.

Beyond Todd, I want to acknowledge a number of others who have been important to this book or in other ways have had an impact on the times I've written about. There's no better place to begin than by singling out Dr. Terry Busch, my senior speechwriter and communications collaborator while I was at Eli Lilly and Company. It was Terry who first urged me to write this book and who then persisted when I refused to take his suggestion seriously. For a long time, I resisted both Terry and Todd with the argument that the world does not need one more book from a retired CEO who thinks he has something different to offer. I now hope I was wrong—that there is room for at least one more, particularly in the context of the dark shadow that's overtaken corporate America during the time I was writing this manuscript. Throughout the

Acknowledgments

book, I have from time to time used words and concepts which Terry first brought to me or which we developed together. I'm grateful for his contributions.

Among those to whom I'm indebted for providing historical perspective and other insights through interviews, conversations, or e-mail exchanges or for providing access to documents, photographs, clippings, and other information, or for other significant assistance along the road I've traveled are Bob Allen, Lisa Bayne, Steve Beering, Jerry Bepko, Tom Berry, Bill Biddle, Ed Bligh, Ed Block, Marty Bronner, Fred Buckingham, Hal Burlingame, Channa Beth Butcher, Helen Butcher, Colin Campbell, Maureen Carroll, Bradley Cook, Jim Cornelius, Mitch Daniels, Jill Danzig, Blaine Davis, Cedric Dempsey, Ron Dollens, Brice Dunshee, Mike Eagle, Mark Ferrara, David Gibson, Ron Gillam, Charlie Golden, Pedro Granadillo, Jenny Graper, Tom Grein, Harold Hackley, Allison Haltom, Tom Hayhurst, Bruce Hazelett, Matt Hazelett, Sheldon Hochheiser, Dick Hoffert, Ray Humke, Jim Irwin, Becky Kendall, Nan Keohane, Jim King, Jim Kittle, Candice Lange, Marilyn Laurie, Clyde Lee, Sara Lentz, Chuck Marshall, Patty Martin, Kathy Martine, Jeff May, Mary May, Gerhard Mayr, Carol Anne Schantz McDougal, Alice Medley, Mei Wei Chang, Jim Morris, David Nadler, Katharine O'Moore Klopf, Tom Peck, Ted Planje, Anna Pratt, Maureen Radigan, Paul Reinken, Gail Rentsch, Sally Rose-Fisher, Mike Russo, Laurie Sachtleben, Curt Simic, John Smart, Jack Sogard, Andy Steffen, Jennifer Stotka, Morry Tanenbaum, Sidney Taurel, Eric Tobias, Roger Tobias, Channing Vosloh, Kathy Wagoner, August Watanabe, Ed West, Sam Willcoxon, Diane Willis, John Zeglis, and others who were helpful but for one reason or another wish to remain anonymous. My apologies to those others I'm certain I will realize I have failed to indentify only after it is too late to do so.

My thanks to Peter-John Leone and the entire staff at Indiana

Acknowledgments

University Press for their splendid assistance and guidance through-out this project.

Susie Hazelett, the Executive Director of the Tobias Family Foundations, helped in a number of ways, including by reading the manuscript and applying her skills as a former English teacher. She also facilitated a number of other aspects of this project, and for that help I am extremely grateful. The manuscript was also read in whole or in part by several others, and we are very grateful for their many useful comments and suggestions.

Dory Cook, my executive assistant, also provided invaluable assistance. She proofread everything and repeatedly detected errors after both Todd and I had concluded that our work was flawless. Laura Lashmet, who works with her in my office, ably assisted with this work. Amy Williams, an executive assistant who works with Todd at Table Moose Media, also provided invaluable logistical support, particularly in scheduling the interviews and handling the transcripts.

As always, my daughter Page Tobias Button was there with support and encouragement when I needed it, as well as her own important recollections.

Finally, I want to thank my wife Marianne, an author herself, for her support and understanding. On more occasions than I can even recall, she would gently say to me, "Why don't we change our plans." I would suddenly realize that I was supposed to be ready to go out, but I'd lost track of time in an odd moment I'd found to spend on the book and the words were suddenly flowing. Thing is, she really meant it. She understood those are rare and elusive times, to be treasured when they come. I'm deeply grateful for that, and for all she has brought to my life.

R.L.T.

Acknowledgments

Marianne and me on our seventh wedding anniversary, on board our boat Dreamer *at our home on Captiva Island, Florida.*

BIBLIOGRAPHY

Allen, Robert E. Interview. Florham Park, N.J., December 3, 2001.

Augustine, Norman R. Interview. Bethesda, Md., December 18, 2001.

Beering, Dr. Steven C. Interview. West Lafayette, Ind., October 30, 2001.

Bepko, Dr. Gerald L. Interview. Indiana University–Purdue University Indianapolis. Indianapolis, November 30, 2001.

Berry, Thomas E. Interview. New Vernon, N.J., November 27, 2001.

Biddle, D. William. Interview. Remington, Ind., August 21, 2001.

Bligh, Edward P. Interview. Howell, N.J., December 10, 2001.

Block, Edward M. Interview. Key West, Fla., December 11, 2001.

Buckingham, Fredrick K. Interview. Punta Gorda, Fla., November 27, 2001.

Burlingame, Harold W. Interview. AT&T, Basking Ridge, N.J., December 3,
2001.

Busch, Dr. Niven T. Interview. Lilly Corporate Center. Indianapolis, September 5, 2001.

Butcher, Channa Beth Vosloh. Interview. Martinsville, Ind., September 26, 2001.

Butcher, Helen. Interview. Remington, Ind., September 17, 2001.

Button, Paige Tobias. Interview. Indianapolis, Ind., October 16, 2001.

Campbell, Colin G. Interview. Williamsburg, Va., December 28, 2001.

Coll, Steven. *The Deal of the Century: The Breakup of AT&T*. New York: Atheneum, 1986.

Cornelius, James M. Interview. Guidant Corporation. Indianapolis, November
2, 2001.

Bibliography

Daniels Jr., Mitchell E. Interview. Washington, D.C., November 3, 2001.

Davis, Blaine E. Interview. Peaks Island, Maine, November 28, 2001.

Dempsey, Dr. Cedric W. Interview. Indianapolis, December 14, 2001.

Dollens, Ronald W. Interview. Indianapolis, October 31, 2001.

Dunshee, Brice H. Interview. Lilly Corporate Center. Indianapolis, October 31, 2001.

Eagle, Michael L. Interview. Lilly Corporate Center. Indianapolis, November 26, 2001.

Fisher, Sally Rose. Interview. Lilly Corporate Center. Indianapolis, October 18, 2001.

Gibson, David D. Interview. Plymouth, Ind., November 12, 2001.

Gillam, Ronald. Interview. Hollywood, Fla., November 14, 2001.

Golden, Charles E. Interview. Lilly Corporate Center. Indianapolis, November 7, 2001.

Granadillo, Pedro. Interview. Lilly Corporate Center. Indianapolis, October 29, 2001.

Grein, Thomas W. Interview. Lilly Corporate Center. Indianapolis, November 7, 2001.

Hackley, Harold. Interview. Remington, Ind., September 17, 2001.

Hayhurst, Dr. Thomas. Interview. Fort Wayne, Ind., November 30, 2001.

Hazelett, Bruce A. Interview. Indianapolis, December 20, 2001.

Hazelett, Suzanne. Interview. Indianapolis, October 30, 2001.

Hoffert, Richard. Interview. Indianapolis, December 12, 2001.

Humke, Ramon L. Interview. Indianapolis, November 26, 2001.

Irwin, James H. Interview. Indianapolis, November 19, 2001.

Kendall, Rebecca. Interview. Lilly Corporate Center. Indianapolis, November 20, 2001.

Keohane, Nannerl O. Interview. Duke University. Durham, N.C., November 20, 2001.

King, James. Interview. Indianapolis, November 19, 2001.

Kittle Jr., James L. Interview. Indianapolis, October 17, 2001.

Lange, Candice P. Interview. Lilly Corporate Center. Indianapolis, November 5, 2001.

Laurie, Marilyn. Interview. New York, December 4, 2001.

Lee, Clyde. Interview. Indianapolis, December 17, 2001.

Lentz, Sara A. Interview. Indianapolis, November 13, 2001.

Magruder, Jeb Stuart. *An American Life: One Man's Road to Watergate*. New York: Scribner, 1974.

Maney, Kevin. "Failure to Define Company's Purpose Led to AT&T's 4-Way Split." *USA Today*, November 1, 2000, page 4D.

Market Wrap. CNBC. New York, August 9, 2000, television broadcast.

Bibliography

Marshall, Charles. Interview. Naples, Fla., November 12, 2001.

Martin, Patricia. Interview. Lilly Corporate Center. Indianapolis, November 2, 2001.

Martine, Kathy. Interview. Far Hills, N.J., December 5, 2001.

May, H. Jeffrey. Interview. Chicago, November 8, 2001.

May, Mary. Interview. Remington, Ind., September 17, 2001.

Mayr, Gerhard. Interview. Lilly Corporate Center. Indianapolis, November 5, 2001.

McDougal, Carol Schantz. Interview. Tucson, November 9, 2001.

Medley, Alice. Interview. Remington, Ind., November 28, 2001.

Mehta, Stephanie N., "Say Goodbye to AT&T." *Fortune*. October 1, 2001, pages 62–63.

Morris, James T. Interview. Indianapolis, October 11, 2001.

Nadler, Dr. David A. Interview. New York, November 19, 2001.

Nadler, Dr. David A. *Champions of Change: How CEOs and Their Companies Are Mastering the Skills of Radical Change.* San Francisco: Jossey-Bass Business and Management Series, January 1998.

Pelson, Victor A. Interview. Chester, N.J., January 7, 2002.

Perkins, Dennis N. T., et al. *Leading at the Edge: Leadership Lessons from the Extraordinary Saga of Shackleton's Antarctic Expedition.* New York: McGraw-Hill, 2000.

Peters, Thomas J., and Robert H. Waterman. *In Search of Excellence: Lessons from America's Best-Run Companies.* New York: Harper and Row, 1982.

Planje Jr., Theodore J. Interview. Lilly Corporate Center. Indianapolis, November 9, 2001.

Quayle, Dan. *Standing Firm.* New York: HarperCollins, 1995.

Radigan, Maureen. Interview. Basking Ridge, N.J., December 4, 2001.

Reinken, Paul. Interview. Indianapolis, November 8, 2001.

Rogers, Everett M. *Diffusion of Innovations.* New York: Free Press, 1995.

Russo, Michael S. Interview. Lilly Corporate Center. Indianapolis, November 8, 2001.

Sachtleben, Laurie. Interview. Clifton, Va., September 17, 2001.

Seifert, Kathi P. Interview. Kimberly-Clark Corporation. Neenah, Wis., January 7, 2002.

Seuss, Dr. *Green Eggs and Ham.* New York: Random House Children's Publishing, 1960.

Shooshan, Harry M. *Disconnecting Bell: The Impact of the AT&T Divestiture.* Elmsford, N.Y.: Pergamon, 1984.

Smart, John R. Interview. Bonita Springs, Fla., May, 22, 2002.

Sogard, R. J. Interview. Indianapolis, October 9, 2001.

Steffen, E. Andrew. Interview. Indianapolis, December 10, 2001.

Stotka, Dr. Jennifer L. Interview. Lilly Corporate Center. Indianapolis, September 27, 2001.

Tanenbaum, Dr. Morris. Interview. Short Hills, N.J., November 21, 2001.

Taurel, Sidney. Interview. Lilly Corporate Center. Indianapolis, November 28, 2001.

Tobias, Eric A. Interview. Indianapolis, November 11, 2001.

Tobias, Randall L. Interview, Clyde Lee. Lilly Corporate Center. Indianapolis, June 30, 1993.

Tobias, Roger H. Interview. Indianapolis, August 8, 2001.

Vosloh, Channing M. Interview. Martinsville, Ind., September 26, 2001.

Watanabe, Dr. August M. Interview. Lilly Corporate Center. Indianapolis, Ind., November 7, 2001.

Welch, Jack and John A. Byrne. *Jack: Straight from the Gut.* New York: Warner Books, 2001.

West, Edward A. Interview. Lilly Corporate Center. Indianapolis, September 20, 2001.

Willcoxon, Sam R. Interview. Highlands Ranch, Colo., November 13, 2001.

Wood, Richard D. Press release. Lilly Corporate Center. Indianapolis, June 25, 1993.

Zeglis, John D. Interview. AT&T. Basking Ridge, N.J., December 21, 2001.

INDEX

Page numbers in *italics* refer to illustrations.

Index

Index

coup, 55
Couric, Katie, 159, *160*
court cases, 44, 45, 46
Crawford, Ann-Marie, 195
credit union, 157
"Cube, The" (Lilly strategy), 180, *180*
Cummins Engine Company, 130
customer premises equipment, 26
customer relations, 94–95
customer service, 89

Daniels, Mitchell E., Jr., 138, 148–149, 164, 207, 231
Davis, Blaine, 11
Dawson, Julia, 115
Deal of the Century, The (Coll), 30
Debenedetti, Carlo, 40
deButts, John, 37, 127, 129
decision making, 139, 192, 252, 260
Dempsey, Cedric W., 140
DePauw University, 87
depression, clinical, 62–66, 234
Depression (1930s), 83, 85, 87, 95–96, 152
Diffusion of Innovations (Rogers), 33
DiMarchi, Richard, 51
Diversified Pharmaceutical Services (DPS), 206, 208
Dollens, Ronald W., 52, 139
Dow Chemical Company, 175, 176, 178
downsizing, 8, 55, 248
dress codes, 200
Drucker, Peter, 170
Dunshee, Brice, 52n

Eagle, Mike, 208–209, *211*, 211–212
Eastwood, Clint, 126
economies of scale, 190
Edison, Thomas A., 33
education, academic, 111, 260
Elanco Animal Health, 8, 15, 52n, 92, 175–176, 178
elder-care services, 157
Eli Lilly and Company, xiv, xv, 42, 134; acquisitions of, 174–180; "board-

room coup" at, 7–8; clinical trial deaths and, 13, 17–19; corporate communications policy, 53–61; corporate culture of, 58, 70, 143, 146–148, 152, 168–169; "Cube" strategy, 180, *180*; FIAU crisis, 13, 55, 56, 148–150; functional organization in, 182–183, 202; Global Management Meeting, 210–212, *211*; history of, 9; human resources programs, 155–157, *158*, 159–163, *162*, 248–249; insulin business, 171–172; Lilly Research Laboratories, 69; mental health issues and, 62; pharmaceutical benefit managers (PBMs) and, 206–207; Prozac patent case and, 44–49; recipe for success and, 150–155; shareholder value creation, *230*, 230–231; stock of, 45–46, 48, 51; succession planning at, 222–226, *224–225*; values of, 70, 142, 168–169; Zyprexa project, 192–198
Elizabeth Arden company, 8, 174
Ellinghaus, Bill, 185–186
e-mail, 38
emerging markets, 196
employees, of AT&T, xii, 5, 27–28, 199
employees, of Eli Lilly, 59–61, 70, 142, 143, 147–148, 229; communications policy and, 54, 55; decision making by, 209; family structures of, 248; flexible hours and, 163–167; human resources programs and, 155–157, *158*, 159–163, *162*; reciprocity and, 152–153, 154; R. T.'s popularity with, 228
"empty suits," 110
Enright, Bill, 77
Enron scandal, 49, 143, 145–146
Erl Wood research facility, 192
ethical standards, 135, 143, 256
Evansville, Indiana, 114, 115
excellence, 142, 147, 168

Index

Index

Index

Index

Index

Index

RANDALL TOBIAS was Chairman and CEO of Eli Lilly and Company from 1993 until his retirement at the end of 1998, when he was named Chairman Emeritus. Before joining Lilly, he had a distinguished career at AT&T, where he was Vice Chairman in the years following the government-ordered breakup of the company in 1984 and negotiated the first-ever telecommunications deal with China. Tobias serves on the boards of a number of major corporations and foundations, and he is an active member of the Indianapolis community. He has a particular interest in the cause of teaching children to read and improving kindergarten through twelfth-grade education in Indiana.

TODD TOBIAS is President and Editorial Director of Table Moose Media, and Founder of *Indy Men's Magazine*.